AF228916

ESCAPE FROM JAVA

To Harry Koziol
US Army – World War II Pacific

ESCAPE FROM JAVA

The Extraordinary World War II Story of the USS *Marblehead*

JOHN J DOMAGALSKI

Pen & Sword
MILITARY
AN IMPRINT OF PEN & SWORD BOOKS LTD.
YORKSHIRE - PHILADELPHIA

First published in Great Britain in 2022 by
PEN AND SWORD MILITARY
An imprint of
Pen & Sword Books Limited
Yorkshire – Philadelphia

Copyright © John J Domagalski, 2022

ISBN 978 1 52678 441 4

The right of John J Domagalski to be identified as Author
of this work has been asserted by him in accordance with the Copyright,
Designs and Patents Act 1988.

A CIP catalogue record for this book is available from the British Library.

Typeset in Times New Roman 11.5/14 by
SJmagic DESIGN SERVICES, India.
Printed and bound in the UK by CPI Group (UK) Ltd.

Pen & Sword Books Limited incorporates the imprints of Atlas, Archaeology,
Aviation, Discovery, Family History, Fiction, History, Maritime, Military, Military
Classics, Politics, Select, Transport, True Crime, Air World, Frontline Publishing,
Leo Cooper, Remember When, Seaforth Publishing, The Praetorian Press,
Wharncliffe Local History, Wharncliffe Transport, Wharncliffe True Crime and
White Owl.

For a complete list of Pen & Sword titles please contact
PEN & SWORD BOOKS LIMITED
47 Church Street, Barnsley, South Yorkshire S70 2AS, United Kingdom
E-mail: enquiries@pen-and-sword.co.uk
Website: www.pen-and-sword.co.uk

Or
PEN AND SWORD BOOKS
1950 Lawrence Rd, Havertown, PA 19083, USA
E-mail: Uspen-and-sword@casematepublishers.com
Website: www.penandswordbooks.com

Contents

Acknowledgments

Writing about a story about World War II – a conflict fought more than seventy-five years ago – is an enormous undertaking. When I began the research for this project, no one who served aboard *Marblehead* during the time in question was still alive – to the best of my knowledge. The project could not have been completed without the help of many individuals. The list is too lengthy to publish in full, but a few are worthy of special thanks. As with any naval history project, the excellent staffs at the National Archives and the Naval History and Heritage Command provided abundant assistance in locating documents and photos. My agent, Ethan Ellenberg, provided great wisdom and support. The fine team at Pen and Sword gave superb guidance throughout the publishing process. Lastly, I want to thank my wife, Sandy. The book would not have been written without her enduring support and encouragement.

Prologue

Marblehead in Peril

Captain Arthur Robinson momentarily struggled to regain his footing after he was knocked to the deck on the bridge of *Marblehead* after the warship violently shuddered from a series of bomb blasts. He immediately knew his ship was in peril. A rising cloud of black smoke quickly drew his attention – fires were raging somewhere aboard. An oil slick trailing behind the light cruiser indicated her fuel tanks had been ruptured. The ship began taking on a list – an ominous sign of serious flooding below deck.

Captain Robinson rapidly began shouting orders to determine the extent of the damage. His most immediate concern was the wellbeing of the engines – the powerplants needed to keep *Marblehead* moving. He asked a nearby crewman with a sound powered telephone, a primitive inter-ship communication system, to contact the engine rooms to determine the current situation. The crewman quickly replied that the circuit was dead. The damage had severed most of the critical communications links to various parts of the ship, hindering Robinson's ability to find out what was happening. Then the helmsman revealed more bad news – the steering was out. There was no way to navigate the ship, and the rudder was jammed to the left. The warship was moving fast, steaming at a clip of over twenty knots, but was now going in circles. It was 10.27 am on February 4, 1942.

The warship had been hit by two bombs and indeed was in great danger. One exploded deep below deck near the very back of the ship. The second was a shallow hit farther forward, detonating one deck below topside. Both caused extensive damage and fires. A third bomb was a near miss, but exploded underwater very close to the side ripping a large gash in the hull below the waterline. The hole allowed a torrent of water to rush into the ship. The air attack was not over – Japanese planes were turning to make another run on *Marblehead*.

Some of the men aboard considered it miraculous the outdated warship was still afloat. Nearly two decades old and obsolete by current standards, fate and perhaps bad luck put *Marblehead* on the front lines in the opening days of World War II in the Pacific. She had put to sea hours earlier as part of a hastily formed task force of American and Dutch vessels seeking to attack approaching Japanese ships. The strike plans were thwarted when the group was struck by Japanese bombers northeast of Java.

Captain Robinson's second-in-command, Executive Officer Commander William Goggins, was below deck during the attack. His location in the wardroom, an officers' mess area, was to keep him far from the bridge as protection from having the two top officers incapacitated by a single hit. However, it put him very close to one of the bomb hits.

An explosion suddenly knocked Goggins off his feet. He was immediately surrounded by a feeling of intense heat. A powerful wave of superheated gas from the explosion whipped through the compartment, burning anything in its path. Paint on the metal bulkhead burned away and the linoleum floor was sizzling and catching fire. Goggins was wearing short pants and a short-sleeve shirt. His exposed skin was seared by the heat. Miraculously, his clothes did not catch fire. The wardroom was filling with thick acrid smoke as the officer struggled to his feet. A sailor abruptly appeared and began helping him to find a way out.

Captain Robinson and every other sailor aboard the mortally wounded *Marblehead* now faced a desperate fight. The battle was to keep their ship afloat long enough to make it to a friendly port. William Goggins would soon face his own struggle for survival.

PART I
WAR CLOUDS

Chapter 1

It was with a great sense of urgency that sailors aboard the *Marblehead* made the warship ready to get underway during the morning hours of November 25, 1941. The deteriorating relations between the United States and Japan were certainly weighing heavily on almost every sailor's mind as the light cruiser started slowly moving through the waters of Manila Bay. Navy wives and dependents had already been ordered out of the Philippines and back to the United States – a testament to the seriousness of the situation in the Pacific. War fears were now growing by the day. The atmosphere in the Philippines at the time was later described as 'electric – sultry as the lull before the tempest'.[1] It was 9.10 am and a long day of cruising lay ahead.[2]

Captain Arthur Robinson was among the officers on the bridge as the warship passed through the bay. The anchorage had long been considered one of the best deep-water harbors in the Far East. He could easily see the fortified island of Corregidor looming in the distance ahead. The small rocky land mass, bristling with cannons and an assortment of defenses, was positioned as if a sentry guarding the entrance to the harbor. The city of Manila was slowly fading into the distance off the warship's stern. The sailors were leaving behind the dazzling tropical city with wide streets and white buildings. It was the capitol and seat of American power in the Philippines.

Various courses and speeds allowed *Marblehead* to use a safe passageway to navigate through the defensive minefields protecting the harbor entrance before moving out into the open sea during the early afternoon hours. The Manila area had served as her home port since early 1938. Captain Robinson was aboard the vessel for about a year-and-a-half, having reported for duty on May 5, 1940.[3]

War was much closer than Robinson and most of the *Marblehead* sailors knew. At that very moment, Japanese soldiers, warships, and planes were gathering at various staging points north and west of the Philippines. Invasions plans were in place for the very waters *Marblehead* would be sailing towards. Events in the region were to develop quickly, in the matter of only a few short weeks, and *Marblehead* would never again return to Manila Harbor.

The light cruiser was not the only American warship on the move. She was steaming in company with the destroyer *Paul Jones*, parts of two other destroyer divisions, and their tender *Black Hawk*. Robinson was in command of the whole force. The ships traveled southeast, passing through the Mindoro Strait while moving along the west coast of the moderate-sized island of the same name. The force continued through green-blue colored waterways surrounded by various Philippine islands, both large and small. The late evening hours brought contact with numerous other vessels at sea, including the heavy cruiser *Louisville* and an assortment of merchant ships.

The destination was unknown to most of the sailors aboard the warships moving south, although by the direction of travel it appeared the vessels were either going to the southern Philippines or departing the American territory all together. No cold weather gear was taken out of storage, supporting the widespread belief among the crew that *Marblehead* was staying in tropical waters. Rumors and scuttlebutt abounded as to when and if the war would start and where the ships would be when the fighting began. Some sailors were just relieved to be out of Manila Bay, widely viewed to be a dangerous place during any conflict. A sailor aboard the accompanying destroyer *Stewart* later recalled that no one 'wanted to chance being trapped in the bay by the greatly superior Japanese fleet'.[4] After all, it was with a similar trap that the United States Navy defeated a Spanish armada in Manila Bay during the Spanish-American War of 1898.

The light cruiser was the largest ship of the group, with her length stretching over 500ft, and packed the greatest firepower. Her clipper bow and low freeboard near the stern (distance from the deck to ocean) gave her a sleek and graceful appearance. Ten 6-inch guns served as her main weapons, but were positioned in a somewhat unusual arrangement by contemporary standards. Two twin turrets, one forward and one aft, accounted for four of the main guns. The remaining six were mounted in casemates with four positioned behind the forward turret and two near the after turret. The casemate guns had limited firing arcs – a potential problem in a surface battle. The design was based on British experience emphasizing broadside fire in World War I.[5] The arrangement proved inadequate as time passed and technology advanced. Depending on the location of the target, not all the main guns could be brought to bear on it.

The armor protecting *Marblehead* was much less than what was afforded to newer American light cruisers. A 3-inch-thick belt shielded the sides of the ship. Armor plates 1½ inches thick protected the deck. The two main battery turrets, however, were surrounded with ½-inch-thick covering – only enough to protect against shrapnel and small arms.[6]

The next few days were spent at sea as the voyage took the ships into the open expanses of the Sulu Sea southwest of the Philippines. The destroyer tender *Black Hawk* led the formation with *Marblehead* steaming about 1,000 yards directly behind. The accompanying destroyers were arrayed in an anti-submarine screen.

The light cruiser regularly launched seaplanes to scout the immediate area on reconnaissance missions. The warship carried two Curtis SOC Seagull biplanes on a pair of catapults just behind the smoke stacks in the middle part of the ship. Manned by a crew of two, the seaplane was essentially an aluminum frame wrapped with fabric. Armament was limited to two machine guns and racks under each wing for small bombs. The Seagull had a range of 878 miles.[7] The aircraft were shot into the air by the catapult, but had to land in the water before being hoisted back aboard *Marblehead* by a crane.

Most of the warship's crew was standing four hour watches followed by twelve hours of time off duty. The arrangement, known as condition three, was used when the captain felt the probability of an enemy attack was remote.[8] As a precaution, however, most of the watertight doors and hatches below deck were closed and sealed, except those needed to operate the ship. Sailors off duty could enjoy the warm weather and sunshine topside, or pass time below deck by sleeping, writing letters, or reading. The light cruiser was in darkened condition during the night hours, showing no outside light, to help mask her location. Almost all the warships in the group conducted training exercises during the voyage, including various types of battle station drills held aboard the light cruiser.

Lookouts on *Marblehead* could see little Bongao Island off the port side during the early morning hours of November 28.[9] Course was changed to due south a short time later. Passing among various small islands put the warship in the Celebes Sea – out of Philippine waters and moving away from American territory. The ships were soon off the northeast coast of Borneo. Positioned about 200 miles southwest of the Philippines, the large island was split between Dutch and British control. The English territory ran along the coast on the northern side of the isle, including the northeastern tip jutting out towards the Philippines. The American ships continued past the British territory to a position off the Dutch-controlled east coast of Borneo. About thirty-five miles ahead lay the oil-rich region of Tarakan.

The voyage was temporarily halted when *Black Hawk* suffered engine problems just before 9.00 am; built prior to World War I, she was the oldest vessel of the group. Occasional mechanical issues were not unexpected on the aged vessel. The destroyers formed a circular patrol around their stricken tender. After initially cruising outside of the destroyer ring, *Marblehead* maneuvered to about 1,000 yards off *Black Hawk*'s starboard quarter and then brought her engines to a halt. Captain Herbert Wiley, the commanding officer of Destroyer Squadron 29, came aboard the light cruiser from *Paul Jones* for a short conference with Captain Robinson before proceeding to the *Black Hawk*. The mechanical issues were found to be not serious and the tender was back underway at about 10.30 am.

The force divided into two smaller groups a short time later with *Black Hawk* and some of the destroyers proceeding to the south. The group eventually anchored further down the Borneo coast at the port city of Balikpapan. The destroyers *Paul Jones*, *Stewart*, *Barker*, and *Parrott* remained with *Marblehead*.[10]

All the destroyers were World War I era relics, considered obsolete and outclassed in almost every characteristic by more contemporary warships of similar type. The *Marblehead* was anything but modern as her design was based on experience and technology from the same conflict. The time was long before the dominance of aircraft in naval warfare – when the mighty battleship still ruled the seas and battles were often decided by gunfire. The role of light cruisers, operating in conjunction with destroyers, was to serve as advanced scouts for the main battle fleet.

The warship's location was now a good distance from her support center in the Philippines and far from the large American naval base at

Malay Barrier 1941.

Pearl Harbor, Hawaii. There was no illusion among her crew as to the ship's precarious position – *Marblehead* would almost certainly be on the front lines if – or when – any conflict erupted. Radioman Second Class Raymond Kester had been aboard the light cruiser for about a year.[11] He endured months of exercises and training designed to make operations routine in a time of crisis. The young sailor remembered word circulating around the ship at the time that the next action would not be a drill. 'We were aboard outdated, outclassed fighting ships; but with spirit and good morale,' he later recalled. 'Most of us felt that when the "real thing" came along, we would, at best, fight a delaying action and be rescued by the main fleet.'[12] The 'main fleet' was the battleships of the much larger Pacific Fleet based at Pearl Harbor.

Lookouts aboard *Marblehead* sighted land just after 5.00 am on the morning of November 29.[13] Within an hour a pilot and crewman climbed aboard one of the Seagull planes mounted on the catapult behind the smoke stacks. The engine sputtered to a start, and the loud drone of the propeller could be heard throughout the after part of the ship. With the sound of a sudden crack, the plane was shot off the catapult for a routine reconnaissance mission. Some Dutch planes were spotted a short time later. The warship was approaching the island of Tarakan. Captain Robinson and the rest of the *Marblehead* sailors were about to complete their final peacetime voyage.

Chapter 2

The light cruiser *Marblehead*'s voyage out of the Philippines was one of many preparations underway by American military forces in the Far East for a war with Japan. The term 'Far East' was commonly used throughout the early part of the twentieth century to describe what is today known as East Asia. The region encompasses much of eastern China and all of Japan, moving south to include various other nations and island groups north and northwest of Australia.

A closer look at the area just before the start of World War II reveals a variety of nations with territory and spheres of influence. China was not the unified country it is today, but a nation divided by disorder and civil war with various groups holding influence in different regions. The current nations of Vietnam, Cambodia, and Laos were combined as the French Colony of Indochina. The influence of the British Empire in the region was substantial, with the territories of Malaya, Hong Kong, and Singapore – the latter serving as the centerpiece of the British Far Eastern realm. The present-day country of Indonesia was the Dutch Colony known as the Netherlands, or Dutch, East Indies. Sizable American territory in the Far East was limited to the Philippines. Seized from Spain in the aftermath of the Spanish-American War of 1898, the nation was governed as an American Commonwealth with her future independence already passed into federal law. Only Thailand stood alone as an independent nation.

The United States maintained a steady naval presence in the Far East dating back to the 1850s when Commodore Matthew Perry sailed to Japan on a mission to open ports for American trade. The naval forces were typically limited to a small number of ships. American sailors often referred to warships stationed in the region as being on Asiatic Station and part of the Asiatic Squadron. The mission of the ships remained the same over the course of many decades – maintain maritime security and protect regional American economic interests, especially in China – essentially 'showing the flag'.[1]

The role of the Far East ships took on greater importance after the Asiatic Squadron defeated a Spanish Fleet in Manila Bay in 1898. The status of the force was eventually upgraded to become the United States Asiatic Fleet, led by an admiral who was of equal standing to those heading the Atlantic, and later, Pacific Fleets. The force typically included a heavy cruiser as a flagship, some destroyers, and a group of small river gunboats primarily for use in China. Asiatic Fleet ships continued to show the flag around the Far East, making regular calls on ports in the Dutch East Indies, China, Japan, Hong Kong, and other regional venues.

***

The warship *Marblehead* was launched on October 9, 1923, at the William Cramp & Son shipyard in Philadelphia after just over three years of construction.[2] She was the ninth ship out of a class of ten, the third naval vessel named after the port city in Massachusetts, and she bore the naval designation of CL-12, denoting her status as a light cruiser.[3] Her sleek lines and four narrow funnels, arranged in two pairs, bore a close resemblance to the American 'flush deck' destroyers built just after the end of World War I – the same destroyers that would decades later accompany *Marblehead* in the South Pacific.

The light cruiser, however, was much larger than the destroyers with *Marblehead*'s hull measuring just over 555ft in length with a beam (width) of 55ft. The forward area of the warship was dominated by a large tripod mast. The perch gave lookouts a position to scan the horizon far and wide in the days before radar. Immediately behind were four smoke stacks, or funnels, numbered one through four as counted from forward to aft. A less imposing single mast stood behind the funnels near the after part of the ship.

Twelve boilers allowed four Westinghouse steam turbines to turn a like number of propellers giving *Marblehead* speeds up to thirty-five knots.[4] The design was the first American warship to feature an alternate arrangement of boilers and turbines – a feature subsequently made standard in all cruiser plans going forward to protect from having all boilers knocked out by a single shell or torpedo hit.[5] She weighed 7,100 tons before fuel, crew, and supplies.[6]

The main firepower came from *Marblehead*'s ten 6-inch guns. Two 3-inch dual-purpose guns comprised the secondary armament. Six torpedo tubes, mounted three on each side in triple batteries, rounded out the weapons as built. The underwater weapons were subsequently removed from most cruiser designs going forward.

The two decades prior to World War II brought some subtle improvements to *Marblehead*. The increased importance of aircraft led to more air defense guns with the 3-inch secondary battery increased to eight, and the adding of eight 50-caliber machine guns. The addition of catapults and seaplanes denoted the increasing role of aircraft in the scouting role once done by ships. Enhanced radio and fire control equipment was added, although she was never fitted with radar while in the Pacific. The extra weight of the various additions added to the stability problems already inherent in her top-heavy design.

After commissioning on September 8, 1924, *Marblehead* left Boston for a shakedown cruise in the English Channel and Mediterranean.[7] The next fifteen years took her to points across the world. The remainder of the 1920s found the warship cruising to Australia, spending time off Nicaragua, and at Shanghai, China. The 1930s brought duty with both the Atlantic and Pacific Fleets, before eventual assignment to the Asiatic Fleet.[8]

***

Relations between the United States and Japan were already tense when *Marblehead* arrived in the Far East in late 1937. The two nations were on a slow collision course as the militarists in the Japanese government sought to gain additional territory over the span of several decades. Japan was an industrial national, the first in Asia, but her home islands lacked much of the critical resources needed for her economy to become self-sufficient – most notably oil. The Japanese Empire controlled Formosa (Taiwan) since just before the turn of the century, and gained influence over the Korean Peninsula in 1910. A greater expansion began in 1931 when troops invaded Manchuria, taking full control of the region in northeastern China before establishing the puppet state of Manchukuo. American leaders denounced the aggression, but did little else, leaving the Japanese to contemplate further moves in China.

An incident between Chinese and Japanese soldiers on the Marco Polo Bridge near Peking (Beijing) on July 7, 1937, served as a pretext for a full-scale invasion of China. Japanese forces swept south capturing key cities, including Nanking and Shanghai, while committing horrific atrocities against the civilian population. Chinese resistance later stiffened and the Japanese were unable to knock out the stubborn defenders, who refused to capitulate.

Japanese leaders had long coveted a resource laden region in southern Asia. Comprised of the Netherlands East Indies, Borneo, and Malaya, the area was rich in oil, rubber, and tin – everything the nation needed to become economically autonomous. The area collectively became known to the Japanese as the Southern Resources Area. Any attack south risked a wider war with the British and Dutch for sure, and possibly the United States.

American President Franklin Roosevelt was in no position to strongly challenge Japan for much of the 1930s. He knew the American public was not willing to support a war in Asia and that his military was unprepared for such a conflict. Most Americans wanted their nation to avoid foreign wars and entanglements in the aftermath of World War I. Many viewed American involvement in the European war as a terrible mistake.[9] That opinion persisted throughout the depression-gripped 1930s when military budgets were cut and the armed services neglected. American policy in the latter part of the decade amounted to publicly denouncing the Japanese aggression backed by some restrained sanctions, while providing limited military assistance to the Chinese. The *Marblehead* would soon be in the middle of the tension-filled Far East.

***

The navy transport *Chaumont* was surrounded by intense activity as she was moored dockside in downtown San Diego on Sunday August 29, 1937. Just over 1,300 soldiers of the 6th Marine Regiment spent about two hours marching to the ship in full battle dress from the Marine barracks. A band led the procession for the entire route. The march was preceded by two days of intense activity, where supplies of all types, including tents, bedding, weapons, ammunition, and provisions, were loaded aboard the transport.[10] The ship made ready for a departure to take place shortly after completion of the embarkation process.

Navy regulation normally did not allow for Sunday departures, except in the case of an emergency. The seriousness of the mission – to protect American citizens in Shanghai, China – was of high importance. The unarmed transport was to be escorted by *Marblehead* for the long voyage across the Pacific, with only a short stopover at Pearl Harbor planned. The light cruiser spent much of the year at Pearl Harbor and moving between various West Coast ports of call. The trip to the Far East would put her under the temporary jurisdiction of the Asiatic Fleet.

A bloody battle for Shanghai was ongoing as the two American ships traveled across the Pacific. Japanese invasion forces had swept south from Manchuria little more than a month earlier to begin a series of brutal attacks against the big cities of eastern China. Chinese forces were currently fighting a losing battle for Shanghai, one of China's largest cities. Americans and other foreign citizens hurriedly moved to an area known as the International Settlement. The enclave was a neutral zone in Shanghai under the control of Western powers.

Foreign warships of several countries, most notably the United States, were regularly stationed in the immediate area. It was perilous duty for sailors as the battle raged nearby on land. The heavy cruiser *Augusta*, flagship of the Asiatic Fleet, remained in the Shanghai area even after a shell (which could have been either Chinese or Japanese) exploded on her deck as sailors gathered for an evening movie. The August 20 incident killed one sailor and wounded seventeen others.[11]

The aggressive Japanese actions brought reinforcements to the International Settlement from various nations aside from the United States, most notably Britain and France. The marines aboard *Chaumont*, along with the escorting *Marblehead* and some Asiatic Fleet destroyers, represented the American contribution. The American ships arrived at Woosung, an area of Shanghai, on September 19.[12] There were soon nearly 9,000 additional soldiers and sailors in the area to protect Western interests.[13]

The situation around the International Settlement remained tense as Japanese occupiers and Western servicemen stood in close proximity. The first high-profile shooting incident between Japanese and American forces took place not long after *Marblehead* arrived on Asiatic Station. The American gunboat *Panay* was sunk by Japanese planes while on the Yangtze River near the Chinese city of Nanking. The attack on December 12, 1937, killed three Americans and wounded forty-eight, including three civilian passengers.[14] Japanese authorities later apologized, ruling the attack an accident, and payed reparations.

The light cruiser spent the last months of 1937 moving among various ports in north-eastern China as violence continued to escalate ashore. She rushed to Tsingtao during late December in company of the destroyer *Pope* and gunboat *Sacramento* to provide assistance to some 300 American citizens in the area.[15] Various voyages subsequently took her to numerous ports of call across China and the Far East as she sailed among the South and East China Seas and the Sea of Japan. The warship later became a permanent member of the Asiatic Fleet and was assigned Manila as a home port.

Machinist's Mate Second Class James Riddle joined *Marblehead*'s crew in October 1938. He was aboard as she moved among various parts of the Far East. The visits to Chinese ports often put *Marblehead* sailors in close contact with Japanese soldiers. 'You go in the channel and a huge bay back there, and the Japanese encampment was right over on the beach, just right there. We could see them from ship board. We'd pull in there and lay anchor,' he later recalled of a visit to Shantou. 'We'd run in … go in on liberty at the Shantou, and the liberty ships and all go in. And we'd run into Japanese soldiers on the streets, armed Japanese soldiers.'[16] Fortunately, the encounters were peaceful.

One of *Marblehead*'s final duties in Chinese waters was a rescue – not of people ashore, but of another warship. The old gunboat *Ashville* departed Amoy, China on July 5, 1941, bound for Manila, only to run into typhoon conditions. She subsequently became dead in the water after the single screw turning her only propeller broke. *Marblehead* was dispatched from Manila to tow the gunboat back to the Philippines, arriving on July 11.[17] A new American leader was about to take command of the Asiatic Fleet and the mission of the ships would soon be changing.

Chapter 3

Admiral Thomas Hart was near the end of a long and distinguished naval career when he assumed command of the Asiatic Fleet on July 25, 1939.[1] He gained extensive experience while serving in various ranks and positions over a period of forty-two years. The span included activities during the two most recent American conflicts – Spanish-American War and World War I. Hart had spent time aboard everything from battleships to torpedo boats and held extensive experience with submarines. He was known as an efficient administrator and a strict disciplinarian.[2]

The Asiatic Fleet command at the time of Hart's appointment included an assortment of ships scattered between the Philippines and Chinese waters – the most noteworthy being the heavy cruiser *Augusta*, *Marblehead*, and thirteen destroyers. Other assets were a squadron of PBY patrol planes, six old submarines, a contingent of marines stationed in Shanghai, various coastal and support vessels.[3] The command also included the Sixteenth Naval District. The area command encompassed the entire Philippines and included the naval base at Cavite in Manila Bay – the largest American naval facility in the Pacific west of Pearl Harbor.

Hart initially used the heavy cruiser *Augusta* as his flagship, later moving to her sister ship *Houston* on November 22, 1940.[4] Many of the warships under his command were aged and considered obsolete by current standards. The Asiatic ships often operated in the shadow of the much larger American Fleet, soon to be divided into the separate Atlantic and Pacific Fleets. As commanding officer of a fleet, albeit a small one, Hart reported directly to Chief of Naval Operations Admiral Harold Stark in Washington. He essentially had the same status as the other fleet leaders.

The ongoing conflict in China was the initial focus for the new leader intent on upholding the traditional Asiatic Fleet mission of showing the flag and protecting American interests. Hart set up his command in Shanghai. World War II in Europe began on September 1, 1939, less than two short months into his tenure. The admiral was soon to be focusing on a more ominous mission – preparing for a war with Japan.

***

The situation in the Pacific dramatically changed after the war broke out in Europe. The fighting pitted Britain and France allied against Germany and later Italy. The conflict was at a critical stage by the summer of 1940 when France, Belgium, and the Netherlands fell in rapid succession to the swift German advance across continental Europe. Britain was isolated and under attack from the air with her seaborne supply line threatened by German submarines. British Commonwealth forces were also fighting in North Africa.

President Roosevelt held a strong belief in internationalism. He knew that if Britain fell, the United States would be trapped between two menacing world powers to the east and west – Germany and Japan. The fall of France began swinging public opinion toward Britain, but the United Sates was still not ready for war. The American economy was starting to gear up for war production, with materials and supplies going to Britain. However, the United States officially remained neutral in the conflict.

The conditions in Europe created new opportunities for the Japanese to expand in Asia. Of the three European nations with significant territories in the Far East – Britain, France, and the Netherlands – two were under German control and one was fighting for survival. Japan formally joined in alliance with Nazi Germany and fascist Italy with the signing of the Tripartite Pact on September 27, 1940. Each member pledged to assist if any other was attacked by a 'power at present not involved in the European War'.[5] By excluding the Soviet Union in the wording of the agreement, the pact was clearly aimed at the United States. The arrangement paved the way for the Japanese to create and expand a 'New Order in Greater East Asia'.[6] The European nations were likely to be hard pressed to stop an attack in the Far East and the United States could be faced with a war on two fronts if it tried to intervene.

A second important event occurred in September 1940 when Japanese forces moved into the northern part of French Indochina, ostensibly to cut off the southern supply route to China. Weak French authorities could do little to stop the advance. The United States responded with an embargo on steel scrap metal. Additional restrictions on other types of metals and products followed over the next five months. President Roosevelt rushed a selective service act through Congress during October in which 16 million Americans registered for military service.[7] America seemed to be drifting closer to war.

The Pacific was fast becoming a dangerous place. The new reality prompted Admiral Hart to shift his focus away from China to preparing for a war with Japan during the Fall of 1940. He foresaw the possibility of his ships being trapped in Chinese waters if hostilities were to start without warning and began moving forces, including his flagship, out of China back to the Philippines. Only a few small river gunboats and an occasional supply ship, along with some marines, remained in China. Hart later established his headquarters in the Marsman Building near the waterfront in downtown Manila. The admiral made the decision late in the year to order Navy wives and dependents to return to the United States. The decision was not popular among the fleets' sailors, but was a necessary precaution during the time of worsening tensions.

The admiral of the Asiatic fleet was in a difficult position as he made ready to prepare his small fleet for war. Almost 5,000 miles separated the Philippines from Pearl Harbor, with the Japanese-held Mariana Islands blocking the most direct route. Other Japanese territories were dangerously close at hand, most notably Formosa (Taiwan). The island was positioned less than 300 miles off the northern tip of the Philippines and was home to large naval facilities and air bases. The location put much of the main Philippine island of Luzon, including Manila Bay, in range of bombers giving the Japanese the potential for a first strike during a conflict.

***

The United States had been planning for a war with Japan for decades. Although evolving through various names starting with War Plan Orange, the basic American plan for a conflict in the Pacific had remained largely unchanged since the early 1920s.[8] Planners assumed the hostilities would start with a Japanese strike on the Philippines, likely by surprise. The initial response was to be defensive, with American and Filipino army units focused on defending the area around Manila Bay. Few American military leaders felt the small Asiatic Fleet could withstand a full attack by Japanese forces – even with some reinforcements. The plan called for the fleet's large warships – cruisers and destroyers – to withdraw south at Admiral Hart's discretion, perhaps operating from Singapore, Australia, or bases in the Indian Ocean. The submarines and smaller craft were to stay in the Philippines for local defense.

A second phase, involving offensive operations, was to be spearheaded by the Pacific Fleet. The force was charged with defeating the Combined Japanese Fleet after advancing west across the Pacific into the Marshall, Caroline, and Mariana Island groups to open sea lanes for troops to be used for a counter attack in the Philippines. The advance was envisioned to be slow, allowing time for American industry to ramp up war production. Time would allow for the United States to out-produce the Japanese in critical military hardware.[9]

American planning culminated with Rainbow 5 in 1941. The final war plan version before America's entry into World War II reflected the current situation of the United States, allied with Britain, fighting multiple enemies on a global scale. The plan took a 'Germany first' approach of prioritizing the war in Europe due to Germany's strong army and vast industrial capacity. A more defensive posture was planned for the Pacific, although the major components remained similar to previous Orange war plans.

A significant part of 1941 found top leaders in Washington and London focused on planning for the war in Europe, but the Far East was not totally ignored. Most viewed an aggressive Japanese move south to secure oil and other natural resources as the most likely starting point of a war in the Pacific, although it was unclear when such an attack could occur. Such a strike was war with the British and Dutch for sure, and the Americans if the Philippines were also attacked.

Discussions among local defense leaders in the Pacific took place to develop a mutual aid agreement and work out tactical arrangements for the region. Few doubted the need for cooperation among the nations, particularly in naval matters. Admiral Hart was known to be a strong proponent of unified strategy for dealing with Japanese aggression.[10] Also seeking a coalition against Japan was Dutch Admiral Conrad Helfrich. The top Dutch naval commander in the region knew his forces alone could not withstand a Japanese assault.

Air Chief Marshal Sir Robert Brooke-Popham, the overall British commander-in-chief of the Far East, hosted a meeting of commanders at Singapore beginning on April 21, 1941. The conference was to build upon previous meetings, taking place over the past year, among the potential allies in a war against Japan. Admiral Hart's chief of staff, Captain William Purnell, was the senior officer representing the Americans. British, Dutch, Australian, and New Zealand officials were also in attendance. Each participating nation had its own primary concerns, often not mutually supportive to the others.

The main British concern was defending Singapore, the cornerstone of their Empire in the Pacific. The island was positioned at the southern end of the Malay Peninsula and controlled the entrance to the strategic Malacca Straits – a narrow waterway connecting the Pacific and Indian Oceans. The British had built coastal defenses, naval facilities, and airfields over the previous two decades to create an island fortress dubbed the 'Gibraltar of the Far East', after the Empire's bastion in the Mediterranean. The British considered Singapore impregnable, a view not shared by the Americans.[11] The main British strategy in case of war was to hold the island until a larger fleet could arrive from Europe to use Singapore as a naval base for operations against Japan.[12]

The ability of the British to send a large fleet to the Far East remained unclear due to the ongoing fighting in the Atlantic and Mediterranean. They were looking for warships from other nations to aid in the defense of Singapore by helping to escort convoys of troops and supplies to the fortress. British leaders previously suggested all or part of the American Pacific Fleet could be based in Singapore, an offer President Roosevelt refused.[13]

The Dutch were primarily concerned with defending their own territory, as the Japanese could stage attacks on the East Indies through multiple routes, but agreed to go along with the British convoy plan on a limited basis. Officials from Australia and New Zealand preferred to keep their naval forces near home waters for local defense.[14] Both British Commonwealth members were currently supplying military forces for the fight in the European Theatre.

The conference lasted for a week, with each side able to air their national views. Conflicting interests among the participants prevented an effective agreement.[15] The meeting ended on April 27 with a loose defense agreement dubbed the ADB Plan. The acronym stood for

American, Dutch, and British Commonwealth. The parties agreed to work together for local defense in the event of a direct Japanese attack. However, the plan lacked substance and all the parties involved were displeased with the result.[16] American leaders in Washington considered the role of the Asiatic Fleet unchanged – defense of the Philippines and withdraw south as deemed appropriate. Admiral Hart was given a wide latitude by his superiors as to what forces should be sent out of the Philippines and when such a move was to take place.[17]

***

Admiral Hart was becoming alarmed over the increasing amount of threatening rhetoric directed at Japan by members of the American press and politicians. He later wrote 'nothing is ever gained by threatening the Japanese, their psychology being such that the threats are likely to prevent their exercise of correct judgement.'[18] By early 1941, he sensed the countries were drifting closer to war.

Hart was sure hostilities could start at any time without warning and was determined not to be 'caught napping'.[19] He moved his heavy ships out of Manila Bay for extensive training in the waters of the southern Philippines during April and May 1941. The warships subsequently spent several weeks practicing gunnery exercises, night cruising, and dodging simulated submarines. Having many of the ships previously spread out among various Chinese ports made organized training activities difficult. 'There had been a dearth of such work because of the usual peacetime duties which had to be met on the Asiatic Station,' he later wrote.[20]

At various times since taking the Asiatic command Hart had campaigned unsuccessfully to his superiors in Washington for reinforcements, particularly larger warships. At one point he was told to prepare for the addition of an aircraft carrier, four heavy cruisers, nine destroyers, and some minelayers, but the transfer of the ships never materialized.[21] 'By May 1941 it had been settled that [the] Asiatic Fleet would not be reinforced with surface ships, but that there was intention to very heavily increase the British Fleet in the Far East,' Hart later recalled.[22] He was eventually able to get a squadron of modern fleet submarines transferred from the Pacific Fleet and some small torpedo boats.

The reinforcements amounted to little more than some minor additions to a small fleet. Although Hart really wanted more heavy surface ships, he appreciated the potential power of the newer submarines and welcomed the addition. Hart was an experienced submariner and knew the boats could play a crucial role in the defense of the Philippines.

The Asiatic Fleet's war preparations were ongoing when relations between the United States and Japan began a downward spiral in July 1941. Late in the month, French authorities were pressured into agreeing to allow Japanese forces to occupy all of Indochina. Forty thousand troops poured into the southern part of the colony in less than a week to establish bases. Japanese warships moved into Camranh Bay and other southern ports.[23] The arrangement provided an ideal staging area for an attack on the long coveted Southern Resources Area and completed the partial surrounding of the Philippines by Japanese territory on three sides in the shape of a horseshoe.

The advance into southern Indochina served to stir many Americans out of their isolationist slumber into thinking that Japan's aggression had gone far enough.[24] President Roosevelt swiftly issued an executive order freezing all Japanese assets in the United States. An important outcome of the order was cutting off oil and other strategic materials that the Japanese war machine needed to operate.[25]

The oil embargo created an immediate and unparalleled crisis for the Japanese, who were heavily dependent on American petroleum. The ban was supported by the British and Dutch, meaning Japan would have to rely on her own limited oil reserves. The crisis could only be resolved through diplomacy or war, and many Japanese leaders favored the latter.[26] Japanese Ambassador Nomura Kichisaburo began negotiations with United States Secretary of State Cordell Hull in Washington. Their meetings continued throughout most of the remainder of 1941 in an attempt to avoid a war. He was joined in November by special envoy Saburō Kurusu. The pair carried out their fateful diplomatic duties, unknowing of the secret war planning already underway in Japan.

Roosevelt made additional moves in the wake of the oil embargo, including sending more supplies into China through Burma and recalling Douglas MacArthur to active service in the United States Army. The retired general and World War I hero was serving as a military advisor to the Philippine Commonwealth president. MacArthur's new role was to oversee a rush buildup of land and air forces in the Philippines.

Chapter 4

Sailors aboard *Marblehead* could see the Tarakan Light Ship shortly after completing a routine crew muster on the morning of November 29, 1941. The beacon served as a guide for vessels nearing the small island off the northeast coast of Borneo. Tarakan Island was home to a town of the same name and a small airfield. The island itself was small, with an area of only about twenty-five square miles, but it contained about 700 oil wells and some related refining facilities. The wells could produce 5,000 barrels of crude a day – a tremendous output for the time.[1] The oil was a high-quality, clean-burning fuel with a greenish tint. The fuel was suitable for large warships with minimal, or according to some oil experts no, refining.

All engines were stopped at 8.35 am to allow a pilot to climb aboard to guide the warship through the outer channel. The long-standing naval custom called for a local sailor, with expert knowledge of a harbor area or waterway, to take over the controls of a large ship arriving at an unfamiliar port. Two additional Dutch harbor guides boarded a short time later.

The light cruiser was soon joined by the Dutch minelayer *Prins van Oranje*. The American ship took up a position about 600 yards behind the smaller vessel.[2] The minelayer guided *Marblehead* past a defensive minefield as the ships navigated the narrow channel separating the island from mainland Borneo. The details of Tarakan slowly became visible has *Marblehead* moved closer to land and eventually into a harbor area. The anchorage was located on the southwestern part of the island adjacent to the town of Linkas. The coastal village served as a small port for loading oil tankers – clearly evident by the numerous oil storage tanks located in the immediate area. Slopes covered with dense jungle gradually rose from beyond the town. The hills were covered with tall trees described

21

in an oil trade magazine as 'magnificent in their stateliness and variety, with brilliantly green foliage'.[3]

By 11.30 am *Marblehead* was settling into a mooring position with sailors using large manila lines to secure her port side to the dock. A local Dutch military officer paid the vessel a short visit about an hour later. It was nothing more than a typical courtesy call commonly made when a ship arrives in a foreign port. In addition to the minelayer and four American destroyers arriving with *Marblehead*, two Dutch submarines were also in the harbor. The light cruiser began loading aboard fuel from the plentiful oil supply a short time later.

A small group of sailors left *Marblehead* just after 4.00 pm to act as a temporary shore patrol. The standard practice was to be repeated nightly while in port to help keep sailors going ashore in line and out of trouble. The movement signaled the start of liberty – an age-old practice of sailors going ashore to spend some time off duty. Larger ports typically offered of variety of recreational opportunities – including drinking establishments and houses of ill-repute. However, it was not to be the case here. The *Marblehead* men going ashore found Linkas to be a small town with limited amenities for foreign sailors. Some of the officers visited the Dutch Navy Officers Club, where the drink of choice was gin and the company included sailors from the two Dutch submarines in port.[4]

Captain Robinson's orders of what to do at Tarakan were somewhat vague. Admiral Hart's instructions were for the ships to travel there 'for fuel, but to have difficulty in obtaining full loads – with a view to occupying the ports, or vicinity, for a protracted period of time'.[5]

How much fuel a warship had the capacity to store and how quickly it was used up played a critical role in naval deployments, especially during wartime conditions. A ship of *Marblehead*'s type could hold a maximum of 2,068 tons of fuel oil giving her a top range of 10,000 miles at fifteen knots.[6] However, the warship normally operated at faster speeds, burning up more fuel. The proximity of friendly ports and tankers was an important factor in every voyage. It was clear Admiral Hart wanted *Marblehead* to be near a ready source of fuel should hostilities begin. The arrangement meant one less thing for Captain Robinson to worry about in the tension-filled Pacific.

The port facilities at Linkas were limited, requiring *Marblehead* to shift births after taking aboard fuel. The American sailors kept busy with daily matters, such as crew musters, routine inspections, liberty, and other training exercises. The coming days saw the destroyers rotating positions at the fuel docks and conducting patrols outside of the harbor entrance.

***

A small group of veteran officers holding *Marblehead*'s senior leadership positions would be responsible for leading the light cruiser into battle should a conflict erupt in the Pacific. At 49, Captain Arthur Granville Robinson was an experienced officer with decades of naval service under his belt, including two stays in the Far East. Robinson was born on May 21, 1892, in Brooklyn, New York.[7] He was appointed to the United States Naval Academy in Annapolis, Maryland, from his home state in 1909.

Robinson's first assignment, after graduating from the academy in 1913, was on a battleship in keeping with a long-standing naval tradition. In the days before the ascent of naval aviation, the big gun ships still dominated the navy and newly graduated officers typically began their naval service aboard one. Robinson was assigned to *Delaware*. He transferred to the armored cruiser *Montana* in May 1917. The old ship was performing convoy escort duty in the Atlantic at the time, operating out of Hampton Roads, Virginia, New York, and Halifax, Nova Scotia.[8] The young officer was serving aboard her when the United States entered World War I in 1918.

Robinson's first ship command was of the destroyer *Robinson* in 1920. She was named after a Revolutionary War era naval hero of unrelated ancestry. The next two decades found the officer serving in a variety of capacities on both land and at sea. He twice spent time in the Far East as part of the Asiatic Fleet. The first duty in the Orient spanned the years 1924 to 1927 when he served aboard the ships *Preble* (destroyer), *Monocacy* (gunboat), and *Palos* (gunboat). After completing several years of stateside duty, he again returned to the Asiatic Fleet in the mid-1930s. Robinson was assigned to *Luzon* in 1934 when the gunboat was conducting patrols on the Yangtze River in China. He slowly rose in rank as he alternated between ship and shore assignments.

Now an experienced mid-level officer, Robinson was given command of *Marblehead* in May 1940 after completing several years of stateside duty in Washington, DC. His only previous cruiser experience came as the navigator aboard the heavy cruiser *Salt Lake City* shortly after she was commissioned near the end of 1929.[9] His new warship was already serving as part of the Asiatic Fleet at the time.

Standing at Robinson's side was a capable executive officer serving as his second in command. Commander William Bernard Goggins was born in the small town of Republic, Washington on September 10, 1898.[10] He attended the University of Washington in Seattle for one semester before accepting an appointment to the Naval Academy in 1916. He was a member of the swim team and participated in track and field during his time at the academy.

Goggins became an ensign upon his graduation in June of 1919. He reported for duty aboard the battleship *Idaho* during the same month. A long list of assignments followed throughout the 1920s and 1930s, including duty aboard several destroyers, additional studies at Yale University, and time aboard the battleship *Arizona*.[11] The assignments gave him a broad level of experience across many functional areas on ships, including navigation and radio operations.

Goggins was stationed at the Naval Academy from 1939 to 1941 before orders sent him to *Marblehead* as the executive officer. The 43-year-old officer had worked his way up to the rank of commander over the previous twenty years. He had completed two stints of duty aboard cruisers, both in the 1930s, spending time on the heavy cruiser *Augusta* and the light cruiser *Trenton*, a sister of *Marblehead*. Goggins was not aboard the warship for long when she made the voyage to Tarakan, having reported for duty on August 3, 1941.[12] The role of executive officer was a position often considered to be the captain's right hand. Goggin's wide variety of experience – both on land and at sea – was to serve him well during the next few months aboard the light cruiser.

***

War fears among the area population were plainly clear to the American sailors ashore in Linkas. It was no surprise, given the backdrop of Pacific tensions. Many locals expected the valuable oil region to be among the first targets for invasion by the Japanese in any upcoming conflict. The area beaches were rigged with cables designed to be barriers against sea-borne invasion. An occasional pillbox and gun emplacement was scattered behind the beach barricades. Perhaps comforting to the local residents, the meager defenses were unlikely to slow a determined invader. War posters were visible at various scattered locations around town. Many featured pictures of British Prime Minister Winston Churchill. The British became hosts of the Dutch government in exile shortly after the Netherlands surrendered to German invaders in May of 1940. Blackout conditions were in place throughout the town during the night hours.

A full-blown invasion scare had already taken place at Tarakan during the middle of November after the Netherlands East Indies government authorities received information the Japanese were planning a surprise invasion of either Tarakan or the Portuguese island of Timor. The latter was positioned just north of Australia, over 900 miles southeast of Tarakan. A high level of vigilance was maintained in the aftermath of the report. Dutch reconnaissance planes swept the waters off the west coast of Borneo after naval officials received information on December 1 of Japanese warships massing off the British side of the island.[13] No sign of Japanese ships was found and the report was deemed to be a false alarm. However, the episode only added to the general unease in the area.

The Dutch had been concerned about a possible Japanese attack for almost a decade. Japanese diplomat Toshio Shiratori bought up the topic publicly in 1933 stating 'the Japanese Navy would seize the Netherlands East Indies oil fields immediately on the outbreak of war, no matter who the enemy might be'.[14] The early December false alarm was enough for Dutch authorities to send an urgent message to all their naval ships in the region advising that the situation in the Pacific was critical. Warships were to immediately prepare for wartime conditions and possible action. The warning noted it was no drill.[15]

The light cruiser *Marblehead* and her four accompanying destroyers remained at Tarakan as 1941 began its final month. All the sailors could do was to wait for developments on the world stage. One destroyer man later recalled the time as 'a sort of suspended animation'.[16] The wait for developments, however, would be a short one.

Chapter 5

Half a world away from *Marblehead*'s location in the Pacific, the negotiations in Washington, DC, between Secretary of State Cordell Hull and Japanese envoys on a possible settlement to the oil embargo were not going well. President Roosevelt was meeting regularly with his team of key military and foreign policy advisors to discuss the crisis in the Pacific. The group included: Hull, Secretary of War Henry Stimson, Secretary of the Navy Frank Knox, Army Chief of Staff General George Marshall, and Chief of Naval Operations Admiral Harold Stark. Roosevelt understood the key principles of sea power and was a strong supporter of the navy. Having served as the assistant secretary of the navy during World War I, he often referred to the service as 'my navy', and knew the ships would likely bear the brunt of fighting in case of a war with Japan.

The American leaders held a secret upper-hand in the negotiations. American cryptanalysts had been deciphering the most secure Japanese diplomatic codes since late 1940. Roosevelt and his top advisors consequently knew the negotiations were likely going to be unsuccessful and that Japan was preparing for war in the near term.[1] However, the information was far from complete and not all the key findings were disseminated to the frontline commanders in the Pacific in a timely manner. The codebreakers had not yet cracked the Japanese military codes, so the details of any attack planning were not known.

In late November, a report of a large Japanese expeditionary force moving south after departing Shanghai reached Roosevelt. Threatening information continued to pour into Washington from various sources of Japanese troop build-ups and ship movements. With negotiations seemingly at an impasse, Admiral Stark sent out a message on November 24 to his commanders in the Pacific – Admiral Hart and Commander in Chief of the Pacific Fleet Admiral Husband Kimmel – warning of 'surprise and aggressive movements' by Japan.[2]

Stark sent a more detailed alert to the same commanders three days later on November 27. 'This dispatch is to be considered a war warning. Negotiations with Japan looking toward stabilization of conditions in the Pacific have ceased. An aggressive move by Japan is expected within the next few days,' the ominous message began.[3] The message also warned of Japanese naval movements afoot and possible amphibious attacks on Thailand, Malaya, Borneo, or the Philippines. Stark directed the naval commanders to 'Execute an appropriate defensive deployment preparatory to carrying out the tasks assigned in WPL 46,' essentially, get ready to employ the war plan. A Japanese carrier force was already at sea en route to Hawaii when the message was dispatched.

The Japanese military was secretly in the final preparations for a series of bold attacks, even as the diplomats continued their meeting in Washington. The preparations were the culmination of months of training and planning. The Japanese war strategy centered on two important tasks: securing the Southern Resources Area and establishing a large defensive perimeter across the Pacific to protect against counterattack.[4] The resources were to adequately supply the military and economy with oil and other critical materials. Japanese Admiral Isoroku Yamamoto, serving as the Commander in Chief of the Combined Fleet, insisted on an opening strike against the United States to keep its navy from hindering the southern operations. He planned a surprise attack to cripple the American Pacific Fleet at Pearl Harbor to be immediately followed by a series of moves against the Philippines, Malaya, the Netherlands East Indies, and elsewhere.

The strategy was highly risky in that it would spread Japanese military assets thinly across the Pacific, while fighting three new enemies simultaneously – the Americans, British, and Dutch. Admiral Yamamoto had first-hand knowledge of the United States from past travels and understood the latent power of the nation.[5] He had no illusions of Japan winning a protracted war with America and knew that the best scenario was to score a series of quick victories before the American industrial capacity could take over. At the same time, Western leaders underestimated Japan's military capabilities. Few believed the Japanese could launch more than one or two major attacks at once.[6] The assumption proved to be a tragic miscalculation.

A mobile strike force built around six large aircraft carriers slipped out of Hitokappu Bay in the Kurile Islands north of Japan disappearing into the foggy sea for the long voyage to Hawaii. The operation was the culmination of months of secret planning. The group adhered to strict radio silence after departing from Japanese waters on November 26. Invasion troops, transports, warships, and aircraft were gathering in Formosa, Indochina, and on Hainan Island off the southern coast of China for the southern attacks.

The Philippines were of no importance to the Japanese in terms of natural resources, but leaving an American territory with military bases unchecked as its forces advance south was not a viable strategic option. The Commonwealth would be subdued, but the operation was largely a sideshow for the main attacks on Malaya and the Netherlands East Indies.[7] Decades of American war planners had been correct in anticipating a Japanese attack on the Philippines, but the Pearl Harbor strike was a complete surprise.

***

Back in Manila, Admiral Hart continued to prepare his small fleet for battle by focusing on logistics, command and control, and reconnaissance. The oilers *Trinity* and *Pecos* were made ready for departure as their services could be critical if the larger warships were to operate far from the Manila area for an extended period of time. Ammunition, spare parts, and other stores were loaded aboard various support vessels, including the submarine tender *Canopus*.

The admiral felt the best way to address the command structure was to separate the strategic and tactical command aspects of the fleet. He decided to handle the overall command and administration duties himself and to keep those functions ashore, even after the hostilities began. Hart planned to continue operating from his headquarters in Manila, where he could work closely with army leaders and keep open lines of communication among his forces and those of potential allies. Rear Admiral William Purnell became his Chief of Staff.

Allied planning in the Pacific remained in a fluid state with no formal mutual defense agreement among the American, British, and Dutch. However, the three nations had exchanged naval liaison officers, with a

British and Dutch naval representative arriving in Manila disguised as shipping control officers. They quickly began working with American counterparts on reviewing cryptographic aids, developing radio procedures, and other tactical strategies.[8]

Hart established Task Force 5, comprised of his larger warships, to better address the tactical issues of his fleet. The force was to move south in wartime for operations, hopefully offensive in nature, with the British and Dutch. Rear Admiral William Glassford was appointed the task force commander. Glassford was in China commanding the remaining small river gunboats and only returned to Manila about a week before the war started.

Patrol planes were one of the few assets not in short supply for the Asiatic Fleet. Admiral Hart's command included a squadron of PBY Catalinas. The large twin-engine seaplanes had limited offensive capabilities, but were ideal for reconnaissance. With army aircraft handling scouting missions north of the Philippines towards Formosa, Hart used his planes to keep an eye on the Japanese to the west, beginning in the first days of December. The slow, but rugged, long-range Catalinas were ideal for the role.

The main area of Hart's interest was Cam Ranh Bay, a deep-water anchorage on the southern coast of Indochina (now in the country of Vietnam), about 830 miles west-southwest of Manila. 'The instructions were to avoid being sighted from the coast, or by Japanese ships, if practical,' Hart later wrote. 'The PBYs were sighted at times by Japanese planes but they were not attacked.' The flights revealed the harbor filled with 20–30 medium or large ships and numerous small craft, with fighter planes patrolling overhead. Hart reported his findings to Washington and noted, 'it became clear that strong Japanese amphibious expeditions were prepared to move'.[9]

Ever cognizant of the deteriorating conditions on the diplomatic front, Hart met with his senior commanders in late November to notify them of his decision to put the initial phase of the war plan into effect – the movement of key ships out of Manila Harbor to safer waters to the south. The plan included issuing orders to Captain Robinson to lead the contingent of warships to Borneo. 'I have secretly informed the Dutch Admiral of this move, but no one else so you should make your visit appear as much as possible to be of a routine nature,' the admiral said. Hart concluded the meeting with, 'If everything goes well in Washington

I will call you back in a couple of weeks. Otherwise, goodbye, good luck and God bless you.'[10]

The deck log records Hart came aboard *Marblehead* during the afternoon of November 24.[11] The visit could have been to speak to Robinson further about his voyage, or just to provide some additional good wishes before the departure. The admiral held *Marblehead* in high regard. 'She was an old ship, but her personal [*sic*] always made the best of what they had and this cruiser could always be depended upon,' he later wrote.[12] The light cruiser left Manila Harbor the next day.

A British admiral came to Manila to visit Hart as the American admiral was continuing preparations for war. The afternoon of December 2 saw the arrival in Singapore of a new group of British ships to the Pacific. Force Z was comprised of the battleship *Prince of Wales*, battlecruiser *Repulse*, and four destroyers under the command of Vice Admiral Sir Tom Phillips. Winston Churchill sent the warships to the Far Eastern Fleet to deter further Japanese aggression. The *Prince of Wales* was a new modern battleship, already famous for dueling with the German battleship *Bismarck* in the Atlantic six months earlier. The battlecruiser *Repulse* was an aged warship of World War I vintage that underwent modernization in the 1930s. The new aircraft carrier *Indomitable* was slated to arrive with the force, but ran aground in the Caribbean and was undergoing repairs.

Admiral Phillips became commander of British naval forces in the Far East upon his arrival in the Pacific. Additional forces were presumably to be sent to the Pacific in the near future. A few days later he traveled by air to the Philippines arriving in Manila on December 5. Hart had a favorable impression of his visitor and later noted Phillips made the visit 'at his own initiative', and that 'his presence in Manila was a carefully guarded secret'. After meeting with General MacArthur, who boasted about his military buildup, growing air power, and ability to turn back a Japanese assault, the two admirals conferred on a range of topics related to the current naval situation in the region. The discussions included the prospect of British ships using Manila Bay as a forward operating base in the future. However, it was unclear if the British were going to move away from their convoy strategy to a more offensive mindset. Phillips asked Hart to send some destroyers to Singapore to operate with his capital ships.[13]

Both naval leaders found the meeting useful and a joint statement was sent to both governments.

A Japanese expeditionary force was already at sea as the two admirals met in Manila. A convoy of fourteen transports, accompanied by escorts, slipped out of Hainan Island off the southern coast of China on December 2. Foul weather helped obscure their voyage south along the Indochina coast. The convoy grew as additional vessels joined over subsequent days, most likely from Cam Ranh Bay. An Australian reconnaissance plane flying from Malaya sighted the group on December 6, radioing that the ships were headed east – towards the Gulf of Thailand.[14] Possible destinations included the Thai capital Bangkok, portions of Thailand further south on the Malaya Peninsula, or Malaya itself.

The conference ended abruptly when Phillips received the alarming news. The British admiral departed for Singapore by seaplane during the evening of December 6. Hart committed to providing the destroyers just prior to Phillips leaving – literally talking to him on the dock. 'I have just ordered my destroyers at Balikpapan to proceed to Batavia on the pretext of rest and leave,' Hart told him. 'Actually, they will join your force.'[15]

The Asiatic Fleet received an unexpected, but most welcome, reinforcement just days before the start of the war in the form of the light cruiser *Boise*. She arrived in Manila on December 4 after escorting a small supply convoy across the Pacific.[16] The light cruiser was scheduled to accompany a tanker back to Hawaii, but was unable to depart prior to the start of hostilities and was temporarily incorporated into the Asiatic Fleet. She was a modern warship, built in the late 1930s, with a powerful main battery of fifteen 6-inch guns, and strong secondary armament. Her 6-inch guns were of a newer design than those on *Marblehead* and could provide an almost continuous rapid fire. Most importantly, *Boise* was the only warship in the Asiatic Fleet equipped with radar.

Admiral Hart had considered deviating from the longstanding strategy of moving his larger ships south when the war started. He instead sought to keep his entire fleet in the Philippines using Manila Bay as an operating base citing, among other reasons, no formal joint operating agreement with the British and Dutch and the ongoing buildup of American forces in the region.[17] However, the change of plans was denied by Admiral Stark in Washington on November 20.

Hart then dispatched *Marblehead* and accompanying destroyers to Borneo. In early December, he sent his flagship *Houston* and the newly arrived *Boise* to waters in the southern Philippines.

***

No notable events took place aboard *Marblehead* during the first week of December 1941 as she remained at Tarakan in the company of her escorting destroyers. Her sailors performed a variety of routine duties – steering gear was tested and found to be in good working order, daily magazine inspections were made to ensure the ammunition storage areas were free of any potential hazards, a general quarters drill was conducted, discipline was handed out to a crewman for a minor infraction, and a catapult was test fired and determined to be problem free. A small group of her officers paid a courtesy visit to the Dutch minelayer *Prins van Oranje*.

An ominous message made its way to *Marblehead* on December 4 from the Chief of Naval Operations office in Washington via the Asiatic Fleet headquarters. It reported 'highly reliable information has been received' of urgent instructions having been sent to Japanese diplomatic posts in various world cities to destroy codebooks, ciphers, and to burn confidential documents. The locations included London, Washington, and Hong Kong. Handwritten notes on the message document indicates only Captain Robinson and Executive Officer Goggins were shown the message that was marked secret.[18]

The information could only mean one thing – war was coming very soon. Captain Robinson took immediate action. Shore liberty was cancelled. He ordered two boilers be kept lit at all times, meaning the ship would have enough available power to get underway on thirty minutes' notice.[19] All gun crews were to be ready to man their weapons within five minutes. Radio communications were carefully monitored around the clock with all messages transcribed, whether addressed to *Marblehead* or not. Communications officers were either sleeping on the bridge or just outside the coding room to be able to quickly interpret any urgent messages.[20]

Lieutenant Commander Nicholas Van Bergen made his regular inspection of *Marblehead*'s guns on the morning of December 5. At 42 years old and with a weathered face, the officer was a career navy man with two decades of service. Van Bergen reported aboard the light cruiser on August 28, 1941, after a stint as the commanding office of the destroyer *Monaghan*.[21] He served as *Marblehead*'s gunnery officer. Sailors manned their gunnery stations as Van Bergen made the rounds about the ship, starting with the 6-inch guns.

The operation of the main battery required a team of crewmen working seamlessly together. Directly below each of the twin 6-inch gun turrets was a barbette (lightly armored tube) connected to a magazine (ammunition storage area) and handling room below. Sailors placed shells and bags of gunpowder onto to a hoist that carried the ammunition up through the barbette. Gunners inside the turret rammed the two components into the guns for firing. Each time a 6-inch gun fired aboard *Marblehead*, a 105-pound armor-piercing shell was sent hurling towards the target.[22] The inspection also included a review of the warships smaller anti-aircraft guns. The gunnery crews passed muster as Van Bergen found all aspects of the guns to be in good working order.

The next day it was time for Captain Robinson to conduct his weekly Saturday morning inspection. The captain's review covered the entire warship, with the commanding officer walking in the company of some senior officers. Chief Boatswain's Mate Harvey Anderson had his deck crew complete a quick cleaning in advance of the inspection. The review was over by the middle of the day and the *Marblehead* sailors filled the mess for lunch.

***

Admiral Hart was exhausted by mid-afternoon on Sunday, December 7, and needed a break (both the Philippines and Borneo were one day behind Pearl Harbor, due to the location west of the International Dateline). He had done everything in his power to prepare his small fleet for a war he knew was coming soon. The admiral fully expected 'the bubble will burst any time'.[23] The tired admiral decided some golf was the best medicine. He traveled to the Manila Golf Club north of the city for a round with Admiral Purnell.

Tropical heat and humidity was in full force as *Marblehead* lay at anchor off the coast of Tarakan in what was to be an uneventful day. Crewmen ate a delicious fried chicken meal with ice cream for desert.

Sailors not on duty idled their Sunday away; two junior officers listened to a classical music record in a cabin. Some enlisted men wrote letters home. Boatswain's Mate First Class Homer Percifield took time to inventory the supply of stamps while manning the ships small post office.[24]

Strong tides in the harbor area had been noted over the last few days, raising concerns about the nearby minefield and prompting a sharp lookout to be maintained over the waters all around the ship.[25] The high level of vigilance paid off when the only excitement occurred late in the day when lookouts sighted a floating mine about 8,000 yards off the warship's starboard side, after apparently having broken free from the nearby defensive field. A Dutch patrol boat recovered it about an hour later.[26] The sailors aboard *Marblehead* were, unknowingly, enjoying their last day at peace.

PART II

PACIFIC IN FLAMES

Chapter 6

The large formation of Japanese planes first appeared off the northern tip of the Hawaiian Island of Oahu at about 7.40 am on December 7, 1941. The sunrise marked the start of a bright and fair Sunday. The first attack wave of 183 planes came from the six aircraft carriers plying the waters about 275 miles due north of the island. The Japanese Strike Force remained undetected while completing the long journey east across the Pacific. The approaching aircraft were discovered by a rudimentary early warning radar, but were dismissed as a scheduled flight of B-17 heavy bombers due to arrive from the United States.[1]

The attackers divided into smaller groups as the planes roared over the lush green island. Forty-nine high-level bombers armed with 1,600-lb battleship shells converted into armor-piercing bombs, forty planes carrying specially modified torpedoes designed to work in shallow water, and fifty-one dive bombers equipped with 500-pound bombs. Forty-three fighters provided cover.[2] The planes approached Pearl Harbor form the north and west. The sprawling naval and air facility was home port to the Pacific Fleet and served as the bastion of American naval power in the Pacific.

The attack began at 7.55 am. The sporadic clusters of clouds did little to obscure the fliers' view of the scores of ships scattered around the harbor below. The morning calm was rapidly replaced by rumbling explosions as American sailors and airmen were taken by complete surprise. A focal point of the attack was Ford Island, centrally located in the middle of the harbor area, home to a naval air station and serving as a mooring point for a variety of warships. Seven battleships neatly anchored along the southeast part of the island, in what has become widely known as 'Battleship Row', made easy targets. The area quickly became the scene of great devastation.

Just minutes into the attack, an armor-piercing bomb glanced off a turret on the battleship *Arizona* before penetrating deep into the innards of the ship exploding the magazines. A catastrophic explosion ripped apart the forward part of the ship and started a raging fire that kept burning for two days. Almost 80 per cent, or 1,177 of the 1,512, sailors aboard perished – more than half of the total casualties for the entire attack.[3] The flagship of the Pacific Fleet, battleship *Pennsylvania*, was damaged in a nearby drydock. Various airfields around the island were also hit, include the army's Wheeler Field and Hickam Field, as well as the Kaneohe Naval Air Station. Most American planes, some clustered together wingtip to wingtip to better guard against sabotage, were destroyed on the ground.

It only took a few minutes for Lieutenant Commander Logan Ramsey to realize Pearl Harbor was under attack. The officer was on duty at the command center on Ford Island when he witnessed a Japanese bomb explode in a hangar area at 7.57 am. He ran to the nearby radio room and ordered all the radio operators on duty to send out a plain language flash message. 'Air Raid, Pearl Harbor. This is not drill.' was sent streaming across the airwaves.[4] The message reverberated around the navy and shook the United States like no time since the start of the Civil War.

Secretary of the Navy Frank Knox was in disbelief when he first saw the message in Washington. 'My God! This can't be true, this must mean the Philippines!'[5] He immediately phoned President Roosevelt with the shocking news. The Japanese had planned to deliver a formal declaration of war to American officials in the capitol just before the strike. However, the message was delayed and did not arrive until Pearl Harbor was already under attack.[6]

A second wave of planes struck Pearl Harbor about an hour after the first. The attackers were met with a higher level of anti-aircraft fire than before, but the subsequent wave did little additional damage.[7] Two critical areas on shore were not targeted by the Japanese and escaped serious damage – oil storage tanks and repair facilities. The three aircraft carriers assigned to the Pacific Fleet were not in port at the time of the attack and escaped destruction.

The overall damage to the American military was devastating. The battle fleet was wrecked and airpower crippled. Nineteen warships, including eight battleships, were sunk or damaged and 2,403 personnel were killed. Total aircraft losses for the army and navy combined amounted 179 planes destroyed and 159 damaged.[8] Japanese losses were minimal compared to the destruction inflicted: twenty-nine planes and five midget submarines. The Japanese carrier force slipped away undetected to the west.

***

The Asiatic Fleet headquarters in the Philippines was lightly staffed during the overnight hours, something not uncommon during peacetime conditions. Marine Lieutenant Colonel William Clement was the duty officer at the center of operations in the Marsman Building during the early morning hours of December 8, 1941. His radio operator received the Pearl Harbor air raid message at 2.53 am. The unofficial message was later followed by an official dispatch from the Navy Department. He immediately phoned Thomas Hart. The admiral was asleep at his residence in the nearby Manila Hotel. 'Admiral, put some cold water on your face. I am coming over with a message,' Clement exclaimed.[9] He arrived at Hart's residence, located about 300 yards away from the Marsman Building, a short time later.

The admiral was sitting bedside as he deciphered the news and quickly drafted a short message for Clement to send out to the entire Asiatic Fleet. 'Japan started hostilities. Govern yourselves accordingly.' The dispatch went out by radio just after 3.00 am.[10] Hart's thoughts immediately went to his scattered fleet. 'Timing was bad for us, still evacuating from China; setting up Glassford in command of cruisers and destroyers – with his outfit scattered over a thousand miles. Reorganizing the submarines, incident to my last reinforcement,' he later wrote.[11]

Hart arrived at his headquarters at about 4.00 am He dispatched Admiral Purnell to notify General McArthur's command, who had not yet heard the news. The admiral and his subordinates then went about getting ready to fight a war.

Most of the ships in Task Force 5, organized to be the fleet's main surface fighting force, were scattered among four locations and the group's leader was still in Manila. Aside from *Marblehead* and her accompanying destroyers at Tarakan, the tender *Black Hawk* and some destroyers were still further south on the Borneo coast at Balikpapan. The groups other heavy units were well south of Manila, but more than 600 miles northeast from *Marblehead*'s position. The heavy cruiser

Houston, designated as the task force's flagship, was at Iloilo on the Philippine island of Panay. The newly arrived *Boise* was at Cebu, about ninety miles southwest of *Houston*. Hart knew it was critical for both warships to get out of the Philippines before Japanese planes struck.

Admiral Glassford had only recently returned to the Philippines from China. He quickly departed Manila Bay with his staff on December 8 aboard a PBY bound for Iloilo, arriving late in the afternoon. The heavy cruiser left port as soon as Glassford and his staff were safely aboard. Lookouts later reported anti-aircraft fire and a vessel on fire in Iloilo Harbor. The Japanese apparently knew of *Houston*'s location and sent planes to sink her, but instead hit a helpless freighter. The enemy missed the cruiser by about an hour. As the warship steamed south during the evening hours, her sailors tuned in as Radio Tokyo boasted of *Houston*'s sinking in Iloilo Harbor.[12] The flagship was later joined by *Boise* after the light cruiser slipped out of Cebu without incident.

Admiral Hart remained in Manila, intent on deploying his submarines and remaining assets in defense of the Philippines. He ordered three large auxiliary ships out of Manila Bay and away from possible damage from Japanese air attacks. The tankers *Trinity*, *Pecos*, and the aircraft tender *Langley* all sailed south to join the forces under Glassford's command. The admiral did not know what the future held for his small fleet, but he vowed, 'we have to do our best and we shall'.[13]

***

Lieutenant (Junior Grade) Jasper MacDonald was sleeping on the deck outside of the radio room during the early morning hours of Monday, December 8, as *Marblehead* lay at anchor in Tarakan Harbor. The assistant communications officer was exhausted after spending the day ashore meeting with Dutch officials. He had previously warned Ensign Robert Fahnestock, who was monitoring communications while on duty just inside the radio room, not to wake him unless the message was very important.

The most important message *Marblehead* was to receive in a long time came through at 3.15 am in the form of Admiral Hart's urgent note about the start of hostilities.[14] After only brief hesitation, he woke MacDonald saying 'Mac, I think this is important.'[15] MacDonald took a quick look before rushing the message down to William Goggins.

The executive officer was up and had been looking over some maps of the area. He ordered the general quarters alarm to be sounded.

The ringing alarm and an accompanying loudspeaker announcement telling sailors to man their battle stations, jolted sleeping sailors awake. The continuous drills had conditioned the men well, so there was no hesitation. Each sailor was assigned a specific post for battle conditions. They rushed to put on shoes and shirts and rubbed the sleep out of their eyes, all while rushing to their battle stations. Hundreds of men were moving across every corner of the ship simultaneously. 'This is it. This is the real thing,' Goggins told some officers arriving on the bridge.[16]

Once all the stations were manned, the loudspeaker broke the news of the war starting by repeating Admiral Hart's message. Sailors all throughout the ship paused to listen. The crew was also notified that *Marblehead* would be getting under way at dawn. Speculation was rampant about what would happen next. Where were they going? Were the Japanese going to attack Tarakan? A radio message from the Secretary of the Navy in Washington came in at 3.48 am 'Execute WPL Forty-Six against Japan.'[17] The American war plan was officially put into effect.

The next couple of hours were spent getting the warship ready for departure. Additional boilers were lit and eventually cut into the main steam line. A Dutch seaplane took off shortly after 5.00 am to investigate the area outside of the harbor. Sailors began loosening the large manila lines holding the light cruiser to the dock and the harbor pilot climbed aboard.

The Dutch minelayer *Prins van Oranje* was the first warship to get underway to lead the American ships past the minefields and safely out of the harbor area. At 5.34 am *Marblehead* started moving directly behind her and through the mine-swept channel.[18] The destroyers *Stewart*, *Parrott*, *Barker*, and *Paul Jones* immediately followed in column.

Captain Robinson's orders were to go south to Balikpapan and await further instructions, but initially his small fleet was sailing into the unknown. A young officer aboard the destroyer *Stewart* later remembered the time: 'It was both scary and exciting,' Lieutenant (Junior Grade) Lodwick Alford wrote. 'For all we knew the whole damned Japanese fleet might be just outside the harbor entrance ready to blow us to kingdom come.'[19] A more realistic threat might have been a Japanese submarine lurking in the immediate area, or the arrival of some enemy planes. There were no Japanese naval or air forces of any type waiting off Tarakan. The Dutch plane slowly passed overhead blinking out 'good luck' as the procession of ships headed out to sea.[20]

After a short stop to discharge the harbor pilot, *Marblehead* proceeded away from Tarakan at a speed of 15 knots. The ships went through a heavy rain squall before passing the Tarakan Light Ship about 340 yards off the port side. The destroyers moved to an anti-submarine screen around *Marblehead* as the formation headed in a south-easterly direction. Speed was increased to 25 knots just before 8.00 am. The destroyers *Barker* and *Paul Jones* left the formation a short time later on orders from Admiral Hart to proceed north to link up with *Houston*.

The news about the Pearl Harbor attack eventually came trickling in as *Marblehead* and the two remaining destroyers moved south, but the full scope of the disaster was not yet known. Tense lookouts intently scanned the sky and sea for any sign of planes, ships, or periscopes. Various small Dutch craft were sighted throughout the day. The ships traveled south, occasionally zig-zagging, to enter the Makassar Strait separating Borneo from the nearby island of Celebes. Passage into the southern hemisphere occurred without fanfare as *Marblehead* crossed the equator at 4.49 pm. There was simply no time for the sometimes lavish ceremony often done during peacetime to initiate the sailors aboard who were making their first crossing. Continuing south, she went to darkened conditions as the light of the first day of war faded.

Chapter 7

The Japanese unleashed a series of simultaneous attacks across the Pacific in the hours and days following the devastating raid on Pearl Harbor. The actions were part of the overall Japanese plan to shield the move into the Southern Resources Area and to establish a defensive perimeter in the Pacific. Three important American and British possessions were struck within hours of the Hawaii attack. The British Crown Colony of Hong Kong was attacked from occupied China. The garrison included British, Indian, and Canadian soldiers, as well as some local volunteers, but the ground troops were without air cover. The outnumbered defenders surrendered on Christmas Day after putting up a stout fight.

Nestled among the Japanese-held Mariana Islands, Guam was the sole American possession in the area and an easy target for invasion. A naval disarmament treaty signed between the world wars did not permit the island to be fortified. The small number of defenders, a mix of American and local forces, were armed with nothing larger than light machine guns. The Japanese took control of the island on December 10 after only a brief fight.

Wake Island was a lonely American possession, barely above sea level, positioned about 2,300 miles west of Hawaii. The small land mass was much closer to the Japanese-held Marshall Islands than any American territory. Unlike Guam, Wake was well defended by a garrison built around a contingent of marines. Defenses included heavy gun emplacements, a variety of machine guns, and a squadron of fighter planes. The initial attack came from the air when a group of twin-engine bombers flying from the Marshalls struck the island. The defenders were ready when the Japanese attempted to land on the morning of December 11. The initial attack was repulsed with two enemy destroyers sunk for good measure. Additional air attacks pummeled the defenders, destroying the last remaining American fighter planes. A second landing resulted in the surrender of the island on December 23, just after an American relief attempt was aborted.

Attacks also took place against American and British property in China. Japanese troops swiftly took control of the International Settlement in Shanghai and the American river gunboat *Wake* – the only American warship to be seized intact during World War II.[1] The latter was one of the few remaining American vessels remaining in Chinese waters. The small contingent of marines still in the area surrendered. Only after Japanese attacks were underway in China, Hong Kong, Malaya, Wake, and Guam, – almost noon Tokyo time – did the Japanese issue a formal declaration of war against the United States.[2]

***

The crew aboard *Marblehead* went to general quarters during the early morning hours of December 9. The exercise, customary in peacetime, took on a greater importance in wartime as a precaution against a surprise attack during the first hours of daylight. She occasionally changed from her base course on the voyage south to zig-zagging as a safeguard against any possible lurking submarines that might escape detection by the two destroyers.

By 8.43 am, *Marblehead* was lying 450 yards off the Balikpapan Light Ship waiting for the harbor pilot to come aboard.[3] The vessel soon entered the harbor area. Captain Robinson ordered the ship to maintain a readiness to be able to get underway in half an hour. A radio broadcast brought the following obvious news just before noon: 'U.S. Congress proclaimed the existence of a state of war between the United States and Japan.'[4] Sailors labored with large manila ropes as the light cruiser tied up her starboard side to the fuel dock. She subsequently began topping off fuel tanks and taking aboard fresh water.

Balikpapan was a much larger city than Tarakan. A series of big mountains stood close behind the town. There was an abundance of lush green jungle foliage nearby. Oil facilities were plainly visible in the distance. The harbor was full of various Allied and Dutch small craft, including some merchantmen. The American ship *President Madison* was docked nearby.

While *Marblehead* was taking aboard fuel, her crew began the process of stripping the ship to get her ready for war. The work involved removing any type of gear or material that was either deemed nonessential or a potential fire hazard during battle conditions. The dock quickly became filled with a variety of items, such as furniture, floor tiles stripped off selected areas, and boxes. Even the captain's gig was removed. The small motor boat served as a sort of personal water taxi for Captain Robinson while the cruiser was in port. Sailors checked and rechecked equipment – guns, range finders, and steering gear – anything that would be needed in battle. The items were placed ashore in the custody of the harbor master.[5]

Raymond Kester remembered the morale was high as crewmen worked to put *Marblehead* in fighting condition. Fear was lurking close by and served as a constant companion to some of the sailors. 'Most of us felt, but did not dwell on the possibility, that we would not survive,' he later recalled. 'We knew the ship was old. We did not realize how bad off we were until we actually fought the ship.'[6]

Sporadic radio reports brought updated information from the Pacific front and the news was not good. At the very time *Marblehead* stood in Balikpapan, the smoke was still rising from damaged and sunken ships in Pearl Harbor as the scope of the disaster slowly became clearer to American leaders, but not necessarily the sailors of the Asiatic Fleet. Additionally, epic disasters were either already underway, or about to befall the Americans further north in the Philippines and the British to the west near Malaya.

***

The strike on the Southern Resources Area began almost simultaneously with the Pearl Harbor attack. The Japanese plan was to first defeat the British in Malay and Singapore to establish a protective flank for moves against the Netherlands East Indies proper.[7] The large invasion convoy that was at sea for almost a week before the start of hostilities rounded the southern tip of modern-day Vietnam on December 6, before changing direction. The ships headed for a point in the center of the Gulf of Siam pointing towards Bangkok. Although the ultimate destination was unknown to the future allies, it appeared the force was heading towards the Thai capital.

The convoy again changed course to the south on December 7. The ships were then moving towards the Thailand-Malaya border area on the narrow Kra Isthmus and later divided into smaller groups. The initial landing took place on the morning of December 8 at Kota Bharu on the northern end of Malaya, more than an hour before the initial wave of planes arrived over Pearl Harbor.[8] Determined air attacks by British and Australian planes and artillery fire were not enough to hinder the invaders. Commonwealth troops put up a determined resistance but were simply outnumbered and unable to stop the invasion. The Japanese quickly had a foothold on Malaya and control of an airfield.

The attack against the British was not limited to Malaya. Japanese troops landed on the British portion of Borneo on December 16 with minimal opposition, and were soon in control of the lightly defended region. Two landings took place further north of Malaya in Thailand with the invaders only meeting token resistance. The nation surrendered after a brief fight.

Admiral Sir Phillips was further south in Singapore, while the initial Japanese landings were taking place in Thailand and Malaya, having just returned from his trip to Manila. The British naval leader was determined to act. The big 15-inch guns of *Prince of Wales* and *Repulse* were a serious threat to the enemy invasion forces. The pair represented the strongest firepower currently available to the American and British in the Pacific. Press reports first alerted the Japanese to the arrival of the British ships in the region, but a reconnaissance plane spotted Force Z in the Singapore area on December 4.[9]

Phillips faced a serious dilemma. Enemy landings were taking place within striking distance to the north, but he had no protective air cover. His own aircraft carrier never made it to the Pacific and the hard-pressed Royal Air Force could offer no air support or reconnaissance assistance. He had very little up-to-date information on the location of enemy naval forces. However, British soldiers at that very moment were in a desperate situation further north and were retreating as Japanese forces advanced. The admiral believed the Royal Navy could not sit idle in Singapore during such a despairing situation. He decided to act. The two capital ships and four destroyers of Force Z departed Singapore late in the afternoon of December 9 in the hopes of finding a Japanese convoy to attack along the coast of Malaya or Thailand. The risky voyage was compounded by the admiral's adherence to radio silence, meaning officials back in Singapore had a difficult time following the force's location.

The force initially went north to a point about 150 miles south of Indochina, a worsening tactical position given the location of Japanese airfields in the former French Colony.[10] The ships were spotted multiple times by enemy reconnaissance planes during the voyage. Phillips then turned south after hearing of a Japanese amphibious operation underway between Kota Bharu and Singapore. He planned to travel at night for a surprise attack at dawn. The information, however, proved to be inaccurate and the force was sighted by a Japanese submarine during the evening.

A swarm of the Japanese land-based bombers operating from the Saigon area found Force Z during the late morning hours of December 10. The planes delivered fatal blows to both big ships, attacking with bombs and torpedoes. The battlecruiser *Repulse* rolled over at 12.33 pm and *Prince of Wales* sank less than an hour later.[11] The destroyers rescued over 2,000 men, but 840 British sailors perished. The dead included Admiral Phillips, who reportedly declined to leave the bridge of *Prince of Wales* just before she went under.[12]

A group of American destroyers narrowly avoided becoming caught up in the disaster. After receiving the updated information, just before the start of hostilities, about the large Japanese convoy on the move off Indochina, Admiral Hart ordered the four destroyers docked at Balikpapan – *Whipple, Alden, Edsall,* and *John D. Edwards* – to proceed at once to Singapore.[13] The ships departed during the evening hours of December 7 with a mission to augment Phillip's Force Z. The tender *Black Hawk* was directed to proceed to Batavia, Java. The destroyers traveled south past Borneo before turning west into the Java Sea, eventually arriving in Singapore. However, the American ships arrived too late – the British force had already departed.

Poor communications and confusion subsequently reigned as the destroyers proceeded north to join the British force, initially not knowing the big ships had already been sunk. Once the facts of the disaster became clear, the American destroyer commander hoped to help rescue survivors.[14] He was quickly ordered out of the area before Japanese planes had a chance to return. A directive from Washington on December 11 ordered Hart to withdraw the destroyers from Singapore and send the group to Darwin, Australia.[15]

The destruction of Force Z brought the grim reality that the most powerful surface force available to the Allies in the Pacific was gone before it had a chance to fire a single shot at the enemy. For the second time in only a few days the mighty battleship, long ruler of the seas, was shown to be no match for airplanes. The Japanese were now free to drive down the Malaya Peninsula towards Singapore with no fear of interference by the Royal Navy.

***

The voyage south from Tarakan put *Marblehead* deeper inside the Netherlands East Indies. The former colony is now the country of Indonesia. The territory is the world's largest archipelago, comprised of thousands of islands, spanning an east–west distance of 3,200 miles and a width of 1,200 miles.[16] When compared to the United States, the distance from east to west is greater than the straight-line mileage between San Francisco, CA and Boston, MA. The archipelago begins in the west with the large island of Sumatra, positioned somewhat parallel to the Malayan Peninsula. Adjacent to the east is Java and the nearby island of Borneo, the largest island of the territory partially under British control. The octopus-shaped island Celebes is next to the Dutch side of Borneo. The island lacks a central body and consists almost entirely of peninsulas. Various smaller islands are positioned to the east and south.

Many of the islands are volcanic in nature with high mountains in the interiors and narrow coastal plains along the water. The location near the equator results in a hot moist tropical environment with monsoons common at certain times of the year, same as in many parts of the Pacific. Lush jungle foliage is abundant on many islands.

A diverse assortment of channels and seas are present throughout the East Indies. The most important is the Java Sea, positioned between Java and Borneo. Ships moving east, from points such as Singapore, Thailand, and Indochina, need to transverse the Java Sea to reach the island of Java. The Flores Sea separates Celebes from a group of smaller islands to the south. Borneo and Celebes are separated by the Makassar Strait, with one portion of the waterway narrowing to about eighty miles. Ships coming from the Philippines must move through the strait to enter the interior of the East Indies.

The first ships from the Netherlands arrived in the East Indies in 1596, in search of spices and exploring trade routes between Europe and Asia.[17] The European nation consolidated their holdings in the region over the next 300 years, largely through its strong navy. The city of Batavia on Java was the seat of political power for the Dutch Colonial Government. The colony was vastly rich in natural resources, including oil, rubber, tin, sugar, kapok, bauxite, and more. The native East Indies population was about 70 million people at the time of World War II.[18] Even after centuries of rule, the Dutch control often only included the larger cities and coastal areas. The thick interior jungles were home to a variety of local tribes who often acted independently of their colonial masters.[19]

The East Indies was defended by its own military forces comprised of both Dutch and local troops. The position of the home country of Holland in Western Europe did not require the need for a large naval presence. Most of the Royal Netherlands Navy was traditionally stationed in the East Indies during the long span of colonial rule. The Dutch leaders were aware of the threat from Japan and sought to maintain a small fleet of high quality warships capable of fighting a holding action against Japan until help could arrive from an ally.[20] The East Indies naval force was traditionally built around a mix of cruisers and destroyers, but also included submarines and minelayers.

The port city of Surabaya, on the northern coast of Java, was the main naval operating base. The military power of the colony was slowly eroding. By the early 1900s the once powerful Dutch Navy had declined in size and effectiveness to the point of being considered a second-rate force by the start of World War II.[21] Defenses in general had lapsed in the decades prior to the conflict with budget cuts, neglect, and pacifist leaders in Europe taking a heavy toll on the local military forces. The defenders facing the Japanese would often do so with obsolete fighter planes, out-gunned warships, and poorly equipped soldiers.

Not all naval components, however, were lacking. The Dutch maintained a small, but powerful, group of submarines. The underwater boats were manned by well-trained crews and were thought capable of inflicting substantial damage against a larger foe. The Dutch were well versed in the use of naval mines and possessed some long-range flying boats. The colony possessed a network of air bases, including a large new airfield at Kendari on the island of Celebes.

The Netherlands East Indies, together with Malaya, Singapore, and New Guinea were often referred to by Allied leaders as the Malay Barrier. The area was considered an imaginary shield standing between Japanese territories to the north and Australia to the south. If the Japanese could break through the position, Australia and additional territories across the Indian Ocean could be threatened. The sailors aboard *Marblehead* were soon to find themselves in the thick of the fight to defend the barrier.

Chapter 8

A steady stream of merchant ships headed out of Manila Bay, almost immediately after the war started, to sail for safer waters to the south. Most of Task Force 5's fighting ships were already out of the area, but Admiral Hart intended to execute the plan of operating his submarine force in defense of the Philippines from Manila Bay. He did not rule out the possibility of bringing his surface force back up to the Philippines as circumstance warranted.

There was no doubt that a Japanese attack was coming. Whether, or when, the Pacific Fleet would sail across the ocean to relieve the garrison on the commonwealth, as prescribed in the war plan, was unknown. Given the extent of damage the force suffered at Pearl Harbor, the full information of the disaster was probably not known to Hart in the first days of the war, no naval help was likely coming.

Hart presumed General MacArthur's air forces would provide a protective cover over the bay. The general's 277 planes included thirty-five new B-17 heavy bombers and about 100 front-line fighters.[1] Contrary to his statements and publicity, MacArthur's forces – both on ground and in the air – were far from adequate to defend the Philippines against the imminent assault.

The growing American military power in the Philippines was seen by the Japanese as a threat to the advance into the Southern Resources Area. Their plan for the conquest of the Philippines was to stage a series of amphibious operations designed to defeat the American ground forces on the main island of Luzon. However, the elimination of American air power was of chief concern and was to be dealt with through a series of immediate air attacks on the opening day of the war. Formidable opposition from the Asiatic Fleet ships was not expected by Imperial planners.[2]

The first Japanese attack on the Philippines was not on Manila, but came at the city of Davao on the island of Mindanao on the southern end of the archipelago. Twenty-two planes from the nearby light aircraft carrier *Ryujo* appeared over Davao Gulf at dawn on the first day of the war and attacked the anchored seaplane tender *William B. Preston*. Two PBY patrol planes were destroyed and one airman was killed, but the tender miraculously escaped damage. She immediately put to sea in search of a safer area to operate.

The news of the Pearl Harbor attack was only hours old when Japanese planes on Formosa were preparing to depart for an early strike on the Luzon air bases, but fog prevented the main force of naval aircraft from taking off. The delay opened a window of opportunity for the Americans to strike first. A controversial series of events at army headquarters in Manila followed, which have never been satisfactorily reconciled, where American air commanders proposed an attack on Formosa but could not get MacArthur's permission to move forward. By mid-morning the fog lifted allowing a massive armada of 192 Japanese naval planes to take off for the Philippines.

The aircraft arrived over their targets, the three main army air bases on Luzon, at 11.35 am to begin a strafing and bombing attack. Despite the delay and the length of time elapsed since the notification of the Pearl Harbor attack, the raiders caught many of the American planes on the ground. MacArthur's air force was dealt a devastating blow with half of its bombers and more than a third of the fighters destroyed in a matter of minutes.[3] Additional attacks again hit the airfields on December 10. Thereafter, Japanese planes appeared uncontested over the Manila Bay area daily. American airpower was no longer able to adequately protect the Philippines or seriously challenge the approaching Japanese invasion forces.

The same day, December 10, British Force Z was meeting its fate off Malaya – Admiral Hart and his fleet received a dreadful blow in the form of an air attack on the Cavite Navy Yard. Fifty-four twin-engine Japanese bombers arrived unopposed over the base during the middle of the day. Flying above the effective range of the light American anti-aircraft guns, the planes divided into smaller groups before unleashing string after string of bombs with deadly accuracy on the targets below. The attack lasted about an hour and virtually demolished the naval facilities leaving behind a fire raging out of control. Admiral Hart was helpless as he watched the raid unfold from Manila on the roof of the Marsman Building. The base was later abandoned after the fires burned out and any salvageable supplies could be safely removed.

A series of small Japanese amphibious operations occurred around the Philippines in advance of the larger invasion. The main landing took place at Lingayen Gulf on the north-western coast of Luzon on December 21. Thousands of Japanese soldiers streamed ashore – the initial waves of what were eventually 43,000 soldiers – to start the drive towards Manila. American and Filipino soldiers, unable to repel the invaders, were soon in full retreat across Luzon – often leaving behind valuable equipment, supplies, and food stores. The capital was abandoned to the approaching Japanese troops in late December without a fight. By early January the defenders settled into last stand defensive positions on the Bataan Peninsula along the western side of Manila Bay and the adjacent fortified island of Corregidor. There they hoped to be able to hold back the Japanese until reinforcements arrived – the timing and composition of which was unknown.

Plagued by bad luck and faulty torpedoes, Admiral Hart's submarine force was no more successful than MacArthur's air and ground forces in impeding the Japanese invasion. All hope of securely basing Asiatic Fleet units of any type, surface or submarine, in Manila Bay or elsewhere in the Philippines was now gone. 'The attack of 10 December made it entirely clear that, as far as security of ships and installations in Manila Bay was concerned, the enemy had control of the air,' Hart later wrote.[4] He eventually notified officials in Washington that Manila Bay was no longer tenable for naval operations.

Operating out of Singapore was no longer a viable option due to Japanese ground forces advancing down the Malaya Peninsula. Admiral Stark in Washington notified Hart to 'retire … in the direction of northwest Australia rather than Singapore'.[5] The move would free up Hart to participate in the defense of the Netherlands East Indies and Australia while also striking Japanese forces as opportunities became available. The admiral ordered his submarine force and remaining large ships to move south out of the Philippines. Hart initially moved his headquarters from Manila to Corregidor before departing with the staff for Java aboard the submarine *Shark* during the early morning hours of December 26.[6] Admiral Francis Rockwell, Commandant of the Sixteenth Naval District, was left in charge of the remaining naval forces in the Philippines, including a squadron of PT boats and an assortment of small coastal defense craft.

***

As the crisis in the Pacific continued to worsen, American and British leaders were holding their first wartime meeting in Washington, starting in late December 1941. President Roosevelt, Prime Minister Churchill, and their respective aides and military leaders discussed a wide range of topics in what was known as the Arcadia Conference. Among the important outcomes of the session was the reaffirmation of the 'Germany first' strategy, with the European side of the war taking greater precedence over the Pacific, putting in place a mechanism for a joint high command structure to include the military chiefs of both nations, and establishing a unified command to confront the Japanese in the southwest Pacific.[7]

The area of the Pacific needing the most immediate attention was the long stretch from Burma in the west to Australia in the east. The middle points included Malaya, Singapore, Netherlands East Indies, the Philippines, and a portion of New Guinea. The Japanese were on the attack across the entire region. Thailand was already out of the war after surrendering to Japan after a short fight. The area was defended by an assortment of scattered United States, British, Australian, and Dutch forces.

The Arcadia Conference established the American, British, Dutch and Australian Command or ABDA to better coordinate the defense of the region. The Dutch and Australians were not at the conference and were never consulted in the arrangement.[8] Australia and adjacent areas to the east were placed under the control of a separate command. Although the Philippines were included in the ABDA jurisdiction, General MacArthur retained an independent command. The arrangement was the first attempt in World War II for a unified command among the various Allied nations.

British General Sir Archibald Wavell was named the overall ABDA commander. His subordinates included Admiral Hart as overall commander of naval forces. Few top officials, including American General George Marshall, believed there was much chance for success in the ABDA area.[9] The command went into effect on the last day of 1941, although it would be a couple of weeks before all the key players were to be on site in the Far East. The headquarters was established in the Lembang area, high in the mountains of the central part of Java.

The geography under ABDA's control was a vast area, with a front line facing the Japanese stretching almost 2,000 miles. The most immediate matters were the Japanese thrust south and a feared Imperial attack on Burma from newly conquered Thailand. The latter could cut off the Burma Road – the main overland supply route into China. Wavell himself was heavily focused on the defense of Malaya and Singapore to the point that he delegated much of the administrative duties to Dutch Admiral Conrad Helfrich, who was also the commander in chief of the Royal Netherlands Navy.

A host of issues were to hamper ABDA in the upcoming battles with Japan – the hasty formation of the command, poor organization, inadequate internal communication in which the activities of the naval, land, and air forces were not coordinated, and too few resources. Diverse national interests and friction among the member nations was present from the start – particularly from the Dutch, whose territory represented a large part of the ADBA area, but their leaders had been left out of senior command positions.[10] Confronted by a superior enemy, who often had control of the air, ABDA was largely doomed from the start.[11]

Admiral Hart remained as Commander in Chief of the Asiatic Fleet, in addition to his status as chief naval officer of ABDA. Although he was the top naval commander, Hart faced a multitude of his own problems and had little actual control over ships of the other nations. Despite the pre-war meetings there were no common communication signals or pre-arranged operating strategy. American ships did not have adequate maps of the area and much of the East Indies was unfamiliar geography. The British and Dutch seemed focused on using warships for convoy escort duties, instead of trying to stop the advancing enemy.

An informal arrangement had the ABDA region divided into three smaller areas for naval operations. The British operated in the sea lanes from Singapore west through the Indian Ocean to Ceylon near India. Dutch warships patrolled the waters around the large islands of Sumatra and Java – essentially the center of the colony. American naval forces were responsible for the area east of Java.[12] The port of Darwin on the northern coast of Australia was established as a service base for ABDA warships, particularly American. It was not the best option – Darwin's existing facilities were poor and the location was far from the frontline operating area – but officials in Washington feared the Malay Barrier might not be held.[13]

***

Radio reports, some from commercial stations, continued to bring war reports to the sailors aboard *Marblehead* at Balikpapan. They heard the disheartening news about the air attacks on the Philippines and the devastating loss of Force Z. The war was getting closer. There had already been a false alarm of an approaching Japanese plane that sent crewmen rushing to air defense stations.[14] A direct confrontation with the Japanese was only a matter of time.

The harbor pilot climbed aboard the light cruiser as she made ready to get underway in a hurry on the late morning of December 11. She moved out of the harbor in company of *Parrott* and *Stewart* after receiving a report of 'enemy ships in the vicinity'.[15] She launched an SOC Seagull to reconnoiter the area ahead. The crew went to general quarters shortly after the warship cleared the harbor and many sailors were wondering if they were about to have their first scrape with the enemy. It was not to be the case as the report proved to be a false alarm.

A day later, *Marblehead* ventured north into Makassar Strait to rendezvous with the tankers *Trinity*, *Pecos*, and the aircraft tender *Langley*. The group was initially accompanied out of the Philippines at the beginning of the war by *Houston*, *Boise* and two destroyers, but the heavy warships later proceeded independently. Captain Robinson's orders were to escort the trio back to Balikpapan. The warship crossed the equator at 8.40 pm on December 12. Long standing navy tradition calls for an initiation ceremony for those aboard who are crossing the line for the first time, complete with costumed characters and overseen by someone dressed as King Neptune. However, as was the case during the last crossing, no ceremony took place due to the war conditions. The war diary woefully recorded: 'Neptunas Rex in bomb shelter and did not come on board.'[16]

The light cruiser reached the appointed meeting spot just before midnight, but lookouts aboard *Marblehead* could find no sign of the approaching vessels. Captain Robinson turned his vessel south to continue the quest. He earlier parted company with the two destroyers, with both proceeding north on their own. A plane catapulted off to conduct an early morning search found the approaching ships the next day.

A second group of American warships came into Balikpapan a few days later. The new arrivals included the cruisers *Houston* and *Boise*, along with some destroyers and auxiliary vessels. Admiral Glassford, aboard his flagship *Houston*, assumed command of Task Force 5.

The *Marblehead* men spoke with some of the newly arrived sailors, who had recently departed the Philippines, to hear their first-hand accounts of the fiery destruction of the Cavite Navy Yard. The harbor was now full of ships and would make an inviting target for Japanese planes.

Captain Robinson again found himself in command of a small convoy when *Marblehead* departed Balikpapan for good on December 16 in the company of *Trinity, Pecos, Langley, Gold Star* and four destroyers. The freighter *Gold Star* was on her way to Guam when the war started. Her cargo of food, beer, and whisky piqued the interest of many *Marblehead* sailors, but was to remain untouched during the ensuing voyage. The light cruiser was approaching the Balikpapan Light Ship when a single 3-inch antiaircraft gun opened fire on an unidentified aircraft approaching off the stern. Eighteen rounds were unleased before the plane turned away and was identified as a Dutch commercial airliner.[17] No hits were scored, perhaps averting a disaster. Chief Boatswain's Mate Harvey Anderson praised the alertness of the gun crew, but pointed out they should not be proud of their aim.[18]

The convoy sailed south for a distance before turning east. The destination was the port of Makassar on the southern end of Celebes. The island roughly resembles the shape of an octopus turned on its left side with four outstretched tentacles, and the port was near the bottom of the southernmost limb. The voyage of over 400 miles ended on December 18 when the ships filtered into the harbor. Makassar appeared to be a clean town having an abundance of white buildings with red roofs. The location proved to be a busy port with various ships entering or departing the harbor during the stay.

The remaining days of December initially saw *Marblehead* sailing in a convoy from Makassar to Surabaya, Java. There was some contact with *Houston* and *Boise* during the time, although the cruisers were moving as part of a different group of ships. The *Marblehead* sailors spent Christmas day 1941 moored in Surabaya. A traditional turkey dinner was served aboard ship with Captain Robinson moving among his crew extolling holiday wishes. Some of the sailors took time to go ashore on liberty where a band was playing Christmas songs.

The warship departed Surabaya on December 27 with three destroyers and a slightly altered group of auxiliaries and merchantmen for an uneventful voyage to Darwin. The ships were at sea as the last hours of 1941 slipped away. Lieutenant (Junior Grade) John Bracken, on duty when the New Year began, started the January deck log with a hopeful entry. 'This starts the year 1942 – may it bring honest pride and success to this ship and its crew.'[19]

***

The New Year brought no changes to the grim situation facing the Allies in the Pacific – the enemy was still on the attack and moving quickly. The risky Japanese plan to start the war with multiple strikes in different directions stretched Imperial resources thinly across the Pacific during the opening weeks of hostilities, it paid off with a series of dramatic victories in the first few days. Aside from incapacitating the Pacific Fleet at Pearl Harbor, Imperial forces sunk the battleships of Britain's Force Z, successfully landed troops in Malaya, and dealt MacArthur's air force a punishing blow in the Philippines. Admiral Hart, his Asiatic Fleet ships, and the brave sailors aboard *Marblehead* would not be getting much help in their looming confrontation with the Japanese.

Chapter 9

The first days of January 1942 found the initial stages of the Japanese war plan going better than expected. The overall objective – the seizure of the Southern Resources Area for oil and other natural resources – had not yet begun in earnest. The preliminaries, however, were well underway and moving ahead of schedule with Thailand out of the war, troops ashore on Malaya advancing towards Singapore, British Borneo attacked, and American forces in the Philippines in retreat. The rapid Japanese advancements typically centered on amphibious operations, land movements through jungle terrain thought to be untravellable by the defenders, and relied heavily on seizing airfields. Once an airfield was under enemy control, land-based aircraft were quickly brought in to cover the next movement.

The Japanese plan to seize the Netherlands East Indies was based on using the initial sudden attacks on Malaya and the Philippines to establish those territories as footholds for two large pincers.[1] Imperial forces also seized the island of Jolo and landed troops in the city of Davao, both in the southern part of the Philippines, in late December 1941 to use as a staging area for further attacks south. Defeating the Dutch involved more than just seizing the various oil ports, it also required conquering Java. Two advances coming from opposite directions – east and west – were to capture various territories throughout the East Indies before finally converging on Java.

Defending the East Indies against a Japanese attack proved to be a difficult undertaking for the local Dutch. The loss of the home country in Europe to German invasion in May 1940 created a host of problems for those in the East Indies. Shipments of reinforcements, new equipment, supplies, spare parts, and even manpower came to an immediate halt after the Netherlands surrendered. The Dutch government in exile, housed in London, was totally dependent on the British. Neither the English hosts nor the United States could spare much in the way of military hardware for the Dutch.

The naval resources of the ABDA commander were simply too little to effectively defend the entire length of the East Indies. The geography of the region was favoring the attackers. The Japanese had two clear routes to the interior of the territory – south from the Philippines through the Makassar Strait and east from Malaya, past Sumatra and into the Java Sea. Although not able to adequately defend the entire colony, the Dutch were determined to hold Java to the very end and to battle the approaching Japanese naval forces wherever possible.[2]

Since the Pearl Harbor attack, when the Dutch declared war on Japan, a state of open hostilities had existed between the Netherlands East Indies and the Japanese. The declaration was not officially reciprocated for nearly a month until Japan formally declared war on the Netherlands East Indies on January 11.[3] An invasion convoy bound for Tarakan was already at sea when the war declaration took place, having departed from the southern Philippines a few days prior. A small air attack by three American B-17s resulted in no damage and ABDA submarines were unable to intercept the force before it appeared off Tarakan on January 10. However, the invaders arrived to find plumes of black smoke towering over the island after alert Dutch officials began the successful destruction of the oil facilities.

The battle for Tarakan lasted less than three days. Japanese troops came ashore at three locations on the east side of the island, opposite most of the beach defenses, before marching through the jungle on the attack. Organized resistance among the 1,200 Dutch defenders broke down on the morning of January 12, and the garrison commander unconditionally surrendered the next day.[4] The Dutch minelayer *Prins van Oranje*, the gracious greeter to *Marblehead* little more than a month earlier, was chased down and sunk by Japanese warships. Some of the Dutch prisoners were brutally murdered in the coming days by the Japanese who were enraged over the destruction of the oil facilities and the sinking of two minelayers by shore guns.[5]

A nearly simultaneous landing took control of Menado and nearby areas on the northern tip of Celebes, where the Dutch defenders were quickly overwhelmed. The Japanese now had a firm foothold on the outer parameter of the East Indies, and the Makassar Strait was wide open for enemy forces to move south. It was only a matter of time – a few days or a couple of weeks at best – before the enemy moved on two important locations – Balikpapan and Kendari. Balikpapan was the second vital oil port on the east coast of Borneo. Kendari was a coastal town located in the southeastern part of Celebes and was home to a large modern airfield – widely considered to be the best in the East Indies. The Dutch had hoped to use the base to provide air cover for naval operations throughout the area.

As the enemy was moving into the eastern part of the East Indies, Imperial troops were making good progress in the west on Malaya. The Japanese were moving down the peninsula as British soldiers retreated towards Singapore. Key British and Dutch warships were busy ferrying convoys to the fortress and were thus in no position to participate in strikes against the Japanese naval forces staging the amphibious operations further east. General Wavell continued to be heavily focused on Singapore, believing the stronghold could hold out long term.[6]

The initial Japanese moves into the Netherlands East Indies did not go completely unchallenged. There were sporadic air attacks and some minor success with submarines – both American and Dutch. The enemy activities were to prompt various Allied attempts to thwart their thrusts with naval action conceived by Admiral Hart.

***

Admiral Hart's arduous five-day journey of nearly 1,000 miles from Manila, much of it submerged for security reasons, ended on January 2, 1942, when the submarine *Shark*, moored at Surabaya, Java. The admiral arrived as the newly appointed ABDA naval commander. He established his headquarters in the Oranje Hotel on the city's waterfront – same as Admiral Glassford who had arrived a few weeks earlier. Hart was immediately thrust into the role of organizing the ABDA naval command. With no information coming from Washington as to when or if naval reinforcements would arrive, it was plainly clear to Hart the 'U.S. forces in the Far Eastern theatre were on their own.'[7]

Hart began to face pressure and criticisms from multiple fronts from the onset. Friction with top Dutch officials, still seething about being left out of the senior ABDA command positions, began almost at once. Admiral Helfrich felt Hart arrived with defeatist disposition and was overly cautious.[8] The Dutch naval leader was unsure if the American admiral was up to the task of assisting in the regional defense or just wanted to retreat to Australia. Isolated back on Corregidor, General MacArthur spared little in expressing his disapproval of Hart. He used every opportunity to criticize the navy's lack of action in the defense of the Philippines, creating 'unfortunate impressions' of the admiral in Washington.[9] Hart was anything but defeatist, but had few resources to undertake the immense job of adequately defending the area.[10]

Convoy escort duty was not what Admiral Hart wanted for his fighting ships. He felt the burden wore down his men and ships at a much faster rate than would otherwise have occurred. The new ABDA naval commander wanted to hit back against the Japanese. He lacked the number of warships among his own forces to do large scale fleet operations, causing him to have to settle for trying some smaller raids. The first attempt came in the middle of January and *Marblehead* was to play a prominent role.

The light cruiser entered the harbor at Darwin during the afternoon of January 2, 1942, having safely delivered her convoy of two destroyers, *Langley*, *Holland*, and *Marechal Joffre*. The latter was a French transport vessel taken over by American sailors at the start of the war in the Philippines. After spending a week in the small isolated town on the northern coast of Australia, *Marblehead* departed on January 8 bound for the island of Timor. Located southeast of Celebes and facing the top of Australia, the island was politically divided between the Dutch and Portuguese control. The warship later moved west to the island of Sumbawa where she dropped anchor with *Boise* and some destroyers on January 12.[11] Admiral Glassford, flying his flag in *Boise*, was overall commander of the small group operating as Task Force 5.

Reports of Japanese shipping at Kema in the far north-eastern part of Celebes prompted Admiral Hart to order an attack. Japanese transports loaded with troops and supplies could be rich and inviting targets. He radioed Glassford on January 14 that 'enemy expected [to] collect forces for another southward advance at Kema Road', and to 'prepare an attack there with one 6-inch cruiser [and] three to four destroyers'.[12] A later message specified *Marblehead* to be the attacking cruiser, an interesting decision given the greater firepower and advanced fire control system of *Boise*. Perhaps the choice was made due to her carrying torpedoes. The location was over 600 miles north of *Marblehead's* current position.

Captain Robinson gathered together the senior officers in his cabin to share the news of the mission. The enemy force was reported to be twenty-three transports accompanied by one heavy cruiser, one light cruiser, and some destroyers.[13] Their ship, along with destroyers *Blumer*, *Pope*, *Pillsbury*, and *Ford*, was to strike under the concealment of darkness on January 18. The attack plan called for the destroyers to make two torpedo runs, allowing the tubes to be emptied on each side, followed by more torpedoes from *Marblehead*. The light cruiser's 6-inch guns would be fired, as needed, to cover the ships withdrawal.

The *Boise* and one additional destroyer were available for additional gunfire support during the escape, if needed.[14] Robinson explained it was a risky and dangerous mission, but it had to be done. He was confident his officers and enlisted men could deliver a superior performance during the upcoming encounter.

Hart left it up to his onsite commanders to make a final determination to press home the attack at Kema based on the 'adequacy of targets to be expected'. The mission was announced to the crew after the warship weighed anchor. Enthusiasm quickly spread among her sailors as *Marblehead* moved north for what was expected to be her first tangle with the enemy. Their hopes, however, were soon dashed.

The mission was cancelled on January 17 after the submarines *Permit* and *Pike* reported no Japanese ships in the immediate Kema area or nearby waters. Captain Robinson announced the news over the loudspeaker system. 'The enemy has moved,' he told his crew. 'Due to the uncertainty of their position we are turning back. I'm sorry. Better luck next time.'[15] The ships returned to Timor to refuel. The ships of Task Force 5 may have been victims of either bad luck or bad planning, for the submarine *Swordfish* found the Kema area full of Japanese shipping only a few days later.[16]

The second attempt to attack the enemy came only a few days later when Dutch sources reported Japanese shipping massed north of Makassar Strait for the anticipated move south against Balikpapan. Some additional destroyers and *Houston* were now available to join the force after arriving too late to participate in the aborted Kema attack. Admiral Glassford altered his battle plan – *Marblehead* and eight destroyers were to stage the strike with *Houston* and *Boise* trailing fifty miles behind to cover the withdrawal.[17]

The opportunity never materialized. The operation was cancelled after Hart learned the contact information 'was wholly false'.[18] The assembled ships scattered for other activities, with *Houston* and two destroyers bound for convoy escort duty.

Hart could considerably strengthen his task force by adding ships from other ABDA members. 'The idea for a cruiser-destroyer striking force was American,' he later wrote. 'Until about January 20, British naval attention was centered on escort and convoy, employing therein also the Dutch surface craft, whose own attention was mostly directed at anti-submarine escort of their own shipping with what destroyers they could get available or could borrow from the Americans.'[19]

Any combined striking force would be hampered by a host of problems, starting with the lack of experience in joint operations and the absence of a common tactical doctrine among the participants. There was a language barrier between the Dutch and the remaining English-speaking navies – always good to add an element of confusion. American maps for the East Indies were outdated, often inaccurate, and of poor

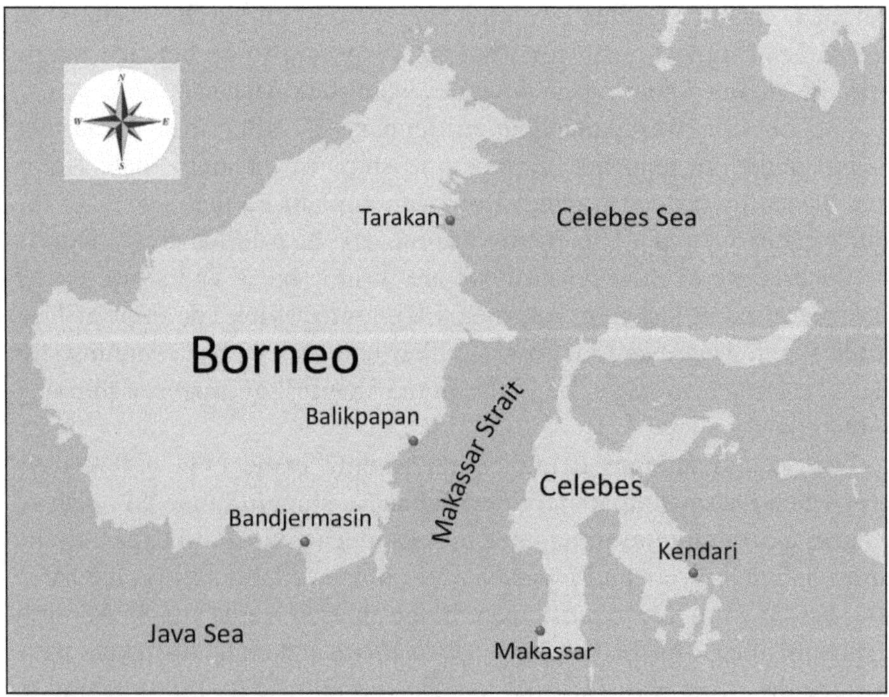

Makassar Strait.

quality – and the American navigators could not read the better maps written in Dutch. There were too few Dutch navigational pilots to go around – or so said Admiral Helfrich. Finally, there was the question of who would command a multi-national strike force.

Admiral Glassford was not Hart's first choice to command his only task force of fighting vessels owing to his lack of experience with large fleet ships.[20] However, he had done good work in commanding the gunboats in China and participating in diplomacy with Japan. The Asiatic commander was short on options and had to appease officials in Washington who considered Glassford as a likely replacement when Hart retired. Glassford took command largely based on the situation and circumstances. The ABDA structure had each participating navy retaining command of their own ships. However, if a combined strike force was assembled, it was Hart who would appoint a task force commander. Before a multi-national strike force was assembled, however, there was a successful attack delivered by an all-American force.

Chapter 10

Admiral Hart was learning painfully that Japanese amphibious tactics were both well suited for the Netherlands East Indies and difficult to counter. Rapid advances over short distances, often in shallow water to thwart submarines, made it difficult to attack the enemy invasion forces. Many of the Dutch islands, outside of Java and Sumatra, had undeveloped interiors, meaning the enemy could gain effective control by seizing a few key coastal points.[1] Japanese advances almost always took place under an umbrella of air cover – land-based fighters and bombers, seaplanes, or in some instances, carrier planes. Air reconnaissance provided regular intelligence information about the movements of Allied warships, while the lack of such was a continuous hindrance for ABDA naval forces. Hart often had to rely on sighting reports from submarines, a form of reconnaissance typically much less effective than from the air.

The admiral was disappointed at the failure of his naval forces to do battle with the enemy. He desperately wanted to break the continuous string of Japanese victories. Hart was also concerned that the ships of the cruiser-destroyer force were stationed too far from the probable area of operations, and worried that the constant movements of the aborted strikes were wearing down his sailors.

Admiral Glassford's Task Force 5 suffered a serious setback during the previous sortie when *Marblehead* met with a mechanical accident. She suffered a turbine casualty late in the day on January 17, causing her top speed to be reduced. The light cruiser was operating on only three engines by the early hours of the next morning.[2] She was an old ship and engineering problems were not uncommon. If such a mishap occurred during peacetime conditions she would have made a trip to the yard for repairs, but that was not the case while on the front lines of a war. Captain Robinson's ship was still moving, and he would have to keep her operating as best possible.

***

Admiral Hart was still determined to counterattack, even with one of his three available cruisers slowed. He soon learned the Japanese were making their move south through the Makassar Strait – an invasion force was heading for Balikpapan. The movement gave the third opportunity for Task Force 5 to attack, although it was now a smaller force. The heavy cruiser *Houston* was out of position, having returned to convoy escort duties. Her powerful 8-inch guns were unable to play any role in the upcoming operation. The light cruiser *Boise*, the hobbled *Marblehead*, and some destroyers were available. Hart knew he needed some additional help and recorded in his diary, 'Oh, for a little LUCK!'[3]

The Japanese were indeed on the move. With Tarakan and the northern part of Celebes under control with minimal losses, they were ready to move against Balikpapan by late January. The city gave the Japanese more than just access to large oil facilities, it also provided a good harbor and an airfield to help secure the southern portion of Borneo and threaten Java. The invasion force departed Tarakan during the night of January 20–21.[4]

The movement of the Japanese convoy was initially detected by American submarines, and PBY Catalina patrol planes later made contact with the ships. The enemy was initially reported as nine transports, four cruisers, and fourteen destroyers moving towards Balikpapan in small groups.[5] The invasion force was actually much larger – sixteen transports and an assortment of patrol boats and minesweepers for close cover and a more powerful escort force consisting of the light cruiser *Naka* and nine destroyers under the command of Admiral Shoji Nishimura.[6] Hoping to avoid a repeat of the destruction that occurred at Tarakan, the Japanese sent advance orders to Dutch authorities on Balikpapan not to damage any of the oil facilities.

Poor weather conditions over the Makassar Strait hampered both Japanese and ABDA air operations, while also serving to partially shield Admiral Nishimura's approach.[7] Various attacks by American and Dutch planes – including fragments of General MacArthur's tattered air force now on Java – caused some damage to Japanese ships during the Balikpapan episode, but did not substantially hinder the invasion operation. Submarines fared little better except for a single Dutch submarine, whose exploits will be noted shortly.

The invasion force arrived off Balikpapan to find the area shrouded with smoke – the Japanese plan to prevent the destruction of the valuable oil facilities by advanced warning had failed. Dutch authorities ordered the oil wells, refineries, and port facilities to be blown up, and then evacuated the engineers who carried out the work.[8] The convoy dropped anchor three miles off the coast late in the day of January 23, and troops were landed early the next morning.[9] The Japanese came ashore without opposition at two locations and proceeded quickly to take control of key positions, including an airfield and bridges. The land battle was of short duration with the enemy soon in control of the entire Balikpapan area. The events at sea, however, did not go as smoothly for the Japanese.

***

The first light of January 20 found *Marblehead*, *Boise*, and six destroyers anchored in Koepang Bay off the island of Timor. The position, south and slightly east of Celebes, was far from the location of the Japanese ships moving through Makassar Strait. Hart wanted an attack like that which had been planned for Kema, but *Houston* was away on convoy escort duty and not available. Also unavailable to strengthen the attack force were two Dutch light cruisers – *De Ruyter* and *Java* – undergoing repairs at Surabaya. The American ships weighed anchor late in the day after the destroyers took what fuel they needed from *Marblehead*. Hart's orders were for the vessels to proceed northwest to the Postillon Islands, a small group south of the town of Makassar on Celebes, at a speed of twenty-five knots.

The engineering problems aboard *Marblehead* were worse than initially appeared and she could only move at a maximum speed of up to seventeen knots.[10] Hart had apparently not received the information of the light cruiser's condition. Admiral Glassford directed *Marblehead* and *Bulmer* to follow behind the other ships at a slower speed. Fate again dealt a bad hand to the Americans as the ships proceeded north. Glassford's flagship, *Boise*, scraped her bottom on an uncharted coral reef while passing through Sape Strait just south of the Flores Sea on the morning of January 21. The unfortunate accident was most likely due to the outdated American maps.

Lieutenant Frederick Bell was aboard *Boise* when the accident happened. 'There was a weird rumbling far below and the ship seemed to hesitate, then shudder again, then pass clear,' he later wrote of the incident.[11] Water was pouring in through the ripped bottom of the ship. The damage was severe with 'all firerooms punctured with some leakage', and was later determined to extend a length of almost 116ft.[12] The flagship could not participate in any additional operations in the area.

Captain Robinson received the news after a plane from *Boise* came in low to drop a message from Admiral Glassford just after 10.00 am '*Boise* hit shoal and cannot proceed as planned. *Marblehead* proceed at best speed to Waworado Bay and be prepared to fuel immediately from port side of *Boise*.'[13] Robinson's War Diary recorded sighting *Boise* 'aground' at 10.31 am.[14] Admiral Hart felt Waworado Bay was too far from the potential action, though he decided not to challenge Glassford's decision.[15]

A pair of destroyers accompanied the two cruisers to Waworado Bay near Sumbawa Island, one of the many small islands nestled between Java and Timor. Glassford and his staff transferred to *Marblehead* after the light cruiser took aboard fuel oil from *Boise*. The warships then parted ways, never to operate together again. The damaged *Boise* retired west to Java in the company of the destroyer *Pillsbury* before later proceeding to British repair facilities at Columbo, Ceylon. She eventually made the long journey back to the west coast of the United States.[16]

The loss of *Boise* was a bitter pill for Hart and Glassford, and yet another setback in their plans to strike back at the Japanese. The admirals were determined to carry out the attack. American sailors had endured weeks of hearing about one Japanese victory after another and were now about to go on the attack. The first American naval battle since the Spanish-American War of 1898 would not be undertaken by the great Pacific Fleet, as was often envisioned by many pre-war planners, but rather by four old destroyers under the leadership of Commander Paul Talbot. The attack was to be delivered by the warships of Destroyer Division 59 – *John D. Ford*, *Pope*, *Parrott* and *Paul Jones* – with *Marblehead* (Glassford aboard) and *Bulmer* staying behind to cover their retirement.

The light cruiser was initially directed to sail for Java after her fueling at Waworado Bay. She was ordered instead to a position off the south-eastern tip of Borneo. All Captain Robinson and his men aboard *Marblehead* could do was to wait for the operation to develop and be ready to assist if the destroyers ran into trouble on the return trip. Commander Talbot received the official order to proceed with the mission from Hart just after noon on January 23, while his ships were to the south of the Postillon Islands. 'Good luck going in…. No further information…. Attack enemy off Balikpapan…. If no contacts by 0400 zone time retire at best speed…. Godspeed coming out.'[17]

Operating in a column the destroyers moved north, passing Makassar town well off the starboard side at 4.32 pm The force then turned to the east in order to give any lurking Japanese planes the appearance of heading towards Mandar Bay off Celebes, before turning back west about an hour after sunset, and skirting Cape Mandar by about six miles for the run across Makassar Strait to Balikpapan at a speed of twenty-seven knots.[18] Stormy weather successfully kept Japanese reconnaissance planes away and the only aircraft sighted proved to be an American PBY.[19] Perhaps the luck Admiral Hart had been hoping for had finally arrived.

Visibility was poor as the ships traveled through foul weather. Crewmen aboard flagship *John D. Ford* occasionally struggled to stay upright as the destroyer was hit by pounding waves. Commander Talbot could not see much through the thick haze as he sat perched on his command chair on the bridge. The mission leader was suffering from a severe case of hemorrhoids and was thought to have lost a considerable amount of blood. He refused to go elsewhere, knowing his place was on the bridge and his responsibility was to lead the men into battle.[20]

The division commander sent instructions for the upcoming engagement to his destroyer captains through a series of messages sent by blinker light. 'Primary weapon torpedoes. Primary objective transports. Cruisers as necessary to accomplish mission. Endeavor launch torpedoes at close range before being discovered.'[21] Talbot gave a variety of additional directions, including information about torpedo settings and retirement plans. He closed by extolling his sailors to 'use initiative and determination'.[22]

The four destroyers sailing towards Balikpapan were obsolete relics of a World War I design commissioned in 1920–21.[23] The main armament consisted of four open mount 4-inch guns and twelve torpedo tubes. Unlike more modern destroyer designs, where the torpedoes were centrally mounted and could be turned to fire off either port or starboard sides, the torpedoes on these ships were mounted in four triple sets of tubes, with two mounts on each side. Only six torpedoes could be fired from each side, meaning if the targets were all clustered in one direction then the ships would have to turn around to bring all the remaining tubes to bear. The Japanese destroyers guarding the invasion force were newer, larger, and more powerful. The enemy also had the 5.5-inch guns of the light cruiser *Naka*.

Talbot's only real possible advantage was surprise and he used it to great benefit. Lookouts sighted what appeared to be distant searchlights shortly after 10.00 pm prompting Talbot to slightly alter course. Lights were again spotted just before midnight, only these seemed to be positioned off shore and were occasionally flickering and flaring up. The lights later proved to be the burning cargo ship *Nana Maru*, damaged earlier by Dutch planes and now an abandoned wreck. The day transitioned into January 24 as the destroyers moved ever closer to Balikpapan.

An eerie situation awaited the American sailors as they began their final approach. The port area was a mass of flames, and burning oil facilities surrounded the area behind. Large clouds of thick black smoke were billowing out into Makassar Strait for about twenty miles. A stench of burning oil lingered in the air.[24] The smoke combined with the thunderstorms to create enough poor visibility to cover the American approach and hinder Japanese lookouts. The fires ashore, burning cargo ship, and occasional Japanese searchlights reflected off clouds to create the dazzling spectrum seen by American lookouts.

The American destroyers narrowly escaped detection at 2.35 am when lookouts aboard *John D. Ford* sighted a column of four Japanese destroyers passing from starboard to port about 3,000 yards ahead.[25] Tense sailors waited for the order to fire torpedoes, but none came as Talbot again altered course. One of the passing ships used a blue light to flash a message in a code unknown to the Americans. The enemy took no action after not receiving a response. The Japanese warships were heading out to sea to search for a lurking enemy. The escorts were not looking for surface ships, but rather a submarine.

Commander Talbot was unaware that an ally was also on the scene in the form of Dutch submarine *K-XVIII*. Operating on the surface due to the poor weather conditions, her talented skipper slipped though the initial ring of escorts before the arrival of the American ships and fired a spread of torpedoes at *Naka*. All the underwater missiles missed the light cruiser. However, one torpedo struck the *Tsuruga Maru*. The transport exploded and later sank, but sources differ as to whether it was from a torpedo aimed at *Naka* or a different spread.[26] The Dutch submarine cleared the immediate area and did not participate in any additional action during the night. Admiral Nishimura then moved his escorts further out from the anchorage to begin an anti-submarine sweep, with some of his destroyers passing in front of the approaching American ships.

The main targets were sighted by American lookouts at 2.46 am – two rows of transports anchored about five miles off the harbor entrance and guarded by an assortment of small escorts.[27] The destroyers sped in for a torpedo attack in a column formation. 'The shore line had not been sighted and visibility was low due to a burning ship at sea and oil fires ashore,' Talbot later wrote. 'It was extremely difficult to distinguish the type of target until close aboard, or to estimate the target angle.'[28] Ten torpedoes were fired at short range during the first pass through the enemy formation scoring no hits. Undaunted, Talbot maneuvered his ships for a second pass, and during the turn *Parrott* unleashed three torpedoes at a target off her port bow. Two minutes later the 3,500-ton transport *Sumanoura Maru* exploded in flames.

The element of surprise was now gone, throwing the Japanese into confusion. Some Japanese captains understood what was happening, though were unable to distinguish between friend and foe in the mêlée, while others – including Nishimura – held to the belief that the attacker was a submarine. The destroyers expended their remaining torpedoes, scoring hits on three additional vessels – transport *Tatsukami Maru*, *PC-37* (a torpedo boat mistaken for a destroyer), and cargo ship *Kuretake Maru* were all sunk. Gunfire damaged at least two other Japanese ships. The only hit on an American warship occurred when a shell landed on the after-deck house of *John D. Ford* starting a small fire and wounding four men.

The battle was over by 3.50 am. With all torpedoes expended, and the Japanese now fully aware the intruders were surface ships, the destroyers sped towards their planned rendezvous with *Marblehead*. The flagship initially lagged behind, but soon caught up with the other destroyers of the force. The light cruiser and her escorting destroyer were about fifty miles south. The first light of January 24 brought the possibility of enemy airplanes, but luck was still riding with Commander Talbot and his strike force was to escape the Japanese all together.

The men aboard the *Marblehead* had no contact with the destroyers coming their way and Captain Robinson ordered a plane launched at dawn. Hours earlier, well before the first rays of morning light crossed the sky, sailors aboard the light cruiser were busy making one of the SOC Seagull planes ready for operations. The plane was fueled up as it sat perched on top of a catapult. A small bomb was attached under each wing – the main weapon should the pilot spot an enemy submarine.

Shortly before dawn, Lieutenant Earl Blessman climbed into the cockpit and began checking critical instruments with a small flashlight. Blessman graduated from the Naval Academy in 1931, later completed flight school in Pensacola, FL, and served as a pilot at various stations, including aboard the aircraft carrier *Lexington*.[29] He was now the senior aviator aboard *Marblehead*.

Radioman Second Class Clarence Jennings was to ride in the back seat to serve as his radio operator and gunner. Both men had parachutes strapped over their Mae West life vests. Jennings clambered around the fuselage to make a last check of the plane before climbing into the cockpit and sliding the canopy shut. The plane's engine started up with a roar. A short time later the aircraft was shot off the catapult. The aircraft began slowly rising into the sky after initially dipping low towards the ocean.

Both men scanned the water for any sign of the approaching destroyers while keeping an eye out for possible submarines. They openly wondered if Japanese planes were shadowing the ships down from Balikpapan. Jennings was the first to spot something, asking over the intercom 'what's that off to the right of the nose?' Blessman looked and replied 'ship wakes'.[30] A message was quickly sent back to *Marblehead*, 'all coming'. Lookouts aboard the light cruiser first sighted the approaching destroyers at 8.05 am. Only after the forces joined together into one group did the tension among the destroyer sailors begin to ease. The destroyers pulled ahead of *Marblehead* with each acknowledging the light cruiser's 'well done' message in signal flags.[31] The combined force steamed south to arrive in Surabaya, Java, before noon.

An official U.S. Navy Department communique released late in the day on January 25 (Washington time) reported, 'United Sates cruisers and destroyers of the Asiatic Fleet have sunk five additional enemy transports, and probably one other, in the Makassar Straits without loss to our attacking forces.'[32] Although the sea battle was not significant in historical terms and largely ignored by the press, it was a much-needed victory for the sailors of the Asiatic Fleet.

Admiral Hart was ecstatic and considered it the best day of the war for him.[33] The encounter, however, only delayed the Japanese invasion operations by one day. Whether the torpedo problems experienced by the destroyer men were the result of foul aiming owing to the high speed and difficult visibility conditions, or the malfunctioning warheads which were plaguing the submariners (or a combination of both) may never be known. Their heroic effort and poise under challenging conditions will be long remembered as having been conducted in the highest tradition of the United States Navy.

***

As the invasion and subsequent sea battle was taking place at Balikpapan, the Japanese undertook a simultaneous operation against Kendari on the southeastern part of Celebes. An invasion force sent from the northern part of the island with six transports and a powerful escort of warships arrived during the first hours of January 24.[34] The unsuspecting American seaplane tender *Childs* was anchored in the vicinity. She made a daring escape aided by a rain squall and a dose of good luck. The important airfield at Kendari fell into Japanese hands after only minimal resistance, although the Dutch destroyed some of the facilities and fuel supply.

Japanese planes were quickly flown into the new forward base for future operations and a naval anchorage was established in nearby Staring Bay. The airfield put Japanese bombers in range of the ABDA naval base in Surabaya, and in a position to hinder reinforcements moving north from Australia. Another ABDA strike force would soon be assembled to thwart the Japanese advance – and this time *Marblehead* would be in the thick of the action.

PART III

FIRE FROM THE SKY

Chapter 11

Positioned on the north-eastern coast of Java, the port city of Surabaya was sheltered from the Java Sea by the adjacent island of Madura, providing an excellent anchorage. Two channels provided access to the harbor area with minefields protecting both. The port was the main operating base for the Dutch Navy in the Netherlands East Indies with facilities to overhaul ships, torpedo workshops, barracks, and a submarine base. The navy yard could make repairs to ships up to 10,000 tones and several floating drydocks were available.[1]

After escorting the victorious destroyers back from the Balikpapan raid, *Marblehead* dropped anchor off Surabaya at 11.21 am on January 25.[2] An assortment of American and Dutch warships along with some auxiliary vessels were scattered about at various points around the harbor. The light cruiser moved a short time later to the Dutch Navy base for repairs to her troubled turbine. A temporary shore patrol departed to make ready for some liberty-seeking sailors. Also leaving the ship was Admiral Glassford and staff who moved ashore to the U.S. Navy headquarters. The light cruiser took aboard fuel and supplies after her turbine was refurbished. The old destroyers were also showing wear, the result of having been almost constantly at sea since the start of the war. The visit to Surabaya would give the weary American sailors and their ships a much-needed break – but it would be a short one.

Admiral Hart, along with members of his staff and a few Dutch officers, visited Surabaya to personally thank some of the destroyer sailors for a job well done. He made an unofficial visit aboard *Marblehead* to see Captain Robinson during the afternoon of January 25.[3] Hart wanted to build on the successful Balikpapan raid with more offensive operations. A tactical victory for sure, and a morale booster during a time when Allied victories were in short supply, the strike did little to slow the advancing Japanese.

Hart felt the 'stage was very well set' for another raid near Makassar Strait where 'some attractive targets' were expected to be found.[4] He conferred with other ABDA admirals after reports indicated Japanese ships were again concentrated in the Makassar Strait area. No large British warships were on hand and Dutch heavy ships were also not available. The strike would again fall to the newly repaired *Marblehead* and four destroyers. The light cruiser slipped out of Surabaya during the late hours of January 30. The next morning found her cruising in company of destroyers *Stewart*, *Edwards*, *Barker*, and *Blumer*. Captain Robinson was in command of the operation as no admiral was present with the force. A possible submarine contact sent *Stewart* off searching for an underwater intruder. However, nothing was found and it turned out to be a false alarm.

A detailed radio message from Hart revealed Robinson's orders were to deliver an attack on enemy shipping off Balikpapan during the evening hours of January 31. A formation of transports close to shore along with two separate groups of destroyers and two light cruisers were reported in the area. 'Final decision to go in, direction and method of attack at your discretion,' Hart noted.[5] Robinson planned a raid like the previous operation – the destroyers were to attack the enemy with torpedoes in a column formation. The light cruiser was to provide support with gunfire and torpedoes and then cover the withdrawal. Surprise was the key element.

The warships moved north while daylight faded to darkness. The sailors aboard wondered if the enemy could again be caught off guard at the same location. If the sighting reports were accurate, then the Japanese escorts were more than double the strength of the small American force. The conditions that helped to successfully mask the attackers' approach during the previous Balikpapan operation were not in place. Gone was the foul weather. The night conditions were to be a full moon with very high visibility – meaning the ships could easily be sighted by keen lookouts.

The American ships were not alone during the day of January 31. A single plane was sighted at 7.00 am flying low while approaching off the starboard bow. The aircraft was later identified as friendly. At 2.00 pm an unidentified plane was spotted in the clouds well aft of the starboard quarter. The aircraft eventually passed to the port quarter before disappearing into a cloud bank.[6] The enemy appeared to be shadowing the ships, forcing Captain Robinson into a critical decision. The Japanese were in control of airbases at both Balikpapan and Kendari, providing easy coverage over Makassar Strait.

Hart sent out a message at 6.35 pm with updated information about the enemy disposition around Balikpapan. The admiral concluded with a hearty 'good luck whatever your decision'. Captain Robinson had all but made up his mind to abort the mission due to the unfavorable conditions, large number of enemy escort ships in the target area, and presence of enemy planes. He gave the order to change course, 'consider the odds to be too great, reverse course to 220 and change speed to 18 knots'.[7] The old *Marblehead* swung around to a south-west heading back towards Java. She was joined by *Houston* around noon the next day. A radio message directed the force to proceed back to Surabaya for a rendezvous with the Dutch light cruiser *De Ruyter*, and a conference of commanders.

Hart was privately concerned that Captain Robinson had not been aggressive enough and the aborted mission could have negative political and diplomatic ramifications with the Dutch leaders on Java.[8] The ABDA naval leaders did not discuss the matter publicly. A new, more powerful force was about to be formed that for the first time would involve warships from more than one nation.

***

During late January, Admiral Hart was contending with the ongoing political pressures emanating from both the local Dutch on Java and others back in Washington. The top Dutch officials were still seething at the senior naval command in ABDA having not been given to one of their admirals and continued to be vocal about it. Much of the criticism of inaction leveled against Hart from the Dutch, and in some cases even British officials, was unjustified. The record of the Dutch admirals later in the campaign would prove to be far from stellar.

The matter came to a head at the end of January when orders arrived from Washington resulting in a somewhat confusing change of command. The remnants of the Asiatic Fleet were reorganized into a new command called U.S. Naval Forces in the Southwest Pacific. Admiral Glassford was promoted and given the command, with Admiral Purnell designated to serve as his chief of staff. Interestingly, the Asiatic Fleet was never formally abolished, and Hart retained command of the nonexistent force.[9] Hart remained ABDA naval commander, but knew his days were numbered.

While Admiral Hart and Dutch officials were worrying about slowing the Japanese advance towards Java, their ABDA counterparts of the British Commonwealth were at the end of a losing battle for Malaya. The initial Japanese landings at the onset of the war, subsequent advances through the jungle, sinking of the capital ships of British Force Z, and the gaining of air superiority, all culminated with the British retreating off the Malaya Peninsula to the island of Singapore on January 31.[10] The British naval base on Singapore was closed and the components of the Royal Air Force still operating were moved east to Sumatra. ABDA Supreme Commander, Sir Archibald Wavell, gave up other tasks to better focus on the defense of Singapore, believing the island fortress could hold out indefinitely.[11] The loss of Malaya had two potential implications for Hart. First, Wavell had less time and attention available for events happening on the eastern side of his command area, meaning the American admiral could continue to have a somewhat free hand in planning and operations. Second, British and Dutch warships previously involved in escorting convoys to Malaya might soon become available to help in offensive operations elsewhere.

Operating with Wavell's approval, Admiral Hart eventually formed a strike force of ABDA warships. However, the American admiral had to deal with a host of issues in putting together the group. Dutch Admiral Helfrich was still coy about committing his surface warships to participate with their American counterparts.

Aware that Japanese naval forces were still massed off Balikpapan and that available American warships were meager, Hart met with Helfrich and Commodore John Collins of the Royal Australian Navy in Batavia on January 26 to discuss pooling resources. He met stiff resistance from the Dutch. Hart later wrote that Helfrich,

> was still found disposed not to be entirely frank as regards [to] the state and readiness of his forces. At this conference, he did not disclose that he could get a considerable force of his own cruisers and destroyers to sea – which would have strengthened our current weakness to the eastward of Java.[12]

The Dutch Admiral sent his warships to search for a Japanese force in Karimata Strait, between Borneo and Sumatra. Hart already knew an enemy force was nonexistent. He eventually sent *Marblehead* and destroyers on the aborted voyage north.

The situation dramatically changed in the span of only a few short days when Dutch warships suddenly became available. Although history records various names, what has commonly become known as the Combined Striking Force was officially formed on February 1, 1942. Hart met with Helfrich, Glassford, and Collins the following day in Lembang to discuss the next steps. Both for political reasons and to keep Glassford out of further operational command, Hart appointed Dutch Rear Admiral Karel Doorman as commander of the Combined Striking Force.

The 52-year-old Dutch admiral had been born in Holland in 1889. After graduating from the Royal Netherlands Naval College in 1910, and serving aboard various naval vessels, he entered the new field of naval aviation. Military aviation was still in its infancy at the time. Doorman would be on the front edge of its development for the Royal Netherlands Navy as both a pilot and flight instructor. Amazingly, he survived thirty-three emergency landings during his time in aviation.[13] Doorman transferred to the Pacific in 1937, was eventually promoted to the rank of rear admiral, and became commander of Netherlands East Indies Seagoing Squadron in 1940. Doorman knew the waters in which his ships would be operating well, perhaps better than any American flag officer. However, he had the disadvantage of having never led a large naval force in battle.[14]

***

The Japanese moves to isolate Java had continued with little hindrance as January drew to a close. The American and Dutch submarine forces scored nothing more than some minor successes since the start of the campaign; ABDA air power was practically nonexistent and played no major role in the fighting.

Both the Japanese and Dutch leaders considered Ambon to be a critical component in the defense of the eastern tier of the Netherland East Indies.[15] The small island sits about half-way between Celebes and New Guinea and was used as a staging area for ABDA submarines and seaplanes. Enemy control would effectively prevent any forces on New Guinea from coming to the aid of Java. Japanese planes bombed Ambon throughout January before naval troops landed on the last day of the month. The mostly Dutch and Australian defenders were defeated within a week, with some of the captured soldiers brutally murdered in

78

a horrific war crime. The city of Makassar on southwestern Celebes and Banjarmasin, facing the Java Sea on the southern part of Borneo were clearly next on the list for invasion. The conquest of the two cities would give the Japanese complete control of both sides of Makassar Strait.

Admiral Hart was still focused on hitting the enemy in Makassar Strait and put in motion plans to do so with his expanded group of warships. On February 1, ABDA air reconnaissance reported a large concentration of Japanese shipping off Balikpapan consisting of twenty transports, three cruisers, and ten destroyers.[16] The ships were presumably assembled as an invasion convoy making ready to sail for Makassar or Banjarmasin. The admiral sought to slow their advance by conducting a raid like the Balikpapan operation. Making an undetected approach north was again seen as the key to a successful operation. Timing was critical as the invasion force could set sail at any time. The ABDA naval leader directed Admiral Doorman and his staff to put together an operational plan while the various ships of the force were gathering off Surabaya.

Captain Robinson guided *Marblehead* into Bunder Roads on February 3 after returning from the aborted mission north.[17] The wedge of sheltered water was positioned between Java and the island of Madura and led directly to the Surabaya harbor to the west. The anchorage was the gathering point of the Combined Striking Force. The ships represented the greatest assemblage of ABDA naval power to date, numbering eleven warships in total. The force was strong enough to inflict significant damage on the enemy. The group included four cruisers – *Houston* and *Marblehead*, along with the Dutch light cruisers *De Ruyter* and *Tromp* – and seven destroyers. The Americans contributed *Stewart*, *Barker*, *Blumer*, and *John D. Edwards*, while the Dutch added *Van Ghent*, *Banckert*, and *Piet Hein*. Admiral Doorman used *De Ruyter* as his flagship. However, the force had no air cover – something a former airman like Doorman certainly knew was risky.

Although the Dutch had a large shipbuilding industry in Holland, with a reputation for high quality work, both Royal Dutch Navy light cruisers under Doorman's command were deficient as compared to their Japanese counterparts. The neutral Dutch saw a vast amount of destruction close to the border of their homeland during World War I in Europe. The post-Armistice anti-war euphoria gained a strong following within the Dutch government, limiting funding for new warships. The economic depression of the 1930s added additional funding constraints. Both factors combined to limit the size and power of *De Ruyter* and *Tromp*.

The design of *De Ruyter* has been heavily criticized due to her small size, thin armor, and light armament.[18] A large narrow forward conning tower was comparable to several types of German capital ships, including the battleship *Bismarck*. She was similar in size and weight to *Marblehead*, although designed and built more than a decade later.

The Dutch flagship's main battery consisted of seven 5.9-inch guns oddly arranged in three double and one single turret. Her ten 40-millimeter anti-aircraft guns were clustered together just forward of the after turrets, limiting the arc of fire and making the guns susceptible to being knocked out in one hit; they did, however, have an advanced Hazemeyer fire control system. The light cruiser *Tromp* was even smaller, mounting six 5.9-inch guns. Neither warship had radar.

Admiral Purnell flew into Bunder Roads aboard a PBY on February 3 for a conference of ship commanders to be held on Doorman's flagship. He first went to *Marblehead*, arriving aboard just after 10.30 am. Only minutes later a report of enemy planes in the area led to rush preparations to get the vessel underway. 'The captain left the ship, went over to the *De Ruyter* and left orders for me to go alongside the *Pecos* and fuel to capacity,' remembered Commander William Goggins, *Marblehead*'s executive office;

> I was making my approach to *Pecos* when the PBY plane, which had taken off after leaving the admiral, reported that the fleet was being attacked by Japanese bombers. There was a high dense cloud over us and we did not see any planes, but the frantic messages from the plane, our own plane, indicated that an attack was imminent.[19]

The ships were not under attack by enemy planes, but the PBY was – by a Zero fighter. When the Japanese plane approached the seaplane, American gunners aboard the slow lumbering aircraft shot it down. The action marked the second time in a three-week span that a Zero fell victim to a sharp-shooting gunner aboard a PBY.[20]

Believing his ship was about to come under attack and hearing a report from *Houston* of a downed plane, Goggins moved away from the tanker and took *Marblehead* through the channel to the outer roads.

'I did not know what the plane was, but thought it might be a PBY,' he recalled. 'We searched around out there for the plane, at the same time keeping a bright lookout for Japanese planes.' The crashed plane likely was the Zero shot down by the PBY.

The aircraft were not coming to attack the ships – the enemy was about to strike Surabaya. The isolation of Java entered a new phase on the morning of February 3, as the Japanese ramped up air operations to destroy remaining ABDA airpower and soften up island defenses for a future invasion. Recent conquests along the Makassar Strait put much of Java in range of Japanese land-based planes for the first time. Some of the Dutch airfields on the island had already been targeted, but the day marked the first attack on Surabaya. The shrieking wail of air raid sirens filled the city during the late morning hours. The approaching armada of twenty-six bombers and fifty fighters from Kendari was one of several air strikes slated to hit targets on the island.[21] The planes passed near Bunder Roads traveling west. Broken clouds allowed the Japanese airmen to spot the assembled warships below.

Sailors aboard *Marblehead* rushed to man air defense stations. Someone aboard the warship remembered seeing one plane lingering behind, likely to send out a detailed contact report.[22] The light cruiser's SOC Seagull seaplanes stayed aboard, though *Houston* launched her planes as a precaution for the vulnerable aircraft to clear the area. The bottled up anchored ships could have made for easy targets. The raiders continued on course to hit targets in Surabaya and destroyed a number of Dutch and American planes both in the air and on the ground.[23] The sighting was an ominous development for Doorman's force. Japanese commanders were certainly alerted to the presence of the sizable ABDA naval group in the area.

Back at Bunder Roads, Admiral Doorman hosted a conference of ship commanders aboard his flagship *De Ruyter*. They reviewed the mission plan in the form of 'Operational Order No 1'. The group was to move against the Japanese fleet off Balikpapan and 'enemy transports will be attacked and destroyed in a night attack'.[24] The document outlined the most current information, including 'enemy aircraft carriers supposed to be at Kendari or south of Celebes'. The order included steaming formations, signal information, and other operational details, all of which were basic, due to the ships having not operated together before.

The cruiser float planes were to maintain a continuous patrol during the daylight hours to act as extra lookouts.

Captain Robinson returned aboard *Marblehead* just before 3.00 pm, from the conference on *De Ruyter*, after his ship had just completed refueling from *Pecos*. The first hour of February 4 saw Sub-Lieutenant Luxemburg of the Royal Netherlands Navy reporting aboard as liaison officer. The warship was underway at 1.13 am moving slowly to clear the minefields protecting Bunder Roads.[25] She continued east into the darkness. Other warships were also departing the area with only *Pecos* and a few destroyers remaining behind.

Lookouts began sighting other ships at about 5.00 am as the group completed a rendezvous at sea before moving into a cruising formation. The flagship *De Ruyter* led a column of *Houston* (with Admiral Purnell aboard), *Marblehead*, and *Tromp* spaced 700 to 800 yards apart. The four American destroyers were positioned on the flanks, while the three Dutch destroyers made up the rear of the formation. The Combined Striking Force was at sea and headed for action.

Chapter 12

The sailors aboard *Marblehead* were treated to an array of red hues that filled the eastern sky and highlighted the bottom of cloud banks as dawn broke on the morning of February 4. The seas were moderate with a slight westerly breeze, visibility was fair, and intermitted clouds covered the sky. The crewmen followed the usual morning procedures – clean up, breakfast, and muster on stations before continuing with routine ship business. Lookouts were keeping a careful watch of the sky and horizon. As the morning progressed they could occasionally see the high mountain tops of Bali and Lombok peeking up through the clouds in the distance off the starboard side. The light cruiser was traveling east following a zig-zag course at a speed of fifteen knots. Five of the eight 3-inch anti-aircraft guns and all machine gun stations were fully manned.

Admiral Doorman's plan was to proceed east into the Flores Sea before turning north towards the town of Makassar on Celebes. His course later came under scrutiny, especially from Admiral Helfrich, who felt it would have been wiser to sail north into the Java Sea from Madura Island towards the southern end of Borneo and then east into the Makassar Strait.[1] The route would have kept the force farther west from the Japanese air bases on Celebes.

Japanese air attacks on Java the day before hit American and Dutch air units hard – both had taken serious losses, and ABDA airpower was not exceptionally strong to begin with on Java. As a result, no fighter cover was expected to be available while the Combined Striking Force tried to make the risky run through the open seas during daylight hours to hit the enemy. Doorman hoped the night departure would help elude the enemy reconnaissance planes expected to be in the air throughout the day.

Captain Robinson was on the bridge as his warship steamed east. Among those clustered with the commanding officer were sailors serving as talkers. Equipped with sound powered telephones connected with various communications circuits, the men were a critical component of the interior communications system aboard *Marblehead*. Robinson could send commands to or get information from almost any part of the ship through the network of talkers.

At 9.35 am Robinson received a radio message from Admiral Doorman, who was notifying his ships that thirty-seven Japanese bombers were reported to be en route to Surabaya, traveling on a southwesterly course. The planes had been sighted just after 8.00 am.[2] At the time the ships were about 180 miles almost due east of Surabaya, and over forty miles north of Bali. Some of the morning clouds were dissipating allowing for a clearer sky.

The admiral's information about the enemy aircraft was not correct. There were far more than thirty-seven Japanese planes in the area and the Japanese were not intending to strike Surabaya, but instead were looking for his ships. A total of sixty bombers had taken off that morning from the newly acquired air base at Kendari, more than 500 miles to the north-east. All were twin-engine bombers – a mix of Nakajima Nells and Mitsubishi Bettys – carrying 132 and 551 lb bombs.[3] A group of seven smaller single-engine planes accompanied the bombers, most likely for reconnaissance purposes. Doorman was likely horror-struck when he eventually realized the planes would be attacking his ships. The long-time student of naval aviation understood, perhaps more than anyone else in the ABDA naval command, the vulnerability of his force and the devastation the bombers could bring upon his ships.[4]

At 9.49 am, less than fifteen minutes after Doorman's message, sailors on *Houston* spotted some unidentified aircraft in the distance. At almost the same time, lookouts aboard *Marblehead* sighted strange planes approaching from the northeast at a high altitude of about 17,000ft.[5] Captain Robinson immediately ordered his crew to prepare for an air attack. He barked out a series of orders that were transmitted by telephone talkers to various parts of the ship. An alarm sounded, followed by an announcement over the loudspeaker system: 'air defense – man your battle stations'.[6]

The klaxon alarm sent men racing in all directions across the ship to reach their battle stations. As sailors ran through passageways and onto ladders, the distinctive sound of clanging steel followed as watertight doors and hatches were swung closed and wheels spun hard to make for a tight seal. The ship went to material condition ZED – meaning all watertight doors and hatches were fully sealed. The conditions allowed for the maximum chance of survivability should the ship sustain damage – especially if the planes were carrying torpedoes. Men who were part of damage control parties went to their assigned stations and prepared to spring into action at the first call of damage.

All the anti-aircraft guns were now fully manned. Magazines were opened to allow for an ammunition train to be formed. Unlike the powered ammunition hoists of more modern warships, it was up to a human chain to move shells from the magazines up to the 3-inch gun stations. Fires were lit under the six unused boilers to give the warship the availability of full speed and power on short notice. Sailors dumped 4,200 gallons of aviation fuel, stored near the after gun turret, over the side lest the highly flammable solution become a raging inferno if hit.

The medical staff made ready to receive casualties. The sick-bay on *Marblehead* was cramped and exposed; the position on the first platform deck, only two levels below topside, did not offer much in the way of protection from hits above. Hospital corpsmen began moving patients and supplies to a larger and safer location – the torpedo workshop.

Cooks put out cooking flames in the galley – one of many precautions taken to get the ship ready for action. 'The men and the gear were dispersed throughout the ship, as well as possible so that there would be no undue concentration,' recalled Commander Nicholas Van Bergen, the ship's gunnery officer. 'We had not manned the 6-inch battery because of its limited elevation and the men for that battery were either disposed passing ammunition, or staying below decks so that they would be less affected by fragmentation bombs.'[7]

The first Japanese planes to close on the force was a group of twenty-seven 'Betty' bombers, followed close behind by nine more of the same type, approaching from the north-east. The Mitsubishi G4M1 began large-scale service in April 1941.[8] The official Japanese name for the plane was the Navy Type 1 Attack Bomber, although the aircraft was commonly known to the Americans as the Betty. The land-based bomber was powered by two engines and featured a long and thin cigar-shaped fuselage. Operated by a crew of seven, the plane was fast, with a long range, and was equipped with an internal bomb bay. The lack of armor and self-sealing fuel tanks made the aircraft susceptible to even a small number of bullets or shrapnel from anti-aircraft guns.

Once nearing the ships, the attackers divided into smaller groups, ignoring the destroyers to move towards the cruisers. Their main targets appeared to be *Houston* and *Marblehead*. Lookouts aboard both ships intently watched as the planes split into smaller groups. 'It is believed that thirty-seven bombing planes were in the formation, which consisted of four groups of approximately nine planes each,' Captain Robinson recalled.[9]

Later in the war, after the number of anti-aircraft guns carried aboard ships was greatly increased, it was standard practice for warships under air attack to cluster together for the protection afforded by the greater amount of fire power. However, it was not the case in early 1942, when policy called for ships to separate to give each vessel room to maneuver. 'At 9.53 am ships scattered in accordance with doctrine and thereafter acted independently until after the completion of the engagement,' Robinson wrote. His ship veered sharply to the right to detach from the other cruisers in the column. A rapid series of events followed as both American cruisers came under attack.

The strongest anti-aircraft guns in the force were aboard the four cruisers. The light cruiser *Marblehead* was ill-equipped for air defense with eight 3-inch guns serving as the primary weaponry. The old guns were hand operated with no modern fire control director to assist in the aiming process and were considered outdated technology. As an additional liability, the shells could not reach high altitude targets. An equal number of machine guns were short range and only capable of close defense. The 6-inch main battery guns were useless during air attacks. The 40-millimeter guns on the two Dutch cruisers were considered good, effective anti-aircraft weapons, though light in number.

The most powerful air defense weapons were the eight 5-inch guns aboard *Houston*. The single-barrel mounts were positioned four on each side of the middle area of the ship and could deliver fire to high altitudes and across wide arches. These guns should have been able to deliver a blanket of devastating fire into the formation of enemy planes with the exploding shells spreading shrapnel among the light-skinned bombers.

The gunners aboard the heavy cruiser were ready for action. A marine gun captain leaning on the rail while chewing some tobacco was carefully watching the approaching planes. 'Well, I know those are not our planes,' he said. 'I think we're gonna have a little bit of trouble pretty soon.'[10] The 5-inch guns opened fire just before 10.00 am. In some extraordinarily good shooting, the first salvo went right into the midst of the enemy formation, but only one shell exploded. The lead plane looked to have momentarily staggered before it continued to move forward. Gunners checked their fuses and settings – everything was correct. A second salvo gave similar results. The sailors were firing defective shells, perhaps the result of old age and a navy policy that prohibited live-fire drills during the pre-war years. The dismal explosion ratio continued as the attack unfolded.

Nine bombers in a shallow V formation reduced altitude to about 14,000ft while approaching *Marblehead* just minutes before 10.00 am. A second group of eight planes was seen in the distance not far behind the first. Commander Van Bergen was still aboard the bridge at the time. The gunnery officer likely would have gone elsewhere if the impending action was a surface fight. 'The captain who was on the bridge at the time took over, and asked me to remain there since it was purely an AA action that was to take place and to give him as much assistance as I could,' he later recalled.[11] Seaman First Class Laughlin Kelly was manning the wheel as helmsman.

Captain Robinson knew the best chance to get his ship safely through the attack was adroit maneuvering. He also knew it was important to make sure the ship was positioned so his gunners had the best shots possible. 'In general the ship was maneuvered to keep the anti-aircraft battery bearing throughout the attacks,' he later wrote. Among the men in the bridge area was Lieutenant (Junior Grade) E.W. Bishop. With no real battle station during an air attack, the junior aviator came to the bridge for a better view of the action. Robinson gave him a pair of binoculars and instructed him to keep a close watch on the bomb bay doors of the bombers. Bishop was to let the captain know when the bombs were about to be released.

The 3-inch guns opened fire as the planes came closer. Yeoman First Class Beauford Gabriel was among the many sailors helping to keep a steady flow of ammunition flowing to the 3-inch guns. He briefly caught a glimpse of the approaching planes while running to his battle station. 'When our firing commenced you remembered very distinctly that this was not a dummy run and a very funny feeling commenced to roll around inside,' he explained. 'However, as soon as you began to work all that feeling disappeared and you only realized that you had certain duties you must do.' He initially started working topside; he continues,

> I had made several trips to the guns with boxes of ammunition when I was told to shift to the line hauling the boxes up from below to the main deck. During the action prior to the bomb hits the loud speaker system was turned on and we could hear what was going on topside. [12]

The work was grueling, but necessary to keep the gunners armed.

Small black puffs began appearing in the sky when the 3-inch guns fired, but the shells were exploding under the bombers. 'They were too high for our 3-inch to meet,' Van Bergen recalled. Speed was increased to twenty knots. As soon as Bishop shouted that the planes were about to release their bombs, Robinson gave the order for full left rudder. Helmsman Kelly spun the wheel and *Marblehead* lurched hard to port. The group of planes passed overhead without dropping any bombs. The guns fell silent at 10.01 am. Either Robinson's tactics were enough to foul the bombardiers' aim in the final seconds of the approach, or the enemy aviators were just eyeing up their target. The formation was seen to be regaining altitude while making a wide circle for another attack.

The light cruiser steadied on a somewhat northerly course. At 10.05 am a group of eight bombers began approaching the ship off her port bow. This time Robinson ordered up emergency full speed and *Marblehead* began to lurch forward at a faster pace. The 3-inch guns once more opened fire as the captain turned the vessel to port. The gunners sweated as they toiled under the hot tropical sun, doing the best they could with their outdated anti-aircraft weapons. Van Bergen explained:

> The procedure on the ship was that the guns would fire until the planes reached their release point, at which time all hands would go down prone, as soon as the planes had passed, the bombs had landed and the planes were in a position where the guns could again fire, the men would be on their feet before the splashes had subsided and the men again opened up.

The planes again passed overhead without dropping bombs. One aircraft was seen to be trailing, smoking as the guns ceased fire.

The vessel was now heading north-northwest. Captain Robinson's quick turns seemed to be working. For a period of about fifteen minutes *Marblehead* successfully escaped the bombers' grip. 'All that we could do would be attempt to out-maneuver them, so they would start a run and if it didn't look good they would turn and make another one,' Van Bergen recalled. The sailors on the bridge certainly must have been wondering how long the process could continue before the vessel's luck ran out or the planes began to run low of fuel and had to depart. The adversaries were essentially in a game of cat and mouse. Every passing minute was critical.

Captain Robinson called for all speed possible and *Marblehead* attained twenty-nine knots at 10.16 am.[13] At almost the same time he ordered a full starboard rudder. The warship was swinging to the right with her bow eventually pointing to the southeast as the planes came around for a third pass at a similar altitude as before. The 3-inch guns started to crackle. The human ammunition train made sure the shells continued to flow to the gunners. Nine bombers were approaching off the starboard bow. This time it was going to be an actual bombing run, but not before the anti-aircraft gunners scored. 'One plane was struck by gunfire, apparently on a bomb, and disintegrated in the air,' Robinson reported. Perhaps the Betty had momentarily dipped into range of the 3-inch guns allowing a shell to penetrate the thin skin of the aircraft.

Just as the planes passed overhead a string of about seven bombs came falling from the sky. Commander Van Bergen could hear a loud swish from the closest bombs as projectiles came speeding towards the vessel. He thought it was going to be close. The call went out for sailors to take cover and brace for impact. A mass of water suddenly rose to great heights off the port bow as the bombs missed *Marblehead* by less than 100 yards. Lookouts stationed in some of the higher positions were drenched as the cascading water came crashing back down to sea level.

The sailors who were not topside were unable to see what was happening, although some knew it was a close call from the sounds of the attack. 'Below the men described the effect as though gravel had been thrown against the side,' Van Bergen recalled. 'There was no jolt.' The light cruiser again escaped unscathed. 'No damage to the ship was noted,' Captain Robinson wrote.

One bomber was hit as the formation passed – possibly from an anti-aircraft gun on *De Ruyter* or from one of *Houston*'s 5-inch shells that actually exploded.[14] The Betty instantly attracted the attention of the gunners, and everyone who was topside, as it trailed smoke while losing altitude. The aircraft was turning towards *Marblehead* as if to make a suicide run in a move later described by one historian as 'a 1942-style kamikaze'.[15] The sailors manning the 50-caliber machine guns opened fire as soon as the plane came into their range. As a standard practice, tracer bullets were mixed in with the machine gun ammunition to help gunners with the aiming process. Captain Robinson watched as the plane was 'spiraling generally towards the ship'. He could see the tracers were hitting home. The plane angled downward, with the pilot apparently killed by the hail of gunfire, before crashing into the sea about 1,000 yards off *Marblehead*'s port bow. The plane 'disintegrated upon contact with the water,' Robinson wrote. 'No survivors were observed.'

The sailors witnessing the short action broke into a spontaneous wild cheer. The celebration, however, was short lived. With little time to spare another group of seven planes appeared on the port quarter in a shallow V formation and the same dizzying sequence of events was repeated. Robinson ordered a left full rudder. The captain thought it was a new group of planes that were not part of the previous waves. Guns opened fire on the attackers. The planes released a stick of bombs, thought to be seven in number, while passing overhead. The trajectory had the falling bombs arching towards the ship. Topside sailors braced for a hit in what looked to be a close call. The bombs straddled *Marblehead* landing all around her with plumes of water rising into the air.

Aviator Walter Winslow watched from his vantage point aboard *Houston* as 'geysers of sea water leaped high in the air to engulf the old cruiser. This time, however, the *Marblehead* did not escape.'[16] The good fortune thus far following *Marblehead* through the attack had run out. The ship shook, shuttered, and seemed to even momentarily jump out of the water.

Sailors all over the ship were tossed about as two bombs scored direct hits. One hit near the stern close to the port side. The other struck forward, just ahead of the first stack, but behind the tripod mast, and near the starboard side. A third bomb was a near miss, exploding underwater not far off the port bow. As Captain Robinson and his crewmen would soon find out, the light cruiser was in serious peril and the next few hours would be critical for her survival. It was 10.27 am.[17]

Chapter 13

The light cruiser *Marblehead* was essentially a small city filled with levels, passageways, and compartments. Her crew routinely moved around many areas of the ship daily, much like an actual city. The warship featured four principal levels of decks with terminology for each that was part of everyday speech for her sailors. To comprehend the scope and extent of the bomb damage and subsequent damage-control efforts, there is a need to have a clear understanding of the deck arrangement.

The upper deck was the area sailors normally referred to as topside – it was long, narrow, and exposed to the outdoors. An imaginary center line running the length of the ship along the upper deck divided the vessel into the port and starboard halves or sides. The main deck was one level down from topside. The deck was fully enclosed for most of the length of the ship – starting from the bow and moving back until just forward of the after 6-inch turret, where it became exposed. The next two decks below were the first platform and the deeper second platform. Both housed various compartments in the forward and after part of the vessel. The two decks were separated in the middle of the ship by the engineering spaces containing the boilers and engines.

Two mechanical components of the warship – pipes and air ducts – were to play an important role in determining how fast and effectively the sailors could deal with fires, flooding, and damage. A critical component of the firefighting apparatus was a piping system commonly known as a fire main. The pipes supplied water for firefighting, pumped in from the sea, to various locations around the ship.

A ventilation system, comprised of a series of air ducts, was used to distribute fresh air around *Marblehead*. Ventilation was of great importance to sailors stationed in the lower decks who were far from topside. The system became a spreader of smoke and noxious gases during a time of fires, causing otherwise undamaged departments to become uninhabitable. No one knew the decks and equipment better than the executive officer.

***

Commander William Goggins was on the bridge when the Japanese planes were first sighted. He was aware of the earlier report of a formation of enemy planes heading towards Java. 'Apparently they were looking for us, and it is my guess that they had noted our presence the day before and were returning to bomb the ships,' he later recalled.[1] The sounding of the air defense alarm meant it was time for the executive officer to leave the bridge for a position below deck in case Captain Robinson became incapacitated. The arrangement was a critical part of the battle stations plan to have *Marblehead*'s two top officers separated.

The executive officer was headed to the wardroom, an officers' mess area. The compartment was positioned one deck down from topside, on the main deck, near the base of the tripod mast and just forward of the first funnel stack. He did not go directly to the wardroom, but wanted to first check on a few things related to the readiness of the ship for combat. He later said,

> I went below and cruised the main deck to see that everything was alright, that people were properly stationed, that ZED was set, and that people were lying down, that is, those who did not have [battle] stations … I checked up particularly to see that the aviation gasoline tanks had been dumped. Had these caught fire, the entire stern of the ship would probably have been lost.

The path traveled by Goggins initially took him along the starboard side of the main deck. He found the men in the immediate area to be in good spirits and briefly stopped to tell a sailor that *Heron* had made it through an extended air attack. The old seaplane tender was damaged, but survived, after battling Japanese planes for the better part of a day back in late December.[2] He may have felt the episode boded well for *Marblehead*'s chances. 'The damage control parties were all at their stations and ready. The men were all lying down,' Goggins later said. 'I went forward on the port side and up to the wardroom.'

The air attack was fully underway, with *Houston* firing her 5-inch guns and *Marblehead*'s own anti-aircraft guns cracking, by the time Goggins arrived in the wardroom. He could feel the vessel moving at high speed. The rapid firing of the 3-inch guns was quickly depleting the supply of shells topside. An ammunition chain was hurriedly formed near the wardroom. Sailors 'began bringing up ammunition from the forward 3-inch magazine group and running it aft on the port side and up No. 2 hatch to the guns,' Goggins continued. 'We had considerable quantity of ammunition in an office which had been the first lieutenant's office, but that was going so fast that it was necessary to get up as much as possible right away.'

Some important duties aboard the ship did not stop even with the vessel under air attack. A petty officer overseeing the ammunition chain was startled when Mess Attendant First Class Wong Hing fell out of line shortly after the process started. The orderly regularly served Captain Robinson meals and coffee. Ignoring calls to return to his post, Hing hurried away telling the officer the captain has coffee every day at 10.00 am. He carried out his duty of bringing Robinson his coffee on the bridge, even returning the cup and tray to the pantry, before returning to his position passing ammunition.[3]

Two other officers joined Goggins in the wardroom – aviator Lieutenant Edward Blessman and Ensign Charles Coburn. The men drank coffee and smoked cigarettes as the ship creaked and groaned while making sharp turns during the evasive maneuvers.[4] None of the officers likely wanted to be sequestered below deck while the action was happening topside. Although unable to know the precise details of what was happening above, they could still hear the air assault unfolding. 'During the attack, a wave of planes would come over and the battery would fire,' Goggins recalled. 'As the planes got almost directly overhead, the fifty-caliber would start firing and the resulting racket was tremendous, even down below in the wardroom.' A chorus of cheers coming from topside was the only indication of when a plane was hit.

The nearby ammunition chain was working diligently to keep the supply of shells flowing to the gunners. 'Just forward of us in the passageway where the ammunition was being whipped up was Lieutenant Goodhue,' Goggins later said. The executive officer made sure everything was operating as smooth as possible. 'They were carrying boxes of four aft at double time.'

Goggins was leaning against a wardroom table when Seaman First Class Clifford Clendenen dashed through the compartment yelling 'All gunners' mates on the AA batteries to set fuses.'[5] The sailor seemed to vanish immediately after making the announcement. Some of the men from the ammunition chain quickly departed to relieve the exhausted sailors working the guns. Everything for Goggins changed in an instant as the bombs hit *Marblehead* only a few moments later.

***

Machinist's mate Second Class Harold Partin was sound asleep in his bunk having recently completed duty on the mid-watch (4.00 am to 8.00 am). The sounding alarm was immediately followed by Chief Machinist's Mate Elliot Annis shouting to anyone in earshot: 'it's a real raid, boys. Get going!'[6] Partin immediately jumped out of his bunk. He caught a brief glimpse of a Japanese plane in the distance whose fuselage was sparkling in the sun.

Partin was a member of the amidships repair party. A large ship like *Marblehead* typically had multiple groups of sailors positioned with equipment at various points around the vessel ready to deal with battle damage. The light cruiser had three repair parties – forward, amidships, and after – ready to jump into action when needed. The disbursement was necessary to ensure most of the men trained in damage control techniques were not wiped out in a single hit.

At about the same time another crewmember involved with damage control was hurrying to his battle station at central station. Lieutenant Commander Martin Drury was serving as *Marblehead*'s first lieutenant. The term, as used in the U.S. Navy, was not a rank but rather the role of chief damage control officer. He arrived at central station at about 9.55 am. The compartment, located at the bottom of the ship directly below the forward base of the tripod mast, was an assembly and command point for coordinating damage control efforts. The room contained the ship's gyro compass and some switchboards. The sphere-shaped gyro compass was a type of non-magnetic compass device able to find true north by using the force of gravity and the rotation of the earth.[7]

Also in the compartment were Lieutenant (Junior Grade) Frank Blasdel and some enlisted men who were part of a repair party. Blasdel was serving as the assistant first lieutenant and would be actively involved in any damage control activities. Reports immediately began flowing into central station, through various communication circuits, reporting the three repair parties were in position and ready for action. A different circuit reported all battle dressing stations were ready – medical triage stations positioned around the ship.

Drury made sure his repair parties had the most up to date information as possible while the action was developing. 'Continuous information over the JA and JZ telephone circuits gave a clear picture of the number and relative locations of the enemy planes; this information was relayed to the repair parties in the routine manner of battle problem exercises,' he wrote.[8] When the first group of bombs – near misses – fell near *Marblehead*, resulting in reports of strange scraping sounds against the hull, some repair men were quickly dispatched to investigate any possible damage.

***

The two bomb hits and one near miss happened virtually simultaneously. The first bomb crashed through the main deck far aft near the stern and slightly to port of the centerline, with the topside point of entry narrowly missing the corner of the 6-inch main battery turret. The projectile traveled approximately 12ft into the ship, passing through the first platform deck, before exploding in the hand steering compartment directly below. The force of the explosion was vented upwards and aft, buckling the main deck behind the turret and causing extensive structural damage. Bulkheads were ruptured, compartments demolished, and watertight doors blown open. The steering gear was completely wrecked, leaving the rudder jammed 30 degrees to the left.[9]

The second bomb ripped through the hull of a small motor launch stored topside on the starboard side before smashing through the upper deck. The point of entry was close to the forward funnel and slightly to starboard of the centerline. The projectile exploded just above the main deck causing extensive damage to crew space, the wardroom, and adjacent passageways. The force of the blast traveled downward, causing additional damage deep into the ship, including demolishing the sick-bay and piercing fuel tanks. Water lines, piping, and electrical circuits were severed. An armored bulkhead kept the damage from extending into the nearby forward fireroom.[10]

A third bomb did not hit *Marblehead* but exploded in the water well forward off the port side – close enough to cause substantial damage. The bomb struck the water at an estimated 70-degree angle at a position just behind the forward main battery turret, passing close to the hull before exploding at a depth of about 16ft. The underwater detonation lifted *Marblehead* upward and to the starboard, while sending a shock wave through the ship.[11] The resulting damage was localized but severe, bending portions of the hull inward. Two large irregular shaped holes, measuring about 2ft by 9ft, were ripped open allowing a torrent of seawater to flow into the ship. The keel was bent and distorted over a length of 8ft. The important backbone of the hull, however, stayed intact.

The weapons of destruction were thought to be 100 kilogram (220 lb) general purpose bombs, a type known to have been used by the Japanese at various times during the early part of the war.[12] Flooding and fires resulted from both direct hits and an extensive intake of water from the near miss. The old warship, whose stability characteristics were poor by contemporary standards, also had the added disadvantage of having a riveted hull.[13] The outdated construction method was less effective at keeping watertight integrity than the welded hulls of newer ships, especially during situations involving battle damage.

***

Those on *Marblehead*'s bridge had a clear view of the bombs falling towards the ship and were sure at least some were going to be direct hits. The moment of impact sent a sudden jolt through the bridge area knocking everyone off their feet except Laughlin Kelly. The helmsman remained upright owing to his firm grip on the wheel. Captain Robinson quickly regained his footing. He could see a cloud of black smoke slowly rising from his ship and a slick of oil trailing her.

Gunnery Officer Lieutenant Commander Nicholas Van Bergen was among those with the captain when the bombs struck. 'No one has been able to describe the noise of the explosion of the bombs,' he recalled of when the ship was hit. He clearly remembered the swift shock. 'As a matter of fact, I don't think anyone heard it.'[14]

Captain Robinson immediately began shouting commands to find out the extent of the damage. He was initially most concerned about harm to the engines – the power plants keeping the ship functioning – and directed the talker with the sound powered telephone connected to the engineering spaces to find out the current situation. The sailor quickly replied the communications with the engine room were out.

Other talkers soon reported their circuits were also dead. The bombs severed critical communications lines, hindering the ability of the captain to get information from various departments and finding out the magnitude of the damage. Most communication systems around the ship were out except for a limited number of sound powered phones. Then helmsman Kelly announced more bad news. 'Steering gear's gone, sir,' he told the captain.[15] The rudder was jammed to the left; there was no longer any ability to steer the ship. The warship was still steaming over twenty knots, but was now going in circles.

***

Members of the ammunition party had just left the wardroom area, disappearing from William Goggins' sight, when the compartment was suddenly jolted by the first bomb hitting near the stern. The executive officer knew the back of the ship had been hit and was starting to move towards a hatch to find out what was happening, when the second bomb struck not far from his location. There was a tremendous explosion followed by the lights going out. 'My sensation was that the whole after end of the ship was coming right at me,' he remembered. 'I do not recall that the noise was particularly loud, but the shock was rather severe and I was struck by something, I don't know what it was, on the left hip.'

The compartment was suddenly transformed into a mass of wreckage. 'I could not see very well on account of the lights having all gone out,' Goggins continued. Although knocked down by the force of the explosion, he made it back onto his feet in a short time. 'At this time, I was standing about 6ft from the forward door of the wardroom and I saw that I was almost completely surrounded by wreckage. Apparently, I had not been hit, but I could feel an intense heat from the flash of the bomb.'

Goggins remembered 'standing in this hot gas and I could feel myself burning. The heat was so intense that the bulkheads, the paint on the metal and the linoleum was sizzling and catching fire.' All of his exposed skin was badly burned, although his clothes did not catch on fire.

The wardroom was filled with strong acrid smoke. 'I did not see anybody around me,' Goggins continued. He did not know the location of the two young officers who had been with him just moments ago. Aviator Edward Blessman suffered multiple injuries and was dead. Charles Coburn was gravely injured with terrible burns on his face, arms, and legs – but was alive. Unknown to Goggins there were two other men in the wardroom at the time of the explosion. Lieutenant Arthur Goodhue was burned across a large part of his body and Boatswain's Mate First Class Glenn Bassinger was killed.[16]

After a short time Goggins found Signalman First Class Douglas Murch, who was positioned between him and the compartment door. Murch had suffered some burns, but was not seriously wounded. 'The door was piled high with debris, but there was a small space above it through which we could climb,' Goggins continued. 'Murch climbed through and I followed him and went up on deck.' They were leaving behind a compartment in flames,

> There was by this time a good fire burning in the wardroom and below steam was escaping from some pipes that had been cut. All the lights in the forward compartments were out. The party previously working on the ammunition apparently started up on deck, taking the wounded with them.[17]

The executive officer was seriously injured, though a combination of shock and adrenaline may have desensitized him to his condition. He wanted to get to the bridge to find out the condition of the captain and what happened to the ship. While passing by his cabin, Goggins spotted a man lying on his own transom while groaning in pain. A doctor or some other medical person appeared to be with the wounded man. The conditions were dark and he could not be sure. Goggins briefly peered in before continuing on his way to the bridge. 'I climbed up to the bridge and found that the captain was alright,' he later recalled. He saw the rudder indicator was full to the left. Captain Robinson told him there was no steering control and communications were out. 'The ships around us were keeping clear and were also circling and were firing at the planes overhead,' he noticed after taking a quick glance out on the horizon.

The executive officer decided to go by himself to find out what was wrong with the steering gear. He climbed down the ladder to the main deck. 'I could see a number of wounded, mostly burns, being taken aft, some of them were lying on the main deck,' Goggins continued. 'I recall particularly one of the Chinese boys lying there who appeared to be in a pitiful condition, but there wasn't anything that could be done for him at the time.' It may have been Mess Attendant First Class Shao Ching Yin, who suffered terrible burns across his face and body. He had been in the Chief Petty Officer's Quarters near the back of the ship and his wounds would soon prove to be fatal.[18]

After moving past the wounded on deck, still in the forward area of the ship, Goggins noticed the damage control parties were already at work. 'I went aft on the deck – someone asked me what was the matter with my neck and I then learned that a piece of shrapnel had clipped the back of my neck and that blood was running down my uniform,' he recalled. He replied that he was 'all right', but he was, in fact, far from alright.[19] 'I had been burned in all areas not covered by my clothing,' he later said. Scorched skin was hanging in folds from his arms and legs.

The location of the forward bomb hit was close by. Goggins could see the hole in the deck. He went past a hatch that was emitting smoke, steam, and flames. 'I can recall this particularly because the flame and smoke was hot and burned me as I went by,' he said. 'The anti-aircraft battery was intact and was still firing and they were apparently doing alright.' Goggins was not intending to slow down or stop to get aid for his wounds – he was determined to help save his ship.

Chapter 14

Lieutenant Commander Martin Drury was ready for action. His location was deep below deck near the bottom of the ship in central station. His role as *Marblehead*'s chief damage control officer would be taking center stage in the coming hours as the effort began to assess the damage, make repairs, and determine if the ship could be saved. Drury was monitoring the topside action as best he could and trying to keep his men informed as to what was happening during the ongoing air attack. All he could really do, however, was to wait until some damage took place.

The wait abruptly ended when central station was violently shaken by an intense explosion. 'The gyro compass collapsed and the switchboards were dislodged,' Drury wrote of the aftermath.[1] 'The electrician's mate was directed to pull all switches on the boards. Almost immediately thereafter word was received that the I.C. room was flooding rapidly.' Drury then dashed out of central station on his way to the flooding compartment.

The internal communications room (commonly referred to as the I.C. room) was a critically important compartment containing motor generators and a series of main switchboards connecting various parts of the ship. It was nestled near the bottom of the ship on the port side, not far from central station. Drury arrived to find the watertight hatch to the compartment closed and sealed. He ordered a nearby sailor to open it, 'hoping to be able to enter and possibly prevent the total flooding,' he wrote. 'As the scuttle was loosened, air started to blow out under considerable pressure; the scuttle was then securely dogged down. A hasty inspection of the surrounding area revealed no damage, but the hiss of escaping air could be heard further forward.' There was nothing more he could do now for the compartment.

The first lieutenant briefly returned to central station where he heard reports of the two bomb hits. 'All battery powered communications were dead and communications with amidships and after repair stations (sound powered) had gone out apparently from a severed or burned cable,' he explained. Unable to communicate from central station, Drury again left the compartment to go directly to the repair parties to learn the extent of the damage first-hand. He left Frank Blasdel in charge of central station.

Drury moved up and towards the back of the ship after departing central station. He encountered the sick-bay – demolished and on fire – with a large rupture in the deck exposing a fuel oil tank directly below. There was burning clothing and debris scatted about with steam leaking out of a broken pipe. Fortunately, the compartment was evacuated before the explosions. He stopped in at the amidships repair station. Based on the brief observations he was satisfied everything possible was being done to help the ship. Drury then made his way up to the bridge and reported to Captain Robinson the 'extent of the damage was yet undetermined, but probably serious.'

***

The effort to save *Marblehead* was truly a herculean undertaking, involving many sailors spread across the ship from senior officers to enlisted men. The work required a mix of heroics, determination, and persistence. Saving a badly damaged ship can be considered a process or a series of steps. After ascertaining the extent of the damage and making sure the caring of the wounded was under way, the next – and perhaps most important – step was to keep *Marblehead* from sinking. Her sailors needed to deal with the two most serious threats to be successful – extinguishing fires and stemming the flooding. In many ways, it was two separate damage control battles happening at the same time – one forward and the other near the back of the ship.

The forward bomb hit and near miss happened almost simultaneously and resulted in extensive damage below deck. A dangerous situation existed beneath the waterline where the hull was ripped open by the near miss explosion. The holes were creating suction to pull water into the ship as *Marblehead* moved through the sea. Captain Robinson explained:

> The buckling of the bottom plating acted as a water scoop,
> causing water at high pressure to enter the hull through the

actual ruptures in the bottom plating, forcing water and fuel oil into spaces well above the water line through ruptured vent ducts, sounding tubes, etc.[2]

The effect seemed to be heightened when *Marblehead* was moving at twenty-five knots or more – a speed she needed to evade the ongoing air attacks.[3] Compartments were fast taking in large amounts of water, forcing the bow to dip lower into the ocean. The draft of a ship is the distance measured from the bottom of the keel to the waterline, essentially the amount of the hull that is underwater.[4] The normal draft for *Marblehead* was just over 15ft. Flooding in the forward part of the ship gradually increased the draft to a maximum of 30ft.[5] The increased weight could be enough to pull the forward part of the ship underwater if the flooding was not stopped.

Directly below the forward main battery turret was a series of compartments that were part of the gunnery apparatus. The spaces included a handling room, where sailors moved shells and gunpowder bags up into the turret directly above, and a magazine area for the storage of the ammunition. A separate magazine, holding 50-caliber ammunition, was adjoining the outside of the hull just forward of the internal communications room. The hull was torn open to the sea with belts of bullets hanging out of the hole. The inside decks and bulkheads in the same area were ruptured, allowing water into the magazines for the 6-inch shells and gunpowder bags. Both watertight doors leading to the handling room had been blown off their hinges, allowing water to freely flow into the compartment.

Many other rooms in the general vicinity were either partially or fully flooded because of seawater pouring in through the frayed hull or being forced up by suction through ruptured decks, broken bulkheads, and loose rivets. Some severed water mains also contributed to the flooding. A fuel oil storage tank was among the long list of damaged compartments, the likely cause of the oil slick trailing the ship.

Fires broke out immediately after the bomb explosion. The severe flooding in the lower compartments reduced the amount of space vulnerable to fire, but also increased the hazard. The suction caused by the open hull, coupled with the ruptured fuel tank, was pushing oil upward to feed the flames.[6] Fortunately, the primary water line used for firefighting remained intact.

Harold Partin was one of many sailors thrust into the forefront of the damage control efforts in the forward part of the ship. The machinist's mate and other members of the amidships repair party were in their battle station position on the starboard side of the main deck and were bracing for a hit when the bombs struck. Lying flat on the deck of the repair station, he was violently tossed around by the blast, although he was not hurt. Partin immediately jumped into action after the call came for his group to move forward to fight fires. He led a team of five sailors through a maze of ripped and twisted metal. They encountered a grizzly scene with scattered body parts embedded in various parts of the wreckage. They were walking on a deck awash with mixture of seawater and blood.

The sailors made it through the labyrinth of wreckage to find the forward fire pump – and to their amazement, it was still in working condition. They wasted no time in uncoiling a hose, hooking it to the pump, and turning on the water to start spraying nearby flames. Partin noticed another crewman was using the steam shooting out of the end of a broken pipe to fight a nearby fire.

Back in central station Frank Blasdel and a small group of men were doing their best to keep in contact with various damage control parties, even with limited communications. Blasdel was 26 years old with a boyish-looking face and had only been aboard *Marblehead* for about six months. Initially he thought *Marblehead* had been hit by a torpedo, judging from the movements of the shock. The young officer found himself in an increasingly perilous position. The hatches to the compartment were closed and sealed to maintain watertight integrity. Water started pouring into the compartment from a tube connected to the nearby interior communications room shortly after the bomb hit. The water level was now slowly rising.

Blasdel had no way of knowing the bulkhead and deck of the internal communications room were buckled and the compartment had filled with water immediately after the explosion. The flooding of the room destroyed all direct internal communication circuits. Only a small number of the sound powered phone circuits remained working. There was some smoke in central station and heat was coming from above, indicating the area one deck higher was likely on fire.

Some pounding was suddenly heard on a hatch located on the side of the compartment. Five sailors unexpectedly came rushing in from an adjacent magazine after the hatch was opened. The water was now knee deep. Blasdel knew he had to find a way to get out before they became trapped without any hope of escape. He wetted down his clothes before going through an escape hatch up to a passageway on the deck above. Crawling on his knees he saw fire blocking every direction and quickly went back down into central station, closing and sealing the hatch behind him.

There was only one way out. The front leg of the tripod mast ended at the top of the compartment. The circular steel tube may have originally been designed as an escape path because it had ladder rungs inside, but it now contained assorted wires and communication tubes. 'We'll abandon station by means of the tripod leg,' Blasdel told the sailors.[7] The men would have to crawl about 40ft to safety once inside the tube. Luck was riding with Blasdel on that day, for the tripod leg above central station was the only one of the three not filled with smoke.

There was only one problem with the escape plan – Fireman First Class Joe DeLude was robust in girth and did not think he would make it through the opening. 'You guys better go first,' he told the others. 'I might get stuck and look where you'd be!'[8] One by one sailors were boosted up to the hatch with small and skinny sailors going first. Each pulled themselves through once they were close enough to grab a hold of the ladder rungs. Before long everyone had made a successful escape, including Blasdel, leaving only Joe DeLude behind.

He was desperate, alone, and knew nobody was available to help him.[9] Working in waist-deep water he positioned furniture under the opening allowing him just enough height for his out-stretched arms to grab ahold of the first ladder rung. He slowly pulled himself up to grab another and then another, until he was finally on his way to safety. DeLude made it through the tube, with some difficulty and little width to spare.

Shipfitter Second Class Clarence Aschenbrenner first came aboard *Marblehead* in September 1940. He was well-known to other crew members by the nickname 'Bull', due to his muscular build. The sailor possessed a thorough knowledge of all aspects of damage control. Aschenbrenner rushed to the damaged areas right after the explosions. 'Immediately upon his arrival he became the key man at the scene,' Captain Robinson wrote. 'His splendid physique enabled him to perform tremendous feats of lifting and moving heavy wreckage and to continue to work ceaselessly for a period of about forty-eight hours.'[10] The sailor fought fires with anything possible, including using fire extinguishers until empty and then resorting to smothering flames with blankets.[11]

Chief Boatswain's Mate Harvey Andersen oversaw the forward repair party. He was injured when the shock of the forward bomb blast threw a 6-inch shell out of its storage rack, hitting him in the ribs and ankle. The chief could only move with great pain and had difficulty getting around, but was not entirely put out of action. With the aid of an improvised crutch, Andersen assisted with the damage control efforts in the forward part of the ship by directing firefighting parties, overseeing the rescuing of the wounded, and helping to keep watertight integrity.[12] Lieutenant Hepburn Pearce served as a spotter for the 6-inch guns during battle conditions. Once it became clear his services were no longer needed, and seeing that Harvey Andersen was injured, he leaped into action to take charge of the forward repair party.

Without receiving any specific orders, Chief Shipfitter Hale McCully left the forward repair station with a small group of sailors immediately after the bomb hit. The party moved throughout the forward part of the ship to check hatches and make quick estimates of damage. He assisted in evacuating sailors from various flooded compartments, including the magazines, before eventually taking charge of the firefighting efforts in the sick-bay. McCully did the latter despite oily decks, smoke, darkness, and hazardous broken steam pipes.

The damage control effort in the forward part of the ship, part of the larger struggle to keep *Marblehead* afloat, included stopping the inflow of water. Submersible pumps were typically used to drain water in these types of situations. 'Every conceivable means was used in trying to check the rise of water and to clear water from compartments that we thought might be tenable,' Nicholas Van Bergen said.[13]

The sailors rapidly found the pumps were not able to do the job. 'Submersible pumps were inadequate even after we were able to rig portable leads to them from amidships where there were still a few electrical leads,' Van Bergen explained. 'They were of an old type submersible pump and soon went completely out of commission due to the strain that was put upon them. Thereafter bailing was our principal source of getting rid of water.' Bucket brigades were quickly formed with sailors using anything that could hold water – including buckets, dishpans, and even coffee pots.[14] As men battled fires and flooding in the forward and amidships areas, a separate battle was being waged near the stern of the ship.

Chapter 15

Limited internal communications initially hindered Captain Robinson's ability to determine the magnitude of the damage to his ship. A clearer picture of the situation began to slowly emerge a couple of hours after the damage. The captain had to rely heavily on the verbal reports of various officers and messengers. It was becoming clear to him that *Marblehead* was near her death throes. The ship was leaving a trail of oil and was without control of her steering. Fires were burning inside the vessel both forward and aft, with smoke billowing from the base of the tripod mast. She was listing 10 degrees to starboard and down by the bow – both indicators of serious flooding.

Some damage was not close to the position of the bomb hits. Violent vibrations from the explosions could travel around the insides of a vessel. Shock from the blasts disabled the forward director (part of the fire control system), knocked off-line three single 6-inch guns and the after main battery twin turret, wrecked the forward range finder, and destroyed the radio room batteries.

Robinson later confided his feeling at the time was that *Marblehead* had less than a fifty-fifty chance of staying afloat during the next eight to ten hours.[1] The captain initially sent a short radio message to Admiral Doorman. 'This ship damaged.' He sent a second message at 10.41 am after the situation became a little clearer. 'Damage is serious.' The message also included *Marblehead*'s exact position.[2]

The Dutch light cruiser *Tromp* and two destroyers edged closer to *Marblehead* less than an hour after the bomb hits. Her captain signaled the damaged cruiser by blinker light. 'We are standing by to take off your crew.'[3] Captain Robinson, however, would have none of it – he was determined to save his ship. He waved off the Dutch vessels while shouting through a megaphone. 'Thanks, but I'm going to put her through as she is. Stand away.'[4]

The potential rescue ships stayed in the immediate area. Gunnery Officer Van Bergen later said:

> The *Tromp* and the destroyers gave us considerable reassurance by dashing over towards us from time to time to find out if we were going to sink or capsize and then standing away again so that we realized that if we did go over there would be somebody around to pick up survivors.

Aside from keeping the ship afloat, the most immediate concern of *Marblehead*'s top officers was the ongoing air attack.

The Japanese planes continued relentlessly to press home their attacks on the ABDA ships, even as sailors aboard *Marblehead* were working feverously on damage control efforts to keep the stricken vessel afloat. The short lull between the bomb hits and next wave of aircraft ended when lookouts sighted a group of planes approaching the starboard bow at 11.04 am. Robinson ordered maximum speed – twenty-five knots. The warship was only able to turn in small circles due to her jammed rudder.[5] The formation did not attack – perhaps the Japanese pilots felt the ship was already close to sinking and wanted to find a new target. The planes disappeared into a cloud bank about two minutes after the initial sighting. 'The Japanese plane movement was most repetitious,' Van Bergen explained. 'They'd make a run, which was either a firing run, or a dummy run depending on our movements, and then fly well clear, assemble, come back for another run.'

Less than ten minutes later two groups of planes were sighted approaching the port bow. Robinson again ordered maximum speed. The 3-inch guns quickly resumed firing when the planes reached the port beam. However, the target was not Captain Robinson's ship.

The flagship *De Ruyter* now attracted the attention of the approaching Japanese bombers. A group of planes closed on the light cruiser just before 11.30 am.[6] Sailors manning her five 40-millimeter gun mounts were furiously working to keep fire on the enemy as the aircraft came closer. The nearby deck was filled with cases containing about 3,000 shells, courtesy of a lift that kept a continuous supply of ammunition coming up from below.[7] One plane began trailing smoke after appearing to have been hit. Gunners saw it pass close to *Marblehead* before crashing into the sea.

A string of four bombs straddled the Dutch flagship so closely that gun crews were drenched with water and fragments temporarily knocked out the Hazemeyer fire control system.[8] Quick attention put the director back in working order after only a short period of time. Skillful maneuvering by her commanding officer helped keep *De Ruyter* free of bomb hits during the attack.

Admiral Doorman still hoped he could get some air cover sent out to his position. The admiral knew friendly planes could not arrive in time to help with the current situation. He wanted to have fighter coverage in case of additional Japanese attacks later in the day. Doorman urgently radioed Admiral Glassford to 'send fighters', conveying that the attack was still under way with 'wave after wave of bombers'. Unfortunately, there were no planes available to help his ships.[9] The ABDA force was to remain on their own and without air cover.

Aboard *Houston*, Captain Rooks was ready for evasive maneuvers when nine bombers had approached his ship earlier in the morning. The commanding officer was lying flat on the deck intently observing the planes through his binoculars waiting to guess their bomb release point. He ordered the heavy cruiser hard to port after sensing the time was right, and watched as a phalanx of bombs careened towards the ship. Towering cascades of water rose on both sides as *Houston* seemed to be momentarily lifted out of the sea. The violent shaking knocked out the main anti-aircraft fire control director causing the 5-inch guns to shift to local control. A seaplane sitting on the catapult was damaged and had to be pushed over the side.[10] The towers of water quickly descended revealing no direct hits. The *Houston* sailors regained their footing and prepared for the next attack. The heavy cruiser thus far escaped damage, but her luck was about to run out.

After seeing *Marblehead* was in peril, Captain Rooks ordered his ship to move closer to the stricken vessel so her 5-inch guns could better provide an umbrella of protection.[11] Multiple groups of planes were still lurking in the immediate area. Captain Robinson initially thought the bombers were making another run on his *Marblehead* and the warship's 3-inch guns resumed firing. 'Attack was broken off at position angle about 45 degrees but bombs were released, landing about 2,000 yards away,' Robinson explained. 'Nine planes observed on the port quarter, apparently not making an approach.'[12] The target of choice was now *Houston*.

Crewmen aboard the heavy cruiser were watching the smoking *Marblehead* when their attention suddenly shifted to a formation of planes spotted off the port side. A group of bombers approached *Houston* at 11.38 am flying in what appeared to be an almost perfect V formation, except for one plane slightly lagging the rest.[13] Gunfire was resumed as if an automatic response. Gunners sent up a wall of 5-inch shells with the faulty ammunition preventing some from exploding.

The thick fire was not enough to stop the attackers from completing a bombing run. A string of bombs fell towards the ship and exploded off the starboard side, drenching the 5-inch gun crews, but causing no damage. The warship, however, had not fully escaped.

One bomb was released late from the lagging plane. The missile spiraled down towards *Houston* at a considerable angle, appearing to be on a dead aim. A delayed fuse likely kept the bomb from exploding when it glanced off the top of the main mast, passed through a searchlight platform and machine gun station before slicing through the leg of the tripod mast and cutting diagonally through the roof of the after-radio compartment. It finally detonated a few feet above the main deck near the after main battery turret.[14]

A tremendous blast shook the ship from bow to stern. 'From the manner in which the *Houston* groaned and shuttered, we knew it was bad,' Walter Winslow later wrote. The after turret was turned to the port side at the time, ready to fire into the water ahead of any planes making a torpedo attack – a practice later determined to be ineffective.

The angle exposed the thinner side-armor of the turret to the full force of the blast. Pieces of shrapnel ripped into the turret and through the bodies of the crewmen inside. The bags of gunpowder on the hoist from the handling room below quickly ignited, adding to the carnage. Most of the sailors stationed in the turret and handling room were killed instantly.

The bomb left a gaping hole in the deck measuring about 12ft wide. The explosion nearly wiped out a damage control party directly below. A serious fire immediately erupted near the location of the hit, and not far from the after magazine. If the flames were not contained quickly, and were able to reach the ammunition storage area, a devastating explosion large enough to sink the ship could follow.

Two sailors stationed below the turret jumped into action. Gunner's Mate Second Class Czeslaus Kunks and Seaman Second Class Jack

Smith were both knocked down by the force of the explosion. The powder handling room directly above them was on fire. The pair struggled back to their feet and used emergency lighting to kick close a blast door to the nearby magazine. They then turned on an internal water sprinkling system. 'We didn't have any orders to do any of that, but it seemed like the right thing to do,' Smith said.[15] Their heroic action likely saved the ship by preventing an internal explosion.

The *Houston* suffered extensive damage. Teams sprang into action around the ship to begin caring for the wounded and performing damage control activities. The heavy cruiser could no longer help *Marblehead*. She needed to address her own wounds with dozens of sailors killed and wounded, her after turret out of action, and a raging fire burning.

Many of the men aboard *Marblehead* were in no position to watch the remaining stages of the air attack unfold over the rest of the task force. Nicholas Van Bergen was among those able to catch a brief glimpse of *Houston*, *De Ruyter*, and *Tromp* under attack. 'From the bridge and from the main deck we could see them some miles off passing in and out of great bomb splashes,' he later recalled.[16]

The attack on *Houston* turned out to be the last bombing run of the morning attack. Sailors aboard *Marblehead* spotted another plane and her guns quickly opened fire. There was no attack this time. 'At 11.42 am one enemy plane circled ship and approached to approximate range of 4,500 yards, altitude of 3,000ft, on an apparent reconnaissance flight of this ship,' Captain Robinson wrote.[17]

The enemy planes began disappearing into the clouds and were gone from the immediate area shortly after the noon hour. The commander of the Japanese 21st Air Flotilla, Vice-Admiral Tada, debriefed the returning bomber crews. He concluded a total of four ABDA cruisers were hit, including a '*Java* type' sunk, a '*De Ruyter* type' damaged, and two other suffering lesser damage.[18] The enemy authorities later reported sinking two cruisers and damaging two others.[19] Contrary to observations made by sailors aboard various ABDA ships, Japanese sources reported the loss of only one plane during the operation. A second bomber, damaged and trailing smoke, managed to complete a five-hour flight back to Kendari on one engine.[20]

Chapter 16

The damage sustained in the after part of the *Marblehead* was no less serious than the situation farther forward. The bomb narrowly missed hitting the after 6-inch turret before exploding below deck. The main deck topside was ripped open, while the floor plating on the first platform deck one level below was pushed downward by about 7 inches.[1] A seam was opened near the bottom of the hull allowing water to flow inwards. A ruptured fuel tank allowed leaking oil to mix with sea water in some of the flooded compartments – similar to what happened in the forward damaged area. Damaged compartments included a variety of storerooms, living quarters for junior officers and chief petty officers, and the medical office. Fires started immediately after the bomb hit.

An explosion and fire near a main battery turret rapidly created a serious situation. The turret itself was jammed in train, meaning it could no longer be turned, and various critical parts were dented, bent, or otherwise damaged. Of greater concern, however, were the critical areas directly below. A circular-shaped barbette extending down from the bottom of the turret contained the handling room, where sailors sent ammunition up to the gun. The barbette was just forward of the chiefs' quarters. Further down were the magazine storage compartments.

The area stored the 6-inch shells and bags of gunpowder used to fire the main battery guns. The standardized proportions of powder were contained in sealed silk bags. Each bag was held in an airtight metal container. If fires were to reach one of these critical compartments, or the temperature within magazines became too high, a massive explosion could tear off the stern of the ship.

The chief petty officers' quarters, located one deck down from topside near the very back of the ship, was among the most heavily damaged compartments. The area served as living quarters for the senior enlisted men aboard *Marblehead*. The explosion occurred just forward, but the force of the blast went right through the compartment buckling the main deck above. The room was demolished and on fire with lockers, personal gear, and bunks thrown about.

Among the many heroes in the after part of the ship was Seaman Second Class Claude Becker and Turret Captain First Class Paul Martinek. Both were inside the after main battery turret when the bomb exploded. The pair jumped into action after the turret became disabled. 'We all got out of the gun turret, for there was nothing we could do there, but we heard our men hollering down below to come up,' Becker later said. The trapped sailors needed to get through a closed hatch to escape. 'The hatch had been warped by the explosion and was burning hot. I got some towels and rags to wrap around my hands, and was able to rip it up so we could get down the hatch ladder.'[2] His actions allowed the men trapped in the magazine to escape through the chiefs' quarters and the wounded to be evacuated.

Martinek's attention immediately turned to the magazine. Each of the critical storage areas and handling rooms was equipped with a sprinkler system using water supplied by the fire main. Martinek quickly turned on the sprinklers to wet down the gunpowder bags in the ready area, meaning, those that were about to be hoisted up into the turret. The magazines were sprinkled for about a half an hour, long enough to avert disaster. He then ran into the chiefs' quarters.

The room was filled with debris, fire, and a haze of smoke. Most of the sailors in the quarters at the time of the hit were either dead or grievously wounded. Mess Attendant First Class Fook Liang was working in the area as part of an ammunition party when the ship was hit. Laing was badly shaken, and likely in shock, but was alive without serious injury. The mess attendant began evacuating the wounded without any orders or direction. Those capable of walking were led out of the compartment, while others were carried or dragged to a medical station in the torpedo workshop. Liang's efforts continued without stop. He subsequently helped fight fires, clear debris, and assisted medical staff. Captain Robinson wrote of his 'initiative and tireless energy', noting his actions saved 'many lives'.

As Liang was helping the wounded, Paul Martinek was suddenly faced with another immediate crisis. He knew there were eighteen powder containers stored in the chiefs' quarters for ready access in case of emergency action. These were now covered in debris with flames and burning mattresses in close proximity. The cans could not be freed from the wreckage. Shipfitter Second Class Paul Link and Claude Becker jumped in to help. The three men – at great personal risk – opened the cans and carried the powder bags to be tossed over the side.

Captain Robinson later praised these sailors for their actions. He wrote of Becker's 'courage, tenacity and prompt action' during the time of crisis. Martinek was singled out for 'his courage, knowledge, initiative, and prompt and correct actions, coupled with utter disregard for his own safety'.[3] The action of both men greatly contributed to saving the ship.

***

A separate group of men aboard *Marblehead* were waging their own fight, even as other sailors continued their battle against fire and water. The dedicated medical staff were working tirelessly to treat the ship's wounded. A ship the size of *Marblehead* had a medical department headed by a doctor. Lieutenant Commander Doctor Frank Wildebush was the chief medical officer, with Lieutenant Doctor Thomas Ryan serving as his assistant.

The doctors were supported by a group of enlisted men who were either rated as a pharmacist's mate or were a hospital apprentice. The former, the more senior position, served the role of a nurse or physician's assistant, while the latter was more of a paramedic and orderly. Medical facilities included the sick-bay – essentially the ship's hospital – several battle dressing areas that served as triage stations, and some collecting stations to be used as gathering places to bring together the wounded. Supplies were distributed among the various stations so as not to be all clustered in one place.

The sick-bay aboard *Marblehead* was small and not well protected. The medical staff began evacuating patients to a safer part of the ship when the battle stations alarm was sounded. The compartment of choice was the torpedo workshop located on the starboard side of the main deck in the after part of the ship.

The two bombs did more than create a mass of wounded sailors. The explosions also demolished the sick-bay and made other critical compartments unusable. 'Due to the fact that the forward battle dressing station and the forward collecting station were demolished, all casualties had to be collected aft,' Captain Robinson wrote.[4] The collection station in the amidships area was also untenable.

The wounded men in the forward area were initially moved into the officers' quarters, before the area became untenable due to fires and smoke. All casualties in the front part of the ship had to be transported aft. 'There were insufficient stretchers available for such a number of casualties and men not at gun stations or repair parties assisted in transporting them,' Robinson continued. The sailors moving the wounded faced a host of obstacles, including the list of the ship, debris blocking passageways, and wet decks slippery with oil.

The after battle dressing station was not accessible due to damage. The torpedo workshop, located forward of the rear bomb hit and undamaged, quickly became the improvised sick-bay. The area included many pipe-bunks used as sleeping beds. The rectangle frames were made of 1-inch steel pipe with webbing filling in the open middle area. About 100 had recently been installed for use as extra sleeping quarters. These were quickly torn from the bulkheads and pressed into use as improvised stretchers.

About 60 per cent of the medical supplies were destroyed or inaccessible. The remainder were gathered in the torpedo workshop and put to immediate use. Conditions in the makeshift sick-bay were grueling. 'The only illumination available was from portable battery sets,' Robinson explained. 'The entire area was crowded and soaked with oil and water. There was much unavoidable traffic through this area because of repair parties working around the after bomb hit.' The compartment was not without close-by danger. 'There was fire near there so while assembling the wounded, trying to dress their wounds by flashlight, the damage control parties were constantly working back and forth through the area,' added Gunnery Officer Nicholas Van Bergen.

The compartment had no working ventilation system and a pungent smell filled the air as the medical staff did their very best to help the wounded. There was no adequate space or facilities for the doctors to conduct surgeries – those situations could only be addressed after the ship made port … if she made port. The arrangement was the best possible under the difficult conditions and was far from perfect. The wounded soon filled up adjacent compartments with some ending up on deck topside. Medical work expanded into adjacent areas as the makeshift sick-bay filled up.

The medical staff worked feverously to stop bleeding and apply dressings to cover wounds and forestall infections. Morphine shots were given to those in pain. A variety of injuries needed care, ranging from broken bones and shrapnel, most likely sustained during the initial explosions, to a large number of burn patients. Many sailors were wearing short pants and short-sleeve shirts that left arms, legs, and faces exposed to deadly flash burns. The common burn treatment of the day was tannic acid, a product used in the leather industry to stiffen hides. Applied to a burn in a jelly form, the acid was used to cover the wound and start the healing process by creating a scab-like cover.[5] In some instances, sailors lacking tannic acid jelly smeared gun grease on burn sufferers to provide temporary relief.[6]

Chief Pharmacist's Mate Archie Evans was among those working diligently to treat patients. He was operating at almost full capacity while hiding the fact that he had suffered a broken arm.[7] Fook Liang appeared, departed and then reappeared in the sick-bay area as he brought in buckets of fresh water and took away oily rags and other debris.

Many other sailors jumped into action to help the medical staff. Beauford Gabriel's work below deck on the 3-inch ammunition line came to an abrupt stop when the bombs hit. 'When these explosions came, all being at practically the same instance, we were thrown about and jolted considerably,' he wrote. 'I was thrown against the bulkhead and on into one of the officers' staterooms. At this time the air was filled with flying debris and a very large amount of smoke.'[8] Gabriel was not seriously hurt. He rushed forward to assist the medical staff with moving the wounded.

The medical staff and sailors throughout the ship were short on fresh water. The water system, including pipes and pumps, was damaged by the forward hits. The fresh water storage tanks, located near the bottom of the ship in the forward area, were ruptured and contaminated with oil. A limited amount of drinking water was available from the engine rooms, though had to be carried up to the torpedo workshop by hand.

Resourceful sailors found a substitute to the limited supply of water. 'Whiskey in small doses was dispensed to all the patients and found very effective in settling nervous tension and getting them to drink water,' Captain Robinson wrote. 'It was also dispensed with excellent results to the repair parties who were working to exhaustion in burning areas and in areas full of water, fuel oil, and fumes.'[9]

The first information on casualties came to the bridge at 1.00 pm with the medical officer reporting six sailors killed and ten critically wounded. Doctor Wildebush also reported an additional thirty-five men received serious burns or wounds and about forty more had minor injuries.[10] The casualty list would change as the days progressed.

***

One sailor in dire need of medical treatment was William Goggins. The executive officer was badly burned by the forward bomb explosion while in the wardroom. He was operating on adrenaline, somewhat blocking out his condition. Whatever was keeping him going seemed to be running out and a feeling of intense pain was taking over.

Goggins was heading towards the stern of the ship to investigate what happened to the steering gear. He went to battle two, a secondary command center located just forward of the rear 6-inch turret. The compartment was empty and the communications systems were out. He knew the station had a voice tube with a direct connection to the steering compartment. Calling down to the steering room yielded no response. The executive officer decided to go directly to the compartment. He started climbing down a ladder after passing through a hatch.

> I got down to the foot of the ladder and found Dr Ryan there with his people dressing wounded as best they could. He started to put some tannic acid jelly on my leg, but it appeared to me that there were many others who needed it worse than I did, especially some who had some severe wounds from shrapnel and really required his attention.[11]

He soon learned the extent of the damage in the chiefs' quarters when he found his path to the steering compartment blocked. Goggins declined further medical attention with only one concession.

> Dr Ryan gave me two morphine pills – I did not want a shot because I did not want to be immobilized, but he gave me two pills which he said would help relieve the pain a little and he told me to hold them under my tongue, but by this

> time I had swallowed them and when I got up on deck my
> knees gave way under me, probably from the action of the
> morphine.

He briefly sat down to rest before getting back to his feet.

Goggins marveled at the damage control effort underway in his immediate vicinity before starting his journey back forward. 'Everywhere I saw men and officers were proceeding to correct damage and to care for those who needed assistance,' he said. The executive officer made his way back up to the bridge with the intention of reporting what he saw to Captain Robinson, only to find Doctor Wildebush was also on the bridge. The doctor 'saw me and said that I would have to lie down, that I could not proceed further,' Goggins continued. Nicholas Van Bergen was with the captain on the bridge and remembered that Goggins 'was suffering from shock and was rapidly weakening'.[12] Robinson agreed with the doctor's recommendation and made it an order. 'The captain ordered me to go below and lie down, so I went down the ladder from the bridge one level to the conning tower, which was near enough to the bridge so that if I were needed I might be able to render some assistance.'

The battle, for William Goggins, was now over. He sat down in the conning tower. An assortment of people occasionally passing through the area stopped to give him updates on damage control. 'My burns were beginning to become very painful and I trimmed off about two inches of my sleeves and trousers in order to keep them from rubbing on the burned areas,' he later said. At one point Douglas Murch stopped by with a can of gun grease and said it could be used to keep the air off the burns. The sailor had previously helped Goggins escape from the burning wardroom. 'So I rubbed this grease over all my burns and [the] pain stopped considerably and I was much more comfortable.' About all the executive officer could now do was wait. Captain Robinson appointed Van Bergen as the acting executive officer.

***

The engineering department was responsible for generating the power to keep *Marblehead* moving and operating, both in times of crisis and normalcy. The need for operating power increased tremendously during times of combat. Although not necessarily on the front line of damage control, the engineering men played a crucial role in saving the ship. The light cruiser's power system consisted of twelve boilers and four steam turbines, positioned in firerooms and engine rooms respectively, positioned deep within the ship. The equipment provided up to 90,000 horsepower to turn her four screws.[13]

Chief Engineering Officer Lieutenant Commander F.C. Camp arrived at his battle station, the main engine control station, shortly after the general quarters alarm was sounded. Within minutes he had made sure the boilers and engines were ready for action. His men subsequently delivered on Captain Robinson's requests for increased speed as he tried to outmaneuver the Japanese bombers.

His position deep below deck kept Camp from seeing the action topside. The officer felt the string of near miss bombs and immediately checked to see if there was any damage. 'All spaces were checked and reported normal,' he wrote.[14] Camp felt *Marblehead* lurch sharply and violently vibrate when the bombs struck. 'All spaces were checked by sound powered telephones for damage and water,' he wrote. 'All reported normal conditions except [numbers] one and two firerooms.' The two rooms were directly under funnel stack number one and adjacent to the forward bomb hit.

The explosion damaged the bulkhead and uptakes to the stack allowing smoke and fire, along with steam from a ruptured line, to enter the firerooms. Sailors in the two fire rooms reported 'fires blown out and rooms filled with smoke, fire, and debris'.[15] A quick inspection found the compartments to be untenable. Camp directed the boilers in both compartments to be disconnected from the main system before he ordered the crews to evacuate.

Personnel on the bridge knew it was extremely important to re-establish contact with the engine room as soon as possible after the damage was sustained. 'We sent a messenger down to the engine room to tell them to put a man on the voice tube, which fortunately had not been damaged, but for which we had no call bell,' Van Bergen later wrote. 'Both ends of that voice tube were manned from then on until the electricians were able to rig a temporary circuit.' Engineering officer Camp was confident his system could still produce sufficient horsepower to keep *Marblehead* moving at a good clip. He sent a message up to the bridge at 10.50 am notifying Captain Robinson there was enough power to maintain a speed of about twenty-five knots.[16] Camp later ventured out to inspect other damage areas, including the steering gear.

***

The herculean damage control work continued unabated throughout the late morning. 'It seemed like a very well conducted drill,' Nicholas Van Bergen later recalled, marveling about the determined effort. 'Men from all stations were lending a hand where they could do most good. No loud orders were given, but everyone seemed to be going to the place where action had to be taken.' The work was beginning to show some initial signs of success by the middle of the day. The worst of the fires were under control by 11.00 am – about a half an hour after the attack – due to the dedicated efforts of the crew.[17]

Although Captain Robinson may not have known it at the time, his ship had a total of thirty-eight watertight compartments affected by water – twenty-nine fully flooded and nine partially flooded.[18] Sailors below decks tried to slow the intake of water by plugging holes with screens, planks, or any type of debris that could be found.[19] Watertight hatches were closed and dogged down to help stop the water spreading as each flooded compartment was evacuated. The actions could not stop the water flowing through ruptured bulkheads and broken pipes. All available pumps were deployed and quickly became overwhelmed.

Bucket brigades were started early in the damage control effort and increased when more men became available after the fires were brought under control. The human chains twisted through narrow passageways and up ladders as exhausted sailors passed the pails of water to eventually be thrown overboard once topside. The sailors used buckets, dishpans, and anything else able to hold water. Chief Boatswain Harvey Anderson was one of many sailors who helped bail. 'We never gave a thought to abandoning ship,' he later said. 'There were plenty of men to bail, but it was a slow and tedious job.'[20] The dedicated effort greatly contributed to keeping *Marblehead* afloat. However, the warship was still turning in circles and would continue to do so until something could be done about her jammed rudder.

PART IV
ESCAPE

Chapter 17

Admiral Doorman now faced a critical decision. With the element of surprise gone, no air cover, additional enemy air activity possible at any time, and two damaged ships, he decided to cancel the operation. There would be no surface attack on Japanese naval forces. He gave

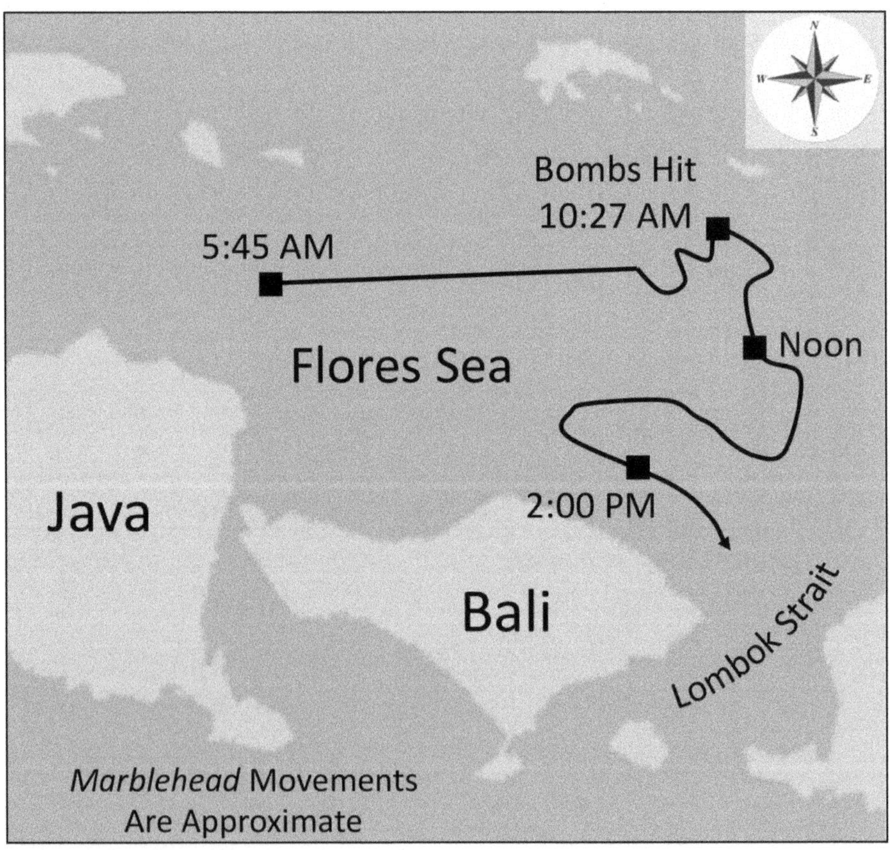

Battle of the Flores Sea & Escape of *Marblehead* February 4, 1942.

the order to retire west at 12.55 pm.[1] The Dutch admiral did not take the decision lightly, knowing history would likely condemn his action. The circumstances, though, really gave him little choice for any other decision.[2] 'Changed course slowly to comply,' Captain Robinson wrote at the time. 'Continued steering with the engines.'[3] Only a minute later, the destroyers *Steward* and *Edwards* approached *Marblehead* to form an anti-submarine screen. The light cruiser was almost directly north of Bali and east of Java as she awkwardly meandered westward with her bad rudder.

At 1.17 pm Robinson sent Doorman a short update on the condition of his ship. '*Marblehead* steering gear wrecked. After part [of] ship badly damaged. Unable to control with engines. Believe will require extensive repairs.'[4] He notified the admiral a short time later of additional damage forward and recommended *Marblehead* be sent south until temporary repairs could be made. Within an hour Admiral Doorman directed her to proceed south through the Lombok Strait and on to the port of Tjilatjap on the southern coast of Java. He advised Robinson to use his discretion for the course and speed, but to 'keep clear of coast as far as possible' as a safety precaution.

Additional destroyers arrived a short time later to assist the damaged warship. Captain Robinson and his escorts were traveling alone. The damaged *Houston* was already en route to the same destination ahead of him. The undamaged Dutch ships were following some distance behind. Moving south into the Indian Ocean offered better protection against air attacks than the current exposed position at sea. Tjilatjap was smaller than Surabaya and about 250 miles southwest of the larger port. The location was the only port of significance in southern Java.

***

Next to keeping the warship afloat, freeing the jammed rudder was critical if *Marblehead* was going to be saved. Even as the current air attacks subsided, she remained in the Flores Sea and exposed to possible further danger. Her chances of making a safe return to port would be greatly increased if her rudder could at least be straightened out from its sharp left angle. Correcting the rudder situation was likely on the minds of every senior officer from Captain Robinson on down the line. 'The principal source of worry was how badly the rudder had been sprung and would we be able to get it clear,' recalled gunnery officer Nicholas Van Bergen. 'It would have been impossible to have controlled the ship in any way until the rudder had been brought amidships.'[5]

The movement of the rudder was controlled by motors in a steering compartment located directly above the actual rudder. The system was operated by a piston and ram mechanism fueled by hydraulic power. Hydraulics use pressurized fluids (hydraulic oil) to make pieces of equipment move – in this case, *Marblehead*'s rudder. Flooding in the room caused the motors to stop working, jamming the rudder at thirty degrees to the left by hydraulic force.[6] The ship immediately lost her ability to control the steering when the hydraulic system ceased operating. Equipment used to steer the ship by hand, an emergency backup system located next to the steering compartment, was demolished in the bomb explosion and looked to be beyond repair.

Damage control men were only able to turn their attention to fixing the rudder once the fire in the chiefs' quarters was brought under control. The flames and burning debris previously did not allow for safe passage to the steering room. After making an initial report of damage to the bridge, head damage control officer Martin Drury went aft to direct the efforts to release the rudder. 'On arrival at the steering gear room, orders were given to cut through the deck above the rudder head in order to reach the rudder yoke directly; the flooded compartment and gas-laden atmosphere made access from below [impractical]' he wrote.[7]

A hasty conference was convened, before much of the cutting work could be completed, to discuss possible alternatives actions. The meeting was headed by Drury and included his assistant Frank Blasdel along with three enlisted men: Quartermaster Second Class Lester Barre, Metalsmith First Class Martin Moran, and Machinist's Mate First Class Dale Johnson. Blasdel came up with a different idea. He thought draining the hydraulic oil from the ram controlling the rudder movement might remove enough pressure to allow it to be straightened out. The group agreed to give it a try and the cutting of the deck over the rudder was immediately stopped. The process required volunteers to go into the steering gear room – a hazardous undertaking – with no guarantee the procedure would work.

The compartment was completely dark and flooded shoulder deep with a mixture of sea water, fuel oil from a ruptured storage tank, and hydraulic oil.[8] Two additional hazards were also present – the chlorine gas produced when water met damaged batteries, and sparks from severed electrical wiring. The room was narrow and crowded with equipment. The two crewmen stationed in the compartment when the bomb hit – Electricians Mate First Class John Owen and Machinist Mate Second Class Orville Sayles – were both killed.[9] Their bodies were still in the compartment. A dreadful stench filled the stale air.

Frank Blasdel was the first sailor to descend slowly into the flooded compartment. Carefully, he went down each rung of the ladder as the water rose ever higher on his body. Sparks from the broken cables occasionally created a brief flicker of light in the darkness. A dead body brushed up against him causing him to pause momentarily. He eventually found a firm footing on the damaged deck. The three enlisted men, Barre, Moran, and Johnson, followed a short time later. Johnson repeatedly dove under the oily water to wrestle with the drain plugs, all the while wondering if the ship would stay afloat. He pondered briefly whether he would ever see his wife again.[10] It was difficult work, under the most trying conditions, but the process eventually succeeded.

The draining of the hydraulic oil slowly reduced the pressure holding the rudder in place. The ship immediately heeled sharply to port after the rudder finally broke free from its jammed position. The sudden jerking movement caused some of the wounded lying topside on deck to momentarily panic thinking *Marblehead* was about to capsize.[11] At 12.47 pm the group managed to move the rudder to a position of 9 degrees left, and it was eventually secured later in the afternoon to a position of 4 degrees right.[12] While not perfect, it was as straight as the men could get it under the difficult conditions. Additional repairs could only be made while the vessel was in port or drydocked.

The rudder was freed from its angled position and now locked in a mostly straight facing. However, it could not be turned in either direction due to the wrecked steering machinery. The accomplishment gave Captain Robinson the capability to move the ship in a straight direction, with some ability to turn by manipulating the engine speeds. By putting the engines on one side of the ship at full speed and slowing or stopping those on the opposite side, he could make *Marblehead* slowly turn in one direction. Robinson had tried the tactic previously, but the jammed rudder only caused the ship to turn in larger circles. The rudimentary arrangement was the best that could be done under the conditions.

Additional steps were taken to stabilize *Marblehead* while the critical work on the rudder was underway. The ship was listing 10 degrees to starboard and down by the bow, both the result of the damage and flooding in the forward areas and possibly aggravated by the high speed maintained during the air attacks. Weight in the form of fuel oil had to be removed to steady her. The warship left port with her tanks nearly full in anticipation of the attack mission. About 300,000 gallons of fuel were subsequently pumped overboard from tanks deep within the forward part of *Marblehead* to correct the list and improve the draft at the bow.[13] The slow process was needed to help save the ship.

***

Captain Robinson set a southerly course as he guided *Marblehead* in the general direction of Lombok Strait at a speed of twenty knots. 'This speed was considered high for the damaged condition of the ship, but was accepted in an effort to get as far as possible into Lombok Strait before darkness set in and to gain distance to the southward for safety,' he wrote. The destroyer *Stewart* took a position directly ahead of the light cruiser to act as a steering guide. She maintained the duty for much of the remaining voyage.

Lombok Strait is positioned about eighty miles east of Java. The narrow body of water separates Bali from the adjacent island of Lombok and measures slightly less than fifteen miles at its narrowest point. Passing through the strait would bring *Marblehead* south of the Malay Barrier and further away from Japanese air bases.

The American ships entered the northern entrance of Lombok Strait at 5.22 pm. Topside sailors could see a tall mountain on Bali about ten miles away off the starboard side. Shortly after 6.00 pm an unidentified plane was sighted to the north. 'Apparently shadowing the formation,' Robinson noted. The aircraft disappeared about ten minutes later, just as the sun began to set ushering in the evening twilight.

The approaching darkness made the passage even more hazardous for the ship with no steering control. 'Rain squalls were setting in, which reduced our visibility, and it was obvious that we would not be able to get through before night fell,' Van Bergen explained. 'Destroyers were told to take station on either bow and in case we got too close to the beach to warn us by their blinker tubes. The destroyers did an outstanding job of work, staying clear of us and still keeping sight contact.'

The ships cleared Lombok Strait at 7.55 pm in darkness and reduced speed to fifteen knots due to heavy seas.[14] The destroyers remained at the head of the formation. 'We managed to get through the night on various courses because the cruiser was all over the lot with her erratic steering by use of her main engines,' remembered Lodwick Alford aboard *Stewart*. 'It was very difficult to do and should never be attempted unless absolutely necessary.'[15]

The ships continued to steam in a mostly southwesterly direction through the night, encountering heavy rain about an hour before midnight. The passage took the warships out of the Pacific and into the Indian Ocean. 'Efforts to maintain watertight integrity and pumping and bailing with bucket brigades continued without intermission,' Robinson wrote. 'At this time twenty-six watertight compartments in the ship were completely [flooded] and eight others partially flooded.'

Captain Robinson knew the ship was afloat largely due to the determined effort of his crew. 'They were called upon to work day and night in fuel, oil, water, and debris,' he later said. 'They worked, ate, and – when they could find a place to lie down – slept in their oil soaked clothing. There was neither time nor fresh water for bathing.'[16]

With limited resources and a damaged galley, the ship's cooks did amazing work to keep the sailors fed – even having hot coffee available within half an hour of when the bombs hits.[17] Robinson explained:

> The greater part of the mess gear and messing facilities of all kinds were destroyed. Fortunately, the galley was able to function, except for the ranges, as soon as steam could be re-piped and water carried by hand. It was necessary to set up an impromptu cafeteria type of mess, using the reduced facilities of the officers' galley as a scullery to clean salvaged mess gear.[18]

Nicholas Van Bergen was among the officers worried about the ability of the men to endure:

> It was extremely hard to get the officers and men to rest because there was so much work to be done, but it was soon

apparent that unless we could get them to lie down and take a little rest several hours at a time, that they would all wear themselves out simultaneously and everything would cease. This was finally accomplished by giving direct orders to the men to lie down on the oily deck and sleep.

Shots of whisky administered by the doctors were also found to help the sleep process.

After determining he could be of no further assistance to *Marblehead*, Admiral Doorman and the Dutch warships ended their distant cover by departing westward at midnight. To keep as far as possible from Japanese planes, he stayed south of Java, traveling the full distance of the coast before turning north to pass through the Sunda Strait to arrive at the port city of Batavia on the northwestern part of the island. He waited to face the consequences of his failed mission.

The morning sunrise of February 5 found Captain Robinson's formation steaming south of Java. The tanker *Pecos* and escorting destroyer *Pillsbury* were briefly sighted about five miles to the east. Lookouts spotted a strange aircraft at 9.55 am in the eastern sky, prompting Robinson to sound general quarters for air defense. 'This plane shadowed the formation until approximately noon and caused the southerly course to be held at the best practical speed in order to conceal the ships' destination,' he wrote of the situation. The formation turned west shortly after 2.00 pm. Tjilatjap was almost 300 miles to the northwest at the time. About two hours later, Robinson ordered the destroyer *Edwards* to proceed ahead to the port 'to confirm our early arrival and entrance arrangements'. The other three destroyers – *Stewart*, *Bulmer*, and *Parrott* – remained with the light cruiser.

As Captain Robinson was slowly nursing his damaged ship towards Tjilatjap, the Japanese were carefully searching for any Allied ships at sea near Java. A case of mistaken identity may have saved *Marblehead* from further air attacks. The American four-stack destroyer *Paul Jones* was dispatched to rendezvous with the Dutch cargo ship *Tidore* south of Sumbawa Island and escort her to Timor. The meeting took place about 150 miles east-southeast of where *Marblehead* had passed through Lombok Strait. The two ships were subsequently attacked by three groups of Japanese bombers during the late morning hours. The destroyer successfully dodged seven bombing runs and about twenty bombs over a nearly two-hour period, while her commanding officer gave a running account of the action over the radio for anyone who could listen.[19] He summed up the action as 'Seven runs. No hits, all errors.'[20]

The Dutch ship did not fare as well as *Tidore*, becoming a total loss after running aground. The destroyer rescued her survivors before departing the area for Tjilatjap. A post-war Japanese document described the planes finding 'the American ship *Marblehead* fleeing ten nautical miles south of Soembawa.'[21] The light cruiser and destroyer shared a similar profile owing to the four stacks that stood out as a dominant feature – especially from a distance.

The wounded light cruiser was in no position to sustain another heavy air attack. The mix-up may have allowed *Marblehead* to live to see another day. 'This undoubtedly saved us because *Paul Jones* was free to maneuver and only had one or two rivets knocked loose, whereas, we with our restricted maneuverability, would undoubtedly have been sunk,' Van Bergen later speculated.

The medical staff diligently continued to treat the wounded all throughout the voyage while operating with limited supplies and under trying conditions. The struggle, in some cases, was a fight to keep the most seriously wounded sailors alive until the ship could reach port and better medical facilities. Among those who did not last the journey was Chief Water Tender George Buckendorf, who died in the last hours of February 4. He was in the chiefs' quarters near the back of the ship when the first bomb hit and sustained serious burns across his head, body, arms, and legs. Mess Attendant First Class Ping Tseng passed away just as *Marblehead* was getting close to Tjilatjap. He was also a victim of the explosion in the chiefs' quarters.[22]

Midnight on February 6 brought squalls and intermittent rain showers. Submersible pumps and bucket brigades were still in action as *Marblehead* inched closer to making port. Lookouts aboard the warship sighted land at 4.47 am, twenty miles off the starboard bow.[23] The small land mass was quickly determined to be Kambangan Island, adjacent to Tjilatjap. The end of the perilous voyage was almost at hand.

***

The Japanese wasted little time in announcing their successful attack on the ABDA ships. Radio Tokyo reported sinking two Dutch cruisers and damaging two more – one Dutch and the other an American '*Marblehead* class' ship. The United States Navy Department in Washington said it had 'no information' about the reported statements. The broadcast also claimed 'the virtual annihilation' of the Dutch Navy from the attack.[24] In a broadcast one day later, Radio Tokyo cited new information, indicating 'the United States light cruiser of the *Marblehead* type and the Dutch East Indies cruiser of the *Java* class which were reported as merely damaged were damaged beyond repair.'

Chapter 18

The port of Tjilatjap was the only deep-water harbor on the south side of Java. The city was positioned on a wedge of land between the east bank of the Donan River and the Indian Ocean. The houses gave way to rice paddies to the north.

The harbor area was sheltered from the ocean to the south by the long narrow island of Nusa Kambangan. A 600-yard stretch of concrete quays, covered by wooden planks, stretched up the eastern side of the river. The water depth next to some of the mooring stations dipped close to 25ft during low tide.[1] Wooden buildings stood near the quays serviced by a road and rail lines. A T-shaped refueling pier, with adjacent oil storage tanks, was about a hundred yards to the north.

To add capacity to the port, a row of mooring buoys for larger ships lined a portion of the Donan River parallel to the piers. Additional buoys were positioned in the channel along Nusa Kambangan Island. A small floating drydock was moored along the coast of the island in the entrance channel.[2]

Dutch harbor pilot G.H. Gerding climbed aboard *Marblehead* at 7.53 am on the morning of February 6. Within a matter of a few short minutes the warship was slowly maneuvering around defense minefields while moving towards the Tjilatjap harbor entrance.[3] The area itself was not a good natural harbor due to having only a single narrow entrance, erratic currents, and large sandbars.[4] The port facilities were small compared to the larger cities on the north side of the island and neither suitable for large scale ship repairs, nor for operating as a supply and logistics hub. The possibility of an enemy taking control of the Java Sea to the north during a time of conflict prompted Dutch authorities to make rushed improvements in the year prior to the start of war – including a limited number of new piers, electric cranes, navigation lights, and mooring buoys.

Getting *Marblehead* into port proved to be a difficult undertaking. The harbor could only accommodate ships with a maximum draft (the amount of hull below the waterline) of 30ft.

The flooded compartments caused *Marblehead* to dip below the threshold. 'At 7.30 am, just prior to entering Tjilatjap, the draft of the ship had been reduced to 20ft forward, 19ft aft, largely by pumping 300,000 gallons (1,000 tones) of fuel oil over the side,' Captain Robinson wrote.[5] It proved to be just enough to allow her to squeeze past a sandbar to enter the port area.[6] The ship was met by two tugs shortly after her arrival. The small boats took up positions forward and aft to ease *Marblehead* into the port area. The process proved to be slow with the towlines parting on three separate occasions.

The wounded *Houston* was already docked in Tjilatjap as *Marblehead* moved closer. The heavy cruiser arrived about one day earlier during midmorning on February 5. A single bomb struck her after deck knocking out the number three main battery turret and causing extensive damage immediately below deck. Forty-eight sailors were killed and scores more wounded. The dead were laid out on the deck near the fantail. A work party promptly went ashore to gather wood for coffins. All they could find was 'that darned rough mahogany and it was harder than hell,' Merritt Eddy remembered. 'We worked all that day and most of the night, the whole carpenter gang.'[7] Others stayed aboard to repair the battle damage and tend to other duties. The wounded were transferred to a Dutch hospital ashore.

The process of burying the dead began early the next morning. The coffins were loaded onto Dutch Army trucks as *Houston*'s band played somber funeral music and sailors from the ship clad in white dress uniforms stood at attention. The ship's chaplain conducted a dock-side ceremony that concluded with a bugler sounding taps. The trucks then moved out, with a contingent of sailors marching behind, for burial in a small Dutch cemetery overlooking the Indian Ocean.

The moving of *Marblehead* into the docking area was almost complete at 12.56 pm as she slowly moved passed *Houston*. Naval tradition called for the *Houston* men to come to attention and salute the incoming American naval vessel. The sailors aboard the heavy cruiser already manned the rails before spontaneously erupting in to a loud cheer. The last they had seen of *Marblehead* she was fighting to stay afloat in the Flores Sea. The exhausted *Marblehead* sailors, some of whom had been manning bucket brigades for two days, did their best to reply. Even Captain Robinson tipped his hat from his position on the bridge.[8] 'It was sort of a miracle that *Marblehead* reached port,' wrote Ludwick Alford of the accompanying destroyer *Stewart*.[9] The statement summed up the belief of many who were surprised to see her arrival.

The tugs nudged *Marblehead* into a dock very close to and just ahead of *Houston*. Her starboard side was bumped up to a pier allowing sailors to begin securing mooring lines. The harbor area was crowded with Allied ships of all types, some from points further north escaping the Japanese advance. Some ABDA auxiliary ships, recently ordered north from Australia by Admiral Hart to be closer to the front, were among the mix.

A series of improvements to the port facilities were located just before the harbor area merged with the Donan River. The new upgrades included new piers with cranes and some additional storage buildings. 'Otherwise Tjilatjap was quite unsatisfactory as a base,' Admiral Glassford later wrote. 'The harbor entrance was difficult to navigate on account of the sharp turns and swift currents. Berthing space alongside piers was very limited.'[10] The admiral described the oil storage facilities as 'meager'.

The town was filled with dusty streets. Aviator Walter Winslow of *Houston* remembered Tjilatjap as 'hellishly hot, fever-ridden, dusty, it's humid air laden with putrid smells'.[11] Recreational opportunities were limited. The visiting sailors would soon come to miss the bars, clubs, and girls at Surabaya.[12]

The light cruiser suffered fifteen dead or mortally injured and eighty-four seriously wounded.[13] Many needed medical attention beyond what could be provided aboard *Marblehead*. The Dutch were ready to help as soon as the ship was securely moored. Army trucks and a hospital train, along with some doctors and nurses, were waiting dockside to transport the wounded to hospitals.

The patients deemed most serious – twenty-one sailors – were to go by train to an inland hospital. The men were carefully carried off *Marblehead* on stretchers. The train had pulled up parallel to the ship at the dock, making for a short trip. The hospital cars were painted white with a red cross on each door.

The movement of patients made for a scene of great contrasts. The members of *Marblehead*'s medical staff carrying the stretchers had been working almost non-stop for nearly two days with little rest. Their clothes were dirty and sometimes blood splattered. Each wounded sailor was turned over to cleanly dressed Dutch doctors and nurses with a brief exchange of information on the status of the patient. The *Marblehead* sailors were not alone. A group of wounded men from *Houston* were loaded aboard the same train cars the night before.[14]

Captain Robinson made a visit to the train to say goodbye to his men and wish them good luck. He may very well have known some of the sailors were not going to live long. Robinson sat dockside with Captain Rooks of *Houston* in silence as the train slowly rumbled away. The train was bound for Petronella Hospital in Jogjakarta, an inland city about 125 miles to the east.

A second group of less critically wounded men, numbering thirty-one sailors, were loaded aboard the trucks to be taken to a local hospital in Tjilatjap. Presumably the men were to be treated and then returned to the ship prior to any departure; the group included William Goggins. The executive officer's wounds were considered serious enough for him to have been sent inland, but he insisted on being able to return to the ship when it departed – whenever that might be. He requested to stay local and his wish was granted, largely in deference to his rank.[15]

Goggins did not leave the ship empty-handed. He was given a bottle of whisky to take along on his journey. Some enlisted men took up a collection of cigars, receiving enough donations to almost fill a box. The container was set on his chest and a lighted cigar put in his mouth as he lay on the stretcher.[16] A mess attendant accompanied him off the boat to help keep him comfortable during the short trip.

A more solemn task aboard *Marblehead* began at 2.20 pm when twelve hastily constructed caskets were carried off to a covered warehouse structure adjacent to the ship. Each was draped with an American flag. An honor guard made up of Marines from *Houston* watched over the building throughout the night. A thirteenth sailor had perished, but the body of Quartermaster Third Class George Rankert was still sealed in a flooded compartment below deck.[17] He was buried later in the day.

Sailors were up early the next morning for a dockside funeral service that began promptly at 5.40 am, with Chaplain George Rentz of *Houston* officiating. The coffins were loaded onto Dutch Army trucks after the conclusion of the ceremony for transport to the beachside cemetery for burial. A group of mostly *Houston* sailors accompanied the trucks to the same cemetery where their fallen shipmates had just been buried. Most of the *Marblehead* sailors were required to return to their ship as she was preparing to get underway.

***

Although *Marblehead* had miraculously made port, she was still badly damaged and unfit for any type of lengthy sea voyage. Her location on the southern coast of Java offered only temporary protection from the advancing Japanese, who were closing in on Java from multiple directions. Many parts of the island were already in range of bombers with air raids on Surabaya steadily increasing by the day. Tjilatjap was an exception, currently out of bomber range – but likely for not much longer. The situation was fast becoming a race against time. Once the bombers came in range, there would be limited advanced warning of attacks and little fighter protection. Ships in the crowded harbor area could become easy targets for Japanese bombardiers.

The two most critical issues facing Captain Robinson, in terms of getting his ship seaworthy enough for a departure to a safer port, were the ruptured hull from the underwater near miss and the broken steering gear. The area had no large shipyard; the only repair facilities consisted of a single floating drydock. The drydock had previously operated in the Batavia area, but had been sent around the island to the southern port.[18]

Better naval facilities existed at Surabaya, but it was too risky to send *Marblehead* back north into range of enemy bombers. 'A conference with local officials disclosed that the repair facilities at this port were very limited and the commercial floating drydock of insufficient capacity to completely dock the ship,' Robinson wrote.[19]

A floating drydock can best be described as a type of floating dock used to repair and maintain ship hulls. The dock, typically U-shaped, is partially submerged to allow a vessel to enter, the water is then pumped out to allow the bottom of the dock to be raised out of the water. The result is a dry platform with the ship completely clear of the water and resting on large keel blocks.

Fortunately, the *Marblehead* sailors had a sort of guardian angel. The Dutch naval architect in charge of the drydock, a man by the name of Adama Van Scheltema, was both skilled and ingenious.[20] He studied the situation in search of a solution. Unable to dock the entire ship at once, he instead came up with a plan to work on only half of the ship at a time. 'It was decided to partially dock, that is raise the forward part of the ship for inspection and repairs, and then tilt the dock in the opposite direction to raise the stern,' Robinson explained. The floating drydock was located directly across the harbor from an area of warehouses and electric cranes.

Captain Robinson was among a small group of senior officers on the bridge when two tug boats arrived alongside the ship just before 6.00 am on the morning of February 7. The harbor pilot was already on board. The vessel was underway within half an hour, slowly moving across the harbor to the small floating drydock. The bow began pushing into the drydock at 7.30 am. The main engines were secured about half an hour later.

The warship's bow began slowly lifting out of the water after the drydock pumps began to operate. As the water level went down, so her bow rose; water poured out from the inside of the ship through holes in the damaged hull. Her stern remained partially afloat in the water. The arrangement put *Marblehead* in a precarious, and sometimes unbalanced, position.

The dangerous undertaking was the only possibility of completing emergency repairs. Robinson later wrote:

> During the time in dock there existed the constant problem of maintaining a condition of stable equilibrium of the overloaded drydock and preventing the ship from launching itself stern first. On several occasions the engineer in charge of the dock found it necessary to flood the dock, and then cautiously repeat the pumping, until the ship was raised sufficiently to continue repairs, and at the same time to allow a small safety factor against a dangerous condition of unstable equilibrium.

Executive officer Van Bergen later explained the situation a little differently:

> It was impossible to keep the ship out of the water long because it was an old drydock, and it was overladen and was constantly in danger of losing its stability, consequently

every few hours it was necessary to submerge the ship again, which would fill it up, pump her out, pump out the drydock and wait until the water drained out of the holes in the bottom before we could continue the welding up forward.

The process slowed the preparatory work needed to be done in advance of the actual repairs. Some of the repairs were not able to be done. Captain Robinson later noted the re-flooding 'ultimately prevented complete stoppage of leaks'. The slow, stop and go process eventually succeeded, allowing for only the most basic repairs to be completed.

American Commander Harry Keith was somewhat of an unsung hero. He arrived in Java from the Philippines after participating in a daring voyage aboard the small schooner *Lanikai*. Keith was serving as the Assistant Material Officer with the American naval contingent in Surabaya, when orders sent him south to Tjilatjap to provide whatever assistance he could to the damaged *Houston* and *Marblehead*. Keith played an invaluable role in helping to source local materials used in making temporary repairs on both ships. Some of the materials were carried out of the jungle by local Javanese using little more than brute force.[21]

***

Admiral Hart was irate over the ending of the attack mission, even though the circumstances would have made it difficult to continue. 'Admiral Doorman still had a considerable force intact, even after providing escorts for the damaged American cruisers, but he immediately withdrew all his ships to the south and west,' Hart later wrote. The movement of the Dutch ships to Batavia was not immediately known to the ABDA naval commander due to the poor Dutch ship to shore radio communications. 'The Striking Force was, therefore, thrown out or taken out of action for the time being.'[22] A good amount of finger-pointing later took place among Hart, Doorman, Admiral Helfrich and others as to the soundness of the attack plan, route taken, etc.

Hart directed his task force commander to return to Tjilatjap and flew down from his headquarters in Lembang for a meeting on February 8. He found Doorman to be 'still shaken' by the events in the Flores Sea and reluctant to venture out again within range of enemy bombers without air cover.[23] Hart understood the concern under ordinary times. He also knew they were facing extraordinary circumstances in trying to defend Java with limited resources against a superior enemy. They could either attack without air cover or do nothing, and Hart favored the former.

The American admiral was also angered by Doorman's plan to refuel his warships about 300 miles south of Java. He felt the location was taking the main fighting force too far away from the front. He considered Admiral Doorman to be overly cautious and considered replacing him as the force commander. Hart took no action because the Dutch were fighting in the defense of their own territory and he felt they should have one of their own commanding the ships at sea.[24]

ABDA intelligent officials believed Bandjermasin on the southern coast of Borneo was the next enemy target for invasion. The move would give the Japanese a base almost directly across the Java Sea from Surabaya. The location was accurate, although some of the details were not – the Bandjermasin operation was still days away from beginning. The coastal city would be captured later.

A group of Japanese ships was emerging out of the Molucca Sea southeast of Celebes as the meeting of admirals at Tjilatjap was ongoing. The unknown destination could be any number of locations, including eastern Java or Bali. Hart saw it as an opportunity for a night attack and ordered Doorman to strike with all his available undamaged ships as soon as possible. The Dutch admiral somewhat reluctantly drew up an operational plan to attack through Lombok Strait with *DeRuyter*, *Tromp*, and ten destroyers. Hart prepared to return to Lembang, satisfied an operation was in the offing.

The Japanese ships were not headed to Java. The invasion force rather stopped off Makassar Town on southwestern Celebes. The Doorman attack was never carried out, possibly due to the admiral becoming disconcerted over the enemy's location.[25]

Admiral Hart needed to decide about what to do with the two damaged cruisers before he could depart Tjilatjap. He toured both ships, coming aboard *Marblehead* at 11.27 am on February 8 while the ship was in drydock.[26] Seeing the crewmen hard at work on repairs aboard both ships made an impression on the admiral. 'Both ships had been severely punished, but the morale and courage of the officers and men seemed in no way to be impaired,' he later wrote.

Bali
Madura
Surabaya
Patjinan
Java Sea
Java
Jogjakarta
Tjilatjap
Indian Ocean
Bandung
Batavia
N
E
S
W

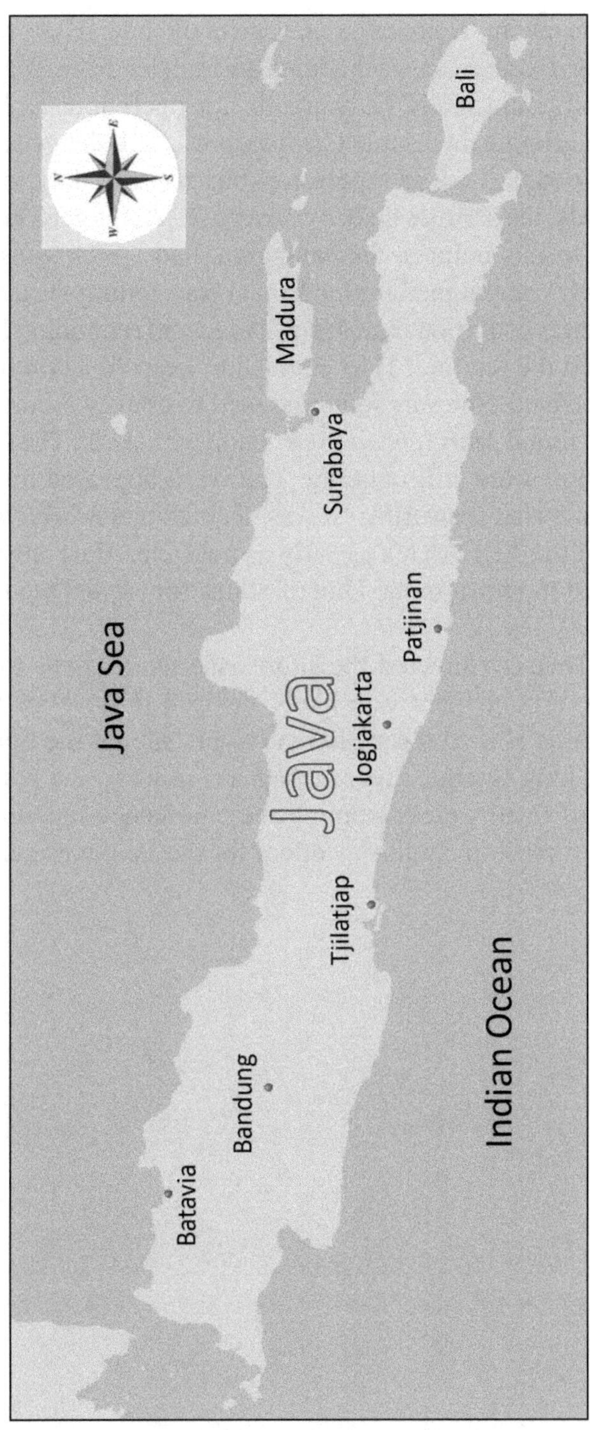

Java.

The decision about *Houston* was a difficult one. Hart was aware the light cruiser *Phoenix* was scheduled to transfer from Pearl Harbor to Australia and could likely be available for operations in his area.[27] 'Although with after turret disabled, *Houston* was still the most powerful cruiser available in the area and quite capable of escort duty, at least,' he later wrote. Only the British heavy cruiser *Exeter*, largely involved in escort duty up to this point in the campaign, had 8-inch guns. Captain Rooks reportedly campaigned for his ship to stay, telling the admiral she was in much better condition than *Marblehead* and reminding him *Boise* already departed the region.[28] Hart decided to keep *Houston* in the area until *Phoenix* arrived. She was soon assigned to convoy escort duty.

The admiral found *Marblehead* to be 'badly wrecked'. The temporary repairs to the hull were still ongoing. The work appeared to make the ship at least somewhat seaworthy. 'It was decided that *Marblehead* must be gotten out of the ABDA area as early as possible,' Hart later recalled. She was ordered to return to the United States for repairs via the Indian Ocean.

The admiral wisely directed the submarine tender *Otus* to serve as her escort. The arrangement was likely devised to have an American ship close by to be able to rescue her survivors should the light cruiser sink during the long voyage. The *Marblehead* sailors were going home. At least, most of them were, assuming the emergency repairs could be completed and their ship could stay afloat for the long voyage.

Chapter 19

Commander William Goggins was among the small group of wounded men carried off *Marblehead* shortly after her arrival in Tjilatjap. The officer was among a small group of wounded sailors who did not go aboard the hospital train. They also did not go to a local hospital. The sailors instead went to a nearby dressing station. Goggins later described the place:

> It was not really a hospital, but it had the facilities for dressing wounds and beds in which we could be placed. We were taken ashore in stretchers and put in ambulances and taken to this dressing station and then as time permitted, our wounds were dressed and we were kept there during the night. I don't remember exactly how many were in this hospital.[1]

Although his wounds were serious, Goggins hoped to be taken back aboard the ship before she departed – whenever it might be. The Chinese mess attendant who accompanied him ashore stayed with him for the night.

> During the evening at the hospital he went out and got some Ovaltine and two bottles of liquor, which he thought I would need. He had all my money, a suit of shorts, my shaving gear, and some underwear and a few little things in a bag which he carried along.

After spending the night at the dressing station Goggins awoke to the news that he, along with several others, was transferring to the same hospital that the more serious patents had been sent to via the hospital train. He unhappily concluded they were too badly injured to be properly cared for aboard the ship when she sailed. A total of fifteen *Marblehead* sailors were making the trip – three officers and twelve enlisted men.[2] The other two officers aside from Goggins were Lieutenant Arthur Goodhue and Ensign Charles Coburn. 'We left Tjilatjap at about 8.00 o'clock in the morning in field ambulances, which are very rough and uncomfortable,' Goggins later recalled. 'The heat was terrific and we had practically no attention, except an occasional drink of water or a sandwich on the way.'

The sailors were learning the hard way that many of the roads on Java were not well developed; unfortunately for the men, most of the better developed roads were along the northern coastal areas of Java, and the city of Jogjakarta was just over fifteen miles inland. A smooth train ride would have been much preferable. The ambulances traveled over rutted dirt roads, rattling and bouncing for the entire trip.[3] 'This was perhaps the most painful and trying part – riding in these ambulances,' Goggins continued. 'There were four in each ambulance and we went in a sort of a convoy, one driver leading who knew the way – they lost the way once.' Much to the sailors' dismay, any questions about the route or amount of time left was always answered with a standard response of 'just a little farther'.

The grueling nine-hour journey ended when the small convoy arrived at Petronella Hospital in Jogjakarta late in the afternoon of February 7. 'We got to the hospital at about 5.00 o'clock in the evening of the Seventh, were carried into the main lobby where the Dutch doctors and nurses were waiting for us,' Goggins said. The grueling trip encompassed a driving distance of about 125 miles.[4] The wounded sailors were about to enter the unfamiliar world of interior Java.

***

The process of getting *Marblehead* seaworthy was a herculean undertaking involving many people working long shifts, including her exhausted sailors, local Javanese workers, and engineers from the destroyer tender *Black Hawk*. The effort continued round the clock with few breaks or stoppages. The attempts to raise her bow in the floating drydock were successful after multiple tries. The front part of the ship was out of the water from her stem to an area about even with the forward legs of the tripod mast.

Once out of the water, the extent of the damage from the near miss was revealed for the first time. There was a large indentation near the very bottom of the hull on the port side, about equal to the area directly behind the forward 6-inch turret. The bomb went deep into the water, later estimated to have been a depth of about 16ft, before exploding slightly below the turn of the bilge – the area between the bottom keel and the vertical side of the ship.

Although it likely was not known at the time *Marblehead* was in Tjilatjap, the keel was distorted and bent upward over a span of about 8ft. The critical beam – often considered the backbone of a ship due to its integral part of the hull – remained intact. Rivets and seams were loosened in the general area, allowing more entry points for water. Engineers later reported the damage from the near miss to be 'among the most severe cases of this character which any U.S. vessels have yet reported'.[5]

At the center of the large indentation were two jagged holes, each measuring approximately 2ft by 9ft, in the hull leading into a series of compartments comprised of the forward magazines.[6] The area housed ammunition of various types. Belts of 50-caliber bullets were visibly hanging out of the hole. All the ammunition had to be removed for safety reasons before any patching work could be started.

The rooms were not only flooded with water, but also some fuel oil from a ruptured storage tank, making for a slippery, messy situation. Captain Robinson explained:

> The force of the underwater explosion had completely wrecked these spaces, and powder cans, shells, and small arms ammunition were scattered throughout the area. Before the water and fuel oil had drained from this space, the ship's force commenced removing the ammunition. When the water and oil level within the ship dropped below the two large ruptures in the ship's bottom, additional handling parties were formed and ammunition was removed through the bottom and side of the ship direct to the drydock floor.[7]

The delicate process of removing the ammunition was easier done through the holes in the hull than carrying it through the maze of damaged compartments leading topside.

Sailors working in the compartments found shells twisted into an assortment of contorted shapes. Fortunately, the magazines did not explode at the time of the bomb hit. Such a tremendous blast, likely resulting in fatal damage, could have ripped off the front part of the ship. Sailors worked to wipe down the oily compartment walls and floors once the ammunition was removed. Javanese workers assisted in the messy process. Late in the night of February 7, the cleaned and emptied areas were deemed safe enough to move forward with patching the ruptured hull.

Local workers created custom steel patches that were welded over the holes in the hull. Caulk was inserted into all seams and rivets in the immediate vicinity. 'Because of the intermittent flooding of the dock, the ship was never completely emptied of water and the forward hull could not be made fully water-tight, but the patching prevented any surge of water from the outside,' Robinson later wrote of the partial repairs.

The repair work was not limited to the front part of the ship. 'While repairs were progressing on the underwater damage, the ship's repair force on a day shift and the local Javanese workmen on a night shift, were engaged in clearing away the fantail deck plating and the mass of wreckage below,' Robinson wrote. The damage from the initial bomb explosion and subsequent fire was extensive. The force of the blast had vented upward, mangling and rupturing the main deck near the fantail. 'There being no crane available, it was necessary to cut the wrecked deck plating and other masses of wreckage into pieces small enough to be handled by manpower.' The cut-up wreckage and decking was carried off the ship in a slow process made worse by the tropical conditions.

Work on the ship's stern proved to be more difficult than the bow. The improvised arrangement in the drydock was not well suited for keeping the stern out of the water. If the ship were to slip off the keel blocks from her precarious position while the stern was raised, she would come down with the propellers, shafts, rudder, and more, crashing on the floor of the drydock.[8] The result of such an accident was irreparable damage – *Marblehead* would be going nowhere. She would be trapped at Tjilatjap to become an easy target for bombers once the port came into range of land-based Japanese planes. 'During this time, the stern was raised as far as possible and held in this position for a short time while the ship's divers and repair force inserted plugs in rivet holes and arc-welded all evident leaks in the after end of the ship,' Robinson continued. One area not able to be repaired was the jammed rudder. There was neither the equipment nor parts available to rebuild the steering motors and other mechanisms needed to make the rudder operational again.

Less visible to the outside world was the large amount of work going on inside *Marblehead*. Repairs included improving the living conditions aboard ship. 'Because of oil and debris through the entire ship, the lack of berthing space and absence of fresh water, the ship was, for the most part, uninhabitable,' Robinson wrote. Many of the men, who lost their toiletries and personnel possessions to smoke and fire, had little more than the clothes on their backs. Replacement items were obtained from any source possible, including other U.S. ships in the harbor and various places ashore, and were distributed to needy sailors at no cost.

The *Marblehead* crewmen were given access to the nearby Dutch cargo-passenger ship *Tjitjalengka* through the efforts of the liaison officer on shore. Sailors could go aboard for rest, food, and even an occasional drink of Dutch beer. John Bracken remembered 'her showers and beds were most welcome'.[9]

Sleep and down-time were both at a premium for the exhausted sailors. The weary men could get a small amount of each, including some liberty ashore. The sparse facilities in the town did not stop some sailors from over indulging on drink and more than one faced punishment after returning aboard intoxicated.[10]

Teams of workers toiled below decks in hot conditions to clear out debris, cut away mangled metal, and clean compartments. Drying waterlogged supplies was one thing, but when the seawater was mixed with oil, it made for a messy and difficult cleaning process. Undamaged supplies were organized and moved to drier compartments when necessary. Some of the flooded storerooms were filled with canned goods. With the labels soaked off or unreadable, cooks could only guess as to the contents, making for some unusual future meals. 'The repair force was engaged in restoring a fresh water system in the forward part of the ship, rigging temporary lighting, power and sound powered telephones throughout the ship, shoring weakened bulkheads and decks, and plugging and welding holes and seams within the damaged areas,' Robinson wrote.[11] The goal was to make *Marblehead* livable again for the sailors who would endure the hopeful voyage to safer waters.

A group of gunner mates worked diligently to service all main battery and 3-inch guns not damaged by the bomb hits. They cleaned and dried any ammunition thought to be salvageable.[12] All the guns were eventually returning to working order, except the after 6-inch twin turret. Crewmen determined it was not repairable under the current conditions. The guns could only operate in local control, meaning each had to be aimed individually by their own crews with no assistance from the fire control directors.

***

Water started flowing into the drydock at 8.20 am on February 10.[13] The harbor pilot soon climbed aboard in preparation for getting underway. The sailors and yard workers had done all they could to make *Marblehead* seaworthy, now her time in the drydock was about to be over. The rising water entered various forward compartments, including the magazines and internal communications room, indicating the patches were not fully watertight. Her bow cleared the sill of the drydock just before 10.00 am. She slowly moved across the harbor, with the help of two tugs, to the starboard side of the tanker *Pecos* at the fuel dock.

***

The sailors aboard *Marblehead* were not the only ones preparing to leave Java in early February. Admiral Hart's time on the island was also nearing an end. It was an open secret his ABDA command was tenuous and filled with tension from the start. Aside from the approaching Japanese, he was facing a growing list of enemies among his allies who were diligently working for his removal.

Among his American peers, General MacArthur was openly critical of the navy's quick withdrawal south at the beginning of the conflict. He was trying to encumber Hart with the loss of the Philippines.[14] The admiral's want of offensive action against the approaching Japanese ran counter to the British desire to use valuable warships primarily for convoy escort duty, mainly for ships bound for Singapore. Their leaders viewed the holding of the island bastion as the key to preventing the enemy from breaking through the Malay Barrier.

Dutch leaders were resentful from the start that one of their admirals did not get the top naval position and were mostly concerned with protecting their own territory from the approaching enemy. Admiral Helfrich was critical of Hart's leadership of the multi-national command and constantly needled him about the performance of American naval ships, especially the poor showing of submarines.[15] Helfrich thought Hart errored in the opening days of the war by sending his cruisers and destroyers too far south to be able to properly fight the Japanese.[16] The Dutch admiral simultaneously held two positions – Commander in Chief of the Royal Netherlands East Indian Navy (military) and the Minister of Marine (civilian). Helfrich felt he was better suited to be the ABDA naval commander.

A behind-the-scenes movement for Hart's removal, well under way for some time, began gaining strength by the end of January. Overall ABDA commander General Wavell sent British Prime Minister Winston Churchill a 'private and most confidential' message on January 29 asking for assistance on the Hart issue, citing the American admiral's pessimistic view and age.[17] He appeared to be seeking a way to remove Hart without offending their critical American ally. The Dutch authorities were much more open on the issue. When diplomat Hubertus van Mook traveled to Washington in mid-January to campaign for additional American military reinforcements, he freely criticized Hart at every opportunity.[18]

The situation was discussed in a mid-February meeting in Washington among President Roosevelt, Secretary of the Navy Frank Knox, and Navy Chief of Staff Admiral Ernest King. The group concluded there was nothing to be gained from the crumbling defense of the East Indies. Admiral King advocated moving the defensive line south to Australia, essentially giving up on trying to save anything to the north.[19] The president was evidently convinced Hart was too tired and unaggressive to continue in the command of the ABDA naval force.[20]

King earlier cabled Hart to forewarn him about an 'awkward situation' developing in Washington, noting he was reluctant to lose his services.[21] King thought it was best if he were to ask for separation based on health reasons. Hart did as suggested, writing at the time, 'I don't now see any forks over the long road back there [where] I feel that I took the wrong turn.'[22]

The situation was officially settled for good on February 12 during the Allied Combined Chief of Staff's meeting in Washington. The group of senior American and British military leaders ordered Wavell to turn over the top ABDA naval command to Admiral Helfrich.[23] The official change was to take place on February 15.[24] Admiral Doorman was to remain commander of the Combined Striking Force. Admiral Glassford, along with the senior British naval commander Admiral Arthur Palliser, became subordinates to Helfrich.

The drama playing out at the high levels of the command structure were of little concern to the *Marblehead* sailors. Their ability to get the ship to a safer port remained their top priority as the light cruiser was precariously sitting part way in the drydock at Tjilatjap. Whether *Marblehead* or Admiral Hart would be departing Java first remained a very open question.

Chapter 20

Java was quickly becoming the last bastion of the Malay Barrier in February 1942; the island was of great importance to the Dutch as it represented the political, cultural, and economic center of the Netherlands East Indies.[1] It was also home to the largest population of the territory and contained most of the sizable cities. The census of 1930 showed the island inhabited by a population of 41.7 million people. A little less than 200,000 were Europeans, with the clear majority of the remainder being native Javanese people. The population was estimated to have grown close to 50 million by the start of the war.[2]

The island was the most developed of the entire East Indies. The Dutch colonial capital of Batavia was located on the far northwestern part of the island. Two major east-west roads, both built by the Dutch, provided transportation on the western side of the island. Surabaya served as a major seaport on the northern coast, along with Batavia.

A long and narrow land mass measuring about 660 miles from east to west, and 200 miles wide across at the center point, Java's total land space (including the closely adjacent Madura Island, administratively controlled by Java) is slightly smaller than the state of Louisiana. A mountain range runs the length of the island with a few high peaks and an assortment of volcanoes. Various rivers and streams flow from the highlands towards the coastal lowlands and a thick jungle covers most of the island's interior. Rich volcanic soil, some of the most fertile in the whole colony, allowed for an abundant variety of agriculture during the days of Dutch rule, including rubber, coffee, sugar cane, and various spices. The weather is generally hot and humid, especially near the coast, with lower temperatures in the higher elevations of the mountainous areas.

The larger island of Sumatra lies to the northwest and the small island of Bali is immediately adjacent to the east. Directly south of Java is the eastern end of the Indian Ocean. The expanse of water, stretching about 800 miles, separates the island from the western side of Australia. The ABDA nations saw the value of defending Java to a point. The Dutch leaders were willing to do almost anything to keep their most important island from falling to the Japanese.

***

Marblehead was still moored next to *Pecos* on the morning of February 11, having taken aboard almost 300,000 gallons of fuel oil the day before. Other American ships in port included an assortment of auxiliaries, half a dozen four-stack destroyers, and the gunboat *Ashville*. Sixteen *Marblehead* sailors returned aboard from the local military hospital during the early afternoon.[3] These were the less severely wounded men who the medical staff thought could be cared for aboard the ship while at sea.

The returning group included two members of the amidships repair party. Fireman Second Class Keith Anstine and Metalsmith First Class Eddie Reagan both suffered burns on their hands and other areas. Seaman First Class Lester Valder was near the sick-bay and suffered lacerations on his face and leg. These lucky sailors were not going to be left behind should *Marblehead* make it out of Java.

The warship moved across the harbor the next morning to moor alongside the submarine tender *Otus*. All the while work continued topside and below deck to get her ready for departure. Much of the main deck near the stern of the ship, mangled from the bomb blast, had been cut out and removed, leaving a large open space. The area stretched from the after main battery turret almost all the way to the stern of the ship.

The area needed to be covered with some type of deck before she could put to sea. The temporary solution was to use wood, the only local material available in abundance. It had to be reinforced from below to provide extra strength. Captain Robinson wrote:

> The local contractor supplied and installed athwartships angle bars at each frame on the open fantail and angle bar pillars to support a temporary deck. Lumber was supplied from ashore and installed by the ship's force. In addition to

The launching of the light cruiser Marblehead *took place on October 9, 1923 at the William Cramp & Son Shipyard in Philadelphia, Pennsylvania. Her U.S. Navy commissioning ceremony took place eleven months later.* (US Navy / Naval History & Heritage Command)

The light cruiser Marblehead *seen at sea in 1924. Designed based on World War I technology, she was obsolete nearly two decades later when the United States was thrust into the Pacific War.* (US Navy / Naval History & Heritage Command)

The heavy cruiser Houston *at anchor off San Pedro, California on April 18, 1935. She was serving as flagship of the U.S. Asiatic Fleet during the opening days of World War II in the Pacific.* (US Navy / National Archives)

Admiral Thomas C. Hart was the Commander and Chief of the U.S. Asiatic Fleet at the start of World War II. He desperately wanted to strike back at the advancing Japanese after the hostilities began. Hart is seen here in June 1939 in Washington, DC. (US Navy / Naval History & Heritage Command)

Captain Arthur G. Robinson was Marblehead's *commanding officer when she was badly damaged in an air attack off Java on 4 February 4, 1942. He led the perilous effort to keep her afloat and subsequent long voyage back to the United States.* (US Navy / Naval History & Heritage Command)

Commander William B. Goggins was badly burned during the Japanese air attack. He was later transferred to a Dutch hospital on Java and eventually escaped from the island with Doctor Corydon Wassell. (US Navy / National Archives)

U.S. Navy Doctor Corydon Wassell was charged with overseeing a group of wounded American sailors from Marblehead *and* Houston *on Java in February 1942. He never gave up trying to find a way to escape the island ahead of the advancing Japanese and ultimately succeeded. Wassell is seen here shaking hands with a Chinese student pilot in Albuquerque, New Mexico in 1944.* (US Navy / Naval History & Heritage Command)

The Mitsubishi G4M was known to the Allies at the Betty. The twin-engine bomber was in the forefront of Japanese advances in the East Indies during the early days of World War II. (US Navy / National Archives)

The five-inch guns aboard Houston, *shown here during pre-war training off China, were the most powerful anti-aircraft weapons of the Combined Striking Force. However, the ship was supplied with faulty ammunition, causing some of the shells not to explode.* (US Navy / Naval History & Heritage Command)

A view from the damaged Marblehead *as she passes close to the heavy cruiser* Houston *while entering the harbor in Tjilatjap, Java. Damaged in the same air attack and arriving in port first,* Houston *sailors erupted into cheers upon seeing the ship many thought had been sunk.* (US Navy / National Archives)

Extensive damage near the wardroom of Marblehead *was revealed after tons of sea water and fuel oil was pumped out of the compartment. Sailors in the compartment suffered serious burns from the initial explosions.* (US Navy / National Archives)

Sailors and local yard hands undertake emergency repairs on the after section of Marblehead *in Tjilatjap, Java. A bomb narrowly missed the after turret before exploding deep inside the ship causing the deck to buckle and extensive interior damage.* (US Navy / National Archives)

Wounded sailors are carried off Marblehead *at Tjilatjap, Java. The most serious cases were taken by train to a Dutch Hospital in Jogjakarta.* (US Navy / National Archives)

The hole on the upper deck of Marblehead *reveals the location where the second bomb landed just below a whale boat and near the base of the tripod mast. Both direct hits penetrated the main deck and exploded inside the ship, causing fires, extensive interior damage, and casualties.* (US Navy / National Archives)

The sick-bay was among the many areas aboard Marblehead *to sustain serious damage during the air attack. The photo is looking down on the wrecked medical compartment.* (US Navy / National Archives)

A wounded and weary sailor takes a break aboard Marblehead. *Wreckage and oil-splattered decks can be clearly seen in the background of the photo taken on the port side of the ship.* (US Navy / National Archives)

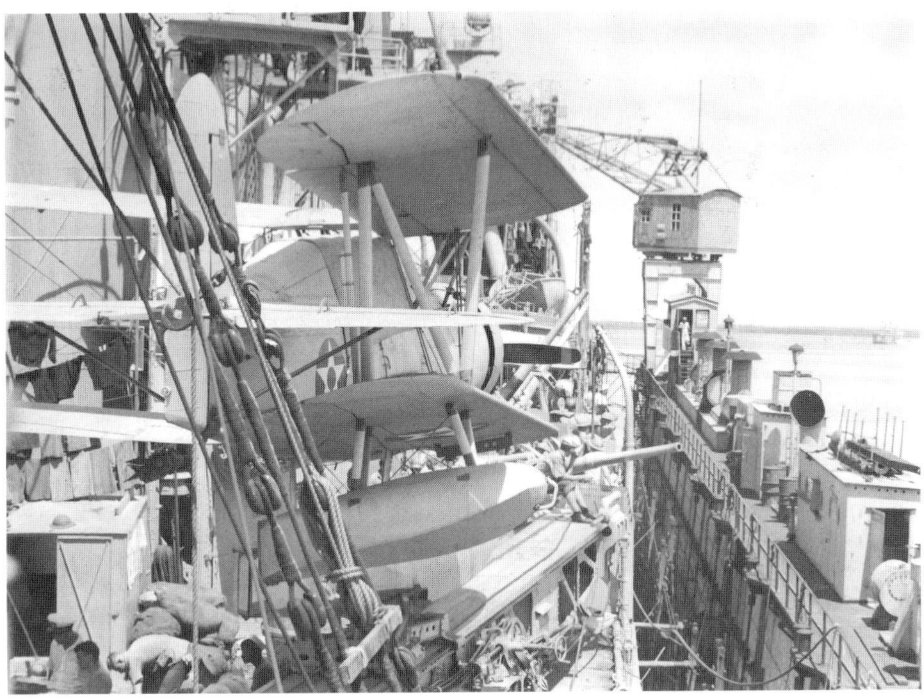

A view of Marblehead's *starboard side looking forward shows an SOC Seagull seaplane perched on a catapult. The picture was taken while the ship was undergoing emergency repairs in a small floating drydock in Tjilatjap, Java.* (US Navy / National Archives)

A view looking over the top of the after turret shows bomb damage at the stern of Marblehead. *The explosion disabled the motors controlling the steering gear, making it impossible to turn the rudder.* (US Navy / National Archives)

A large gash near the bottom of the hull on the port side from a near miss bomb allowed a torrent of sea water to enter Marblehead *below the waterline. The picture was taken while the warship was in a small floating drydock undergoing emergency repairs in Tjilatjap, Java.* (US Navy / National Archives)

An open air canteen on the deck of Marblehead *offers refreshments for a group of sailors. The catering staff went to great lengths to keep the exhausted men fed after losing some of the food supplies and repairing damaged equipment.* (US Navy / National Archives)

Work parties spent weeks aboard Marblehead *removing debris from wrecked compartments below deck, often working in difficult conditions. Slippery fuel oil, as shown in this view of sailors near a main hatch, covered some decks for days after the air attack.* (US Navy / National Archives)

The bent bow of Marblehead *occurred after a collision with a small Dutch tug boat while the light cruiser was departing Tjilatjap, Java. The lack of adequate repair facilities and approaching Japanese required the damaged light cruiser to put to sea from the small port.* (US Navy / National Archives)

A view of Marblehead *under repair at the Brooklyn Navy Yard in June 1942 shows her after main battery turret. The damaged warship sailed nearly 13,000 miles from Java to New York City after a heroic effort by her crew kept her afloat in the Pacific.* (US Navy / National Archives)

A late war picture of Marblehead *shows her at sea on May 12, 1944. Her stay at the Brooklyn Navy Yard in 1942 included repairs of battle damage and a variety of upgrades to armament and equipment.* (US Navy / National Archives)

The Dutch ship Janssens *transported Doctor Wassell and a group of his wounded sailors out of Java just ahead of the advancing Japanese. The small interisland steamer was not equipped for the daring ocean voyage to Australia.* (Australian War Memorial)

the angle bar deck beams, additional tie rods were installed by the ship's force, as all strength members supporting the original deck were completely destroyed.[4]

The final step was to make the temporary deck watertight. Crewmen installed three layers of canvas over the wood, each firmly secured and painted. Robinson considered the after deck to be 'reasonably strong and water-tight' when the construction had been completed.

The important issue of life rafts needed to be addressed prior to undertaking any voyage of substantial length. Many of *Marblehead*'s life rafts were damaged or destroyed in the air attack. Work crews gathered a supply of local bamboo. The stalks were cut into long pieces and tied together to use as temporary life rafts.[5]

The steering situation remained unchanged. 'It had been impossible to accomplish any work toward repairing or improvising steering motors other than salvaging the two damaged panels,' Robinson noted. The engines would continue to be used for steering.

By February 12 it was clear *Marblehead* could not stay in her current location much longer. 'No assistance or material was available in Tjilatjap for further repairs and it was apparent that the port would not be tenable much longer,' Robinson wrote. Nicholas Van Bergen was also ready to depart. 'When as much work had been done by the ship's force and coolie laborers as possible in Tjilatjap, we were very happy to leave there because we realized that this crowded port was soon to receive some more bombings,' he later said.[6] He recalled the ship obtaining a wide variety of materials during the port stay. 'At Tjilatjap we were able to get considerable commissary stores, shoes, clothing, welding rod, and light plate which we needed very badly,' Van Bergen explained. 'Some of this came from ships in the port and some of it came from the beach.'

Captain Robinson radioed to his superiors that *Marblehead* was ready for departure. Admiral Hart previously directed the ship be returned to the United States for permanent repairs. The long journey could only be made in stages. She was to begin the voyage by traveling west through the Indian Ocean to British territory near India. The official orders sent to Captain Robinson simply read 'Proceed with *Otus* to Colombo'.[7]

The light cruiser was about as ready to depart as she could be under the circumstances. The rough patches on the forward hull under the waterline were not totally watertight. The holes were covered enough to prevent the large in-rush of seawater that had caused the rapid flooding while in the Flores Sea. 'When ready to sail, the leakage of water into the ship and within the ship had been reduced to a rate where it was considered that submersible pumps could keep the level under control,' Robinson explained.

Living conditions aboard *Marblehead* improved considerably due to the hard work of her crew and local workers. Robinson continued:

> Most of the crew's living spaces had been made habitable; the installation of bunks, wash basins and cots in the wardroom country provided rough accommodation for the junior officers and warrant officers. A cafeteria system had been improvised for messing the crew; usable parts from various refrigerators and water coolers were salvaged and provided a satisfactory refrigerator for the combined officers' mess.

Sailors from a variety of other American ships frequently visited *Marblehead* during the time, and many lent a hand with the work.

The men down in the engineering compartments began lighting up boilers just before 1.00 pm on Friday, February 13, to build up steam for *Marblehead*'s impending departure. The warship's luck was good thus far in surviving near fatal damage and making port. Fate would, hopefully, now allow her to leave Java on a day noted to be unlucky. Her escort ship *Otus* was already on the move. The harbor pilot climbed aboard as sailors toiled with mooring lines and two tug boats arrived to provide assistance. She was underway at 3.15 pm for what her deck log simply recorded as an 'unknown destination'.[8] Apparently the location of her voyage, known to top officers, had not yet been announced to the crew.

Dutch authorities provided some assistance in advance of *Marblehead*'s departure. An order issued by local authorities earlier in the day was marked both secret and urgent. 'It is hereby ordered, that the airplane, now in the air, be instructed to make a reconnaissance flight south of Tjilatjap in connection with departure of American cruiser and tender today in the afternoon.'[9] Captain Robinson needed some reasonable assurances that waters he was about to sail into immediately south of Java were free of enemy activity. His damaged vessel was in no position to defend against an enemy attack by air or sea. No reports of enemy ships or air activity arrived prior to the start of the voyage.

Sailors aboard a nearby Dutch freighter carried out a final farewell as *Marblehead* slowly pulled away from the dock. They set up a phonograph to play into the ship's public address system, cranked up the volume, and turned a speaker outward towards the departing American ships. The Dutch sailors stood saluting at attention as *Marblehead* passed while the Star-Spangled Banner played over the speakers. John Bracken remembered it as a 'chilling and moving moment'.[10]

The ship was about to begin sailing into the unknown. Weather and sea conditions were not overlooked as important factors in the voyage. Van Bergen later recalled:

> We were so extremely heavy forward due to the flooding there, and so extremely heavy aft due to the flooding there and so weak amidships due to the structural damage done by the hit in that locality, that we were extremely afraid that if we ran into any sea way that the ship would break.[11]

Only time would reveal if the wounded ship could stay afloat long enough to reach her destination.

***

The dining room of the Savoy Hotel in Bandung, Java, served as the setting for a party held on the evening of February 14. The occasion was the retirement of Admiral Hart. The event marked the end of his duty in the Far East. He arose to speak after dinner and drinks, though the officer struggled to find words. 'Well boys, we all have a busy day tomorrow, so we'd better break this up,' he finally told the group.[12] Hart then stood by the door to give a formal farewell and handshake to the sixteen officers who attended the event.

Hart spent a restless night, uneasy about leaving the many men under his command at such a critical time early in the war. He departed Batavia the next morning dressed in civilian clothes. A young lieutenant drove him to the docks in Batavia in a battered sedan, flying a small flag with four stars representing his status as a full admiral. The officer dropped him off at a pier and departed after wishing the admiral good luck and giving him the flag from the car.

Admiral Hart later boarded the damaged British light cruiser *Durban*. The old ship took him to Colombo, Ceylon, on the first leg of a long voyage back to the United States.[13] Hart spent a great deal of time in his cabin objectively analyzing the events of the past two months. The passage recorded in his diary was written in third person: 'I can't find any great and serious fault with Hart. He did function pretty well for an old fellow during those three weeks in Manila; they involved the losing side all through but nothing Hart could have done would have turned the scale.'[14] He later wrote a lengthy narrative as his official report of the events taking place under his command.

Chapter 21

One group of wounded *Marblehead* sailors was getting a good look at Java's interior while the damaged warship remained in Tjilatjap. William Goggins and his companions had arrived at the Petronella Hospital in Jogjakarta on the afternoon of February 7. Founded in 1897, the hospital was the oldest and largest medical facility in the region.[1] The current building had opened in 1901 and subsequently expanded in 1930 to 380 beds. Goggins recalled:

> It had been taken over by the Dutch Army and militarized, all the personnel taken into the Dutch Army, Dutch nurses and the doctors. The hospital is a white stucco building all on one floor, tile roof, beautiful garden, trees around it, very clean, beautiful polished floors, all equipment modern and with plenty of nurses and doctors in attendance.[2]

A group of medical staff were on hand for the arrival of the new patients. 'We were sorted out and taken in to have our wounds dressed,' Goggins continued. He was given a shot that put him into a sound sleep before the medical staff began working on him. His bandages were removed and the burns covered with tannic acid jelly before new dressings were applied. Unknown to Goggins at the time, his wounds were believed to be so critical that his chances of survival were considered slim. There were even questions among the medical staff as to whether he would be able to walk again after many weeks.[3]

The officer woke up the next morning to find himself 'in a very nice room by myself with [a] Dutch nurse and a Javanese nurse looking out for me'. He soon became accustomed to his new surroundings and found the Dutch hosts to be more than accommodating. He later recalled:

> The hospital authorities relaxed their rules about smoking in the wards and permitted our men to smoke, something that had never been done. The local Dutch people heard of our arrival and a number of them called to see us to find out if there was anything they could do. I understand that a collection was taken up locally to buy ice cream and cigarettes for the men.

The new arrivals joined a blend of existing navy men from *Houston* and *Marblehead*. Their addition brought the number up to forty-one sailors in total.[4] All were considered to have serious wounds needing care beyond what could be provided on their respective ships.

The medical staff quickly saw that Seaman Second Class Joseph Leinweber needed urgent medical attention when he arrived at the hospital from *Marblehead* on February 7. The young sailor from Pennsylvania, tall with blond hair, had been in the chiefs' quarters near the back of the ship – very close to one of the bomb hits. His condition was considered critical as he was suffering from extensive burns to the point where his face looked almost black, part of his ear was torn off, and he was riddled with shrapnel.[5]

Coxswain Robert Kraus was in bad shape and lucky to be alive. The Wisconsin native was a member of the gun crew in the wrecked after turret aboard *Houston*. The initial explosion threw him hard against the rammer of an 8-inch gun. Two batches of gunpowder exploded near him as he struggled to get out, one occurring close to his face. He was found hanging in a hatch by other sailors who helped him to safety.[6] The back portion of his knee was ripped out, he had a variety of burns and painful shrapnel wounds; a piece of shrapnel had entered his back, puncturing a lung and those close by his bed could hear his breathing every time he moved.

Most of the *Marblehead* men in the hospital were suffering from burns resulting from the two explosions and subsequent fires. The group included Mess Attendant Second Class Pao San Ho, Signalman Second Class William Anderson, Seaman First Class Benjamin Hopkins, and Seaman Second Class Melvin Francis. Ho had first come aboard

Marblehead in January of 1939 with three-and-a-half years of naval service already under his belt.[7] Anderson had come from the small town of Bayesville, OH; he had been passing ammunition near a hatch on the main deck when seriously burned.

Benjamin Hopkins enlisted in the navy on September 12, 1940, while a resident of Nebraska. He joined the service to learn a trade.[8] A furlough after basic training gave him the chance to return home to see his parents in Plattsmouth before shipping out overseas. Hopkins reported for duty aboard *Marblehead* on February 5, 1941.[9] Fate had put him close to one of the bomb hits during the action in the Flores Sea; he had been on the port side of the main deck aft of the wardroom when the explosion caused burns to his face, arms, and legs. His condition was considered serious.[10]

Melvin Francis was a newcomer to *Marblehead*, having been on the light cruiser for just over a month. He was part of a large contingent of eighty-five sailors who transferred aboard from *Chaumont* on January 7, 1942, in Darwin.[11] The transport had been en route to Manila loaded with navy sailors, civilian workers, and cargo, when the war started. She was initially diverted to Fuji and later to Australia.[12] Francis was near the back of the ship during the attack and was suffering from serious burns.

Seaman Second Class William McCurdy also transferred from *Chaumont*. He was in the wardroom, possibly not far from Goggins, at the time of the forward bomb hit. Unlike most of the *Marblehead* men, who were mainly suffering from burns, McCurdy was hit with shrapnel causing serious puncture wounds, including one to his bladder.[13]

Turret Captain First Class Roger Poirier of *Houston* succumbed to his wounds on February 12, bringing the number of surviving wounded sailors down to forty.[14] Poirier was buried in a local cemetery on a bright sunny day, with the service conducted by a Dutch priest. Local workmen dug the grave and residents provided flowers to put at the grave site.

A group of nurses went to great lengths to help the sailors. Goggins later recalled 'receiving the very finest care and attention from the Dutch' during his stay at the hospital. Two nurses caring for the wounded sailors were particularly popular with the Americans. The first was known by the nickname 'Boilermaker'. Seemingly of European descent, she offered a continuous supply of kindness and compassion. The second was Sister DeKraufre, described as a big, good-looking Dutch girl with dark hair.[15] A group of young Javanese boys assisted the nurses with regular duties in the ward. One boy, small in stature, became known to the Americans simply as 'junior'.

At least one other foreign serviceman was known to be at the hospital – a ground crewman of the British Royal Air Force named P.W. Wears. He was receiving treatment for a 'minor skin complaint' on his face and later recalled hearing 'a lot of noise coming from another ward. On investigation I found it filled with wounded and badly burnt survivors from an attack on the *Houston* and *Marblehead*.'[16] Wears had recently taken up the local language and became a 'self-appointed interpreter', helping to communicate with the Javanese orderlies. He assisted the American wounded in various ways. 'I also cleaned their teeth & shaved a few over the next few days.'

The threat of the Japanese always seemed near and Goggins recalled:

> Frequent air raids in this city were the cause of some alarm, although there was no bombing. Apparently, reconnaissance was going on by the Japanese to locate this [air]field and find out when would be a good time to bomb it. Those who could walk would go into the shelters which were built in the hospital, but those of us who were helpless were put on a mattress and slid under the bed, which was about the only thing that could be done. That was the air raid shelter for those who were unable to walk.

***

Another American navy man appeared at the Petronella Hospital around the same time as the arrival of Goggins and the second group of *Marblehead* sailors. Lieutenant Commander Corydon Wassell traveled to Jogjakarta from Surabaya, where he was a doctor serving as part of the American naval staff in the city. Wassell was directed by his superior to look after the well-being of the American sailors in the hospital and act as a liaison with the local Dutch medical staff. 'I saw him first about the second day after I was in the hospital,' Goggins remembered. He was a man of unassuming stature who spoke with a slow drawl.'[17]

Spending time in a foreign land was nothing new for the 57-year-old mild-mannered doctor. Wassell hailed from Little Rock, Arkansas, having been born on American Independence Day in 1884.[18] He had graduated from the University of Arkansas with a medical degree in 1909 and his post-graduate work included studies at the prestigious Johns Hopkins University in Maryland and the Rockefeller School for Health Unit Directors in Mississippi. Coming from a family with a strong history of public service, Wassell wanted to do more than just work as a local doctor in Arkansas – a potentially lucrative undertaking at the time, often resulting in a luxurious lifestyle.[19]

The doctor became a medical missionary for the Episcopal Church in Wuchang, China. He spent more than a decade there, even marrying a girl from New Jersey during his stay. Wassell joined the U.S. Navy Reserve in 1924 with a rank of lieutenant (junior grade).[20] He returned to Arkansas in 1927 and later worked as a doctor in the Civilian Conservation Corps.

Wassell was called up to active duty in August 1940 as war clouds were slowly gathering over the Pacific. His initial duty was at the naval base in Key West, Florida. Orders in late 1941 directed him to report to the Philippines, but the start of hostilities prevented his travel to Manila.

Doctor Wassell was aboard a merchant ship, most likely *President Polk*, in San Francisco awaiting a scheduled 11.00 am departure on December 7, 1941. The voyage was to begin with a trip under the Golden Gate Bridge. 'Before we could pass under the bridge the news came in that Hawaii had been bombed and we didn't get under the bridge,' he later said. 'We kept turning around in the harbor there and about 2.30 we came back to the pier and unloaded that cargo of people.'[21]

The same ship departed later in December, loaded with soldiers and a cargo of fighter planes. The long voyage took the vessel south from the equator for a stop in New Zealand. 'We had a forty-eight hour stay in Auckland, New Zealand,' Wassell later recalled. 'That is the first point of land we looked at after leaving the Golden Gate.' He harbored good memories of the port stay, most notably of the friendly people.

The vessel made a stop in Australia before heading north to Java with a small group of other ships under escort by *Houston*. Admiral Glassford recalled *President Polk* as the 'only ship to arrive' at Surabaya with supplies and provisions.[22] Wassell arrived on the island in late January for duty as the Medical Officer in Command, U.S. Naval Activities, Surabaya, Java. The doctor had some limited contact with Admiral Glassford shortly after his arrival on the island. 'Wassell in uniform reported to me for duty at Surabaya during the first phase of the defense of the [Malay] Barrier,' the admiral later wrote.[23] 'A most unimpressive appearing man, middle-aged it seemed, slouchy, badly groomed and dressed.' The admiral learned in conversation of the doctor's missionary time in China and of his work in 'combating the dread malaria for which disease he was a specialist'. Glassford thought it was appropriate to send Wassell to the southern coast of Java around Tjilatjap, where malaria was prevalent. 'I though no more of him at the time,' Glassford recalled.

Doctor Wassell didn't make it to Tjilatjap – at least not right away. A new assignment came to him in a somewhat unusual manner. He was organizing medical supplies at the dock in Surabaya when he found a mislabeled box containing torpedo parts instead of iodine as marked. When he reported the error to a superior officer, he was told of the situation at the hospital and was ordered to go to Jogjakarta at once via plane. The flight was leaving in a half an hour.[24]

The doctor checked in to a local hotel after arriving in the area and subsequently spent much of his time visiting the hospital. 'During this time he had been given funds by the admiral with orders to see that all of our wants were taken care of,' Goggins remembered. 'He made the rounds several times a day to see the men and the officers.' The doctor came bearing gifts – cigarettes, long holders for men with burnt lips who wanted to smoke, and equipment to help those who needed assistance walking. Wassell quickly settled into his new role of watching over the wounded flock. At about the same time, the sailors aboard *Marblehead*, about 100 miles to the west, were getting ready to depart Java once and for all.

Chapter 22

Captain Robinson and the navigator were on the bridge as the harbor pilot guided *Marblehead* towards the entrance of the Tjilatjap harbor during the early afternoon hours of February 13. The ship was still without rudder control, but was navigating the channel with the help of two Dutch tug boats, each attached to the light cruiser by a line – the tug boat *Kraus* forward and *Pief* after. Two black balls hung under *Marblehead*'s mast, a warning to other vessels in the immediate area that she was not under control.

The harbor pilot directed *Pief* to cast off and return to port 5.10 pm Only minutes later, as *Marblehead* entered the inner end of the minefield channel, the towline from *Kraus* suddenly broke free. *Marblehead* was quickly drifting near the minefield with no ability to steer the ship. The pilot turned ashen, fully knowing the peril of the situation. 'All right now, let's take it easy and try to hold her in the channel with her engines,' Captain Robinson said to those on the bridge.[1] The pilot then gave commands as to which engines to run, port and starboard.

The tug boat nudged in front of the still moving *Marblehead* as the small craft's captain attempted to get into position to re-establish the towline. 'At 5.17 pm the headway of this ship carried her into the tug,' Robinson explained. '*Marblehead*'s stem struck the tug's starboard guard rail abaft the beam. At this time the speed of both vessels is estimated to have been about three knots.'[2] He now had to contend with some new damage to his ship.

There was neither the time, nor the facilities to make adequate repairs to the bow. 'The space inside was too narrow for access and plugs and caulking were driven into the ruptures from the outside,' Robinson explained. 'The pitching of the ship made this work hazardous and ineffective. The forward peak tank flooded, was secured and shored during the ensuing voyage.'

The collision bent a portion of *Marblehead*'s bow about 8 inches to starboard. The bottom-most forward compartment of the ship, previously undamaged, was flooded. Carpenter R.L. Billman went over the side to take a closer look at the damage. He determined it could not be repaired at the time.[3] 'Damage to the *Kraus* appeared slight,' Robinson added. With no time to reconnect with the tug, *Marblehead* continued to move under her own power. The careful use of engines for steering kept her clear of danger. The pilot departed at 5.55 pm after *Marblehead* safely passed the minefields.[4] The light cruiser continued to steam in a southerly direction at fifteen knots in company of *Otus* and the destroyer *Pillsbury*.

***

Captain Robinson's judgement of needing to leave Tjilatjap as soon as possible could not have been better. The middle of February saw the ABDA defense of the Malay Barrier crumbling fast. A force of Japanese troops on Borneo was taken by barge from Balikpapan to a point near Bandjarmasin on the southern part of the island. The coastal city was captured on February 16, giving the Japanese an airbase directly north across the Java Sea from Java.[5] The news of the operation was largely eclipsed by events happening further west.

Soldiers of the British Empire had been retreating down the Malaya Peninsula in the direction of Singapore since the opening days of the war. The force included Commonwealth troops from Britain, Australia, and India. The Japanese gained control of the air early in the campaign, allowing their planes to endlessly attack the ground forces with bombs and strafing. The Royal Navy fared little better at sea, with their two largest ships – battleship *Prince of Wales* and battlecruiser *Repulse* – sunk on December 10 by bombers during a fruitless attempt to locate an invasion convoy. On the ground, Japanese soldiers under the command of General Tomoyuki Yamashita skillfully avoided defensive positions along the main roads by stealthily advancing in small groups through jungles and swamps – places British commanders thought were impossible for troop movements. British positions repeatedly crumbled and turned into full retreats when faced with Japanese attacks from the front or flanks. Commanders were often unable to rally their fleeing men.[6]

The retreat eventually ran the full length of the Malay Peninsula. Japanese ground forces were approaching Singapore by late January.

British leaders previously thought the island could hold under siege for six months. However, it proved to be a faulty assumption and the reality was far less.

The fortress island was separated from mainland Malaya by the Johore Strait, a wide waterway that should have provided a layer of protection. A man-made causeway spanning more than 1,000ft connected Singapore to the mainland. Engineers failed to fully destroy the causeway after the last British troops crossed over the strait on January 31. Explosives only created a 70ft breech. Nearly 85,000 Commonwealth troops were crammed into Singapore under the command of General Arthur Percival. They faced 30,000 Japanese across the straits.[7] The general's incompetence would weigh heavily in the events that unfolded during the next two weeks.

Defenses across the Johore Strait were poor. Parts of the waterway were very shallow, enough for soldiers to be able to wade across during low tide. In building a fortress to repel attackers from the sea, the British had neglected to create adequate defenses on the backside of the island. Little had been done to improve the situation since the start of the war, even after a visit by General Wavell in January. The large 15-inch artillery guns guarding the harbor area like sentinels faced the sea and could not be trained to fire in the opposite direction.[8] Prime Minister Winston Churchill was astonished at the lack of planning, declaring 'it never occurred to me for a moment … that the gorge of the fortress was not entirely fortified against an attack from the northward'.[9]

Throngs of people – civilian and military – rushed to the docks as the siege began, trying to get on a ship – or anything that could float – bound for Sumatra, Java or Australia. The Japanese had nearly complete control of the air and when their planes attacked there were few British fighters available to stop them. Many of the fleeing vessels were later ruthlessly sunk by enemy planes and ships. Repeating the same mistake General McArthur had made in the Philippines, Percival deployed too many troops at the water's edge and his fresh British soldiers were positioned in the wrong location.[10]

General Yamashita's assault began on the night of February 7 with a diversionary thrust that was followed by the main attack. Groups of Japanese soldiers crossed the strait in small boats under the cover of a heavy artillery barrage. The damaged causeway was soon repaired allowing tanks and troops to swarm across. The situation for the defenders became critical after the Japanese captured an outlying reservoir, cutting off the water supply to Singapore proper.

General Percival surrendered to Yamashita on February 15. He had been beaten by the much smaller force under the direction of an aggressive leader. The fall of Singapore was the greatest defeat in British military history, with 138,708 service personnel of all types lost to the enemy.[11] Many were to face years of brutal captivity in Japanese prison camps. Churchill later wrote of the event as the 'worst disaster' to befall the British Empire.[12]

The loss of Singapore had severe consequences for the ABDA command area. The entire western flank of the Malay Barrier simply collapsed. Nearby Sumatra was threatened with immediate invasion, with Java not far behind. General Wavell notified Churchill one day after the fall that 'Landings on Java in the near future can only be prevented by local naval and air superiority. Facts given show that it is most unlikely that this superiority can be obtained.'[13] The Japanese were now free to complete their conquest of the Dutch East Indies, earlier than the high command originally planned, and with more forces available than expected.[14] The enemy wasted no time in exploiting the opportunity. Events over the next three weeks unfolded at a rapid pace with some operations occurring simultaneously.

The jungle covered island of Sumatra was a rich prize for the Japanese Empire due to its oil fields, refineries, storage tanks, and other natural resources. Key targets were the city of Palembang and the nearby island of Banka in southeastern Sumatra. Although an inland city, Palembang was connected to the Banka Strait waterway on the east coast of the island by the deep Musi River, which was navigable by some types of ships. The area contained some of the island's richest oil fields and large storage facilities, while Banka supplied over 10 per cent of the world's tin.[15]

Plans for the Sumatra invasion were underway even as the last parts of the Singapore episode were playing out. A large convoy put to sea from Camranh Bay in Indochina bound for Palembang on February 9, and was shortly followed within days by two additional groups of ships. The units included a powerful covering force comprised of six cruisers, six destroyers, and the aircraft carrier *Ryujo* under the command of Admiral Jisaburo Ozawa. A variety of shallow draft vessels, no longer needed for operations in Singapore but ideal for river attacks on Sumatra, later joined the armada en route. The advanced echelon arrived at the mouth of the Musi River at dawn on February 15.[16]

Good intelligence gave ABDA leaders advanced warning of the approaching enemy forces. Admiral Doorman was ordered to assemble his ships off Java for an attack. The admiral now commanded a true ABDA force with British and Australian warships joining the Dutch and American forces already participating in past operations. The hastily assembled force included three Dutch light cruisers (one was his flagship *De Ruyter*), British heavy cruiser *Exeter*, Australian light cruiser *Hobart*, and ten Dutch and American destroyers. The Combined Striking Force departed southern Java after refueling on February 13 for transit through the Sunda Strait between Java and Sumatra, losing a Dutch destroyer to a reef in transit. Doorman sailed to a position northeast of Banka Island, arriving on the morning of February 15. He intended to move into the strait to attack the Japanese invasion convoy off the Musi River.

Admiral Doorman was heading into a mass of confusion. The Banka Strait area was crowded with craft of all types, having served as the main waterway for those fleeing Singapore during the last days under British rule. The Japanese invasion forces, moving under heavy air cover, were approaching at about the same time. Enemy reconnaissance planes spotted the ABDA force and reported their movements while carefully staying outside the range of the ships' anti-aircraft guns.

Admiral Ozawa dispersed his invasion forces and planned to first attack the approaching ABDA ships by air before unleashing his powerful surface force. Waves of carrier-based planes from *Ryujo* and land-based bombers attacked throughout much of the day on February 15. This time, however, the air attacks were largely ineffective, causing only light damage to two American destroyers. Admiral Doorman called off his attack, not wanting to further risk his warships without air cover, and retreated east into the Java Sea. He later told Admiral Hart that history would condemn him for the decision.[17]

Admiral Ozawa resumed his invasion operations up the Musi River after the challenge from ABDA naval forces was vanquished. General Wavell ordered southern Sumatra to be abandoned after Japanese soldiers reached Palembang.[18] British and Dutch forces retreated to Java, leaving much of the oil facilities undamaged. The Japanese capture of Sumatra included roughly half of the oil reserves in the Dutch East Indies.[19]

The fall of Sumatra allowed Japanese forces to be pushed right up next to the western end of Java. The Dutch island was becoming more isolated with each passing day of February, as enemy operations ramped up to the east. A series of Japanese operations were carried out over the span of only a few days. The island of Timor, split between Dutch and Portuguese control, came under invasion on February 20. A convoy carrying ground troops to the island, under escort by *Houston*, turned back only a few days earlier after coming under air attack. The island was used as part of a staging route for flying fighter planes from Australia to Java via Bali.[20] The loss severed the supply line and was yet another blow in the faltering effort to keep Java out of Japanese hands.

The small mountainous island of Bali, positioned immediately adjacent to Java on the east, and scene of the damaged *Marblehead*'s escape south from the Flores Sea, was the next target for Japanese seizure. An invasion force under the escort of a single light cruiser and handful of destroyers set sail from Celebes on February 18. The ships arrived the next day in the Badung Strait, a narrow waterway only about fifteen miles wide, off the southeast coast of Bali to start the amphibious assault. Although the American submarine *Seawolf* contacted the force, she was unable to slow the operation. A series of sporadic attacks by a small number of B-17 bombers damaged one transport.

Admiral Doorman was again ordered to attack. The numbers now favored the Dutchman – his Combined Striking Force was strong enough to overpower the Bali occupation group. However, his available ships were too widely scattered, at sea or in different ports, for him to intervene in sufficient force before the landings were completed. Some ships were still retiring from the aborted Sumatra operation, while others were refueling away from the immediate area or on convoy escort duty.

The Dutch admiral did carry out an attack using a hurriedly formed plan. Unable to rendezvous his nearest forces into a single unit, Doorman instead attacked with smaller groups of ships. The plan was not viewed favorably by Admiral Glassford and other American naval officers. In the absence of any viable alternatives, they had little choice but to go along with it.[21]

The Battle of Badung Strait occurred when three small waves of ABDA naval forces successively attacked the Japanese ships off Bali during the night of February 19–20. The first wave was led by Admiral Doorman and consisted of the light cruisers *De Ruyter* and *Java* accompanied by three destroyers. The force attacked during the last hours of February 19. Doorman's firepower advantage over four Japanese destroyers was thwarted by the sharp maneuvering of the Japanese, who gained a tactical advantage.[22] The attack turned into a confusing mêlée that included the arrival of additional enemy destroyers. The Dutch destroyer *Piet Hein* was lost in an exchange of gunfire and torpedoes.

The second group of the Dutch light cruiser, *Tromp*, and four American destroyers raced in as Doorman's ships were departing. Two Japanese destroyers were hit by gunfire from *Tromp* and a third by American destroyers. The Dutch light cruiser was badly damaged by return gunfire and later sailed to Australia for repairs, keeping her out of the remainder of the campaign. The final wave was a group of Dutch torpedo boats. These small vessels missed finding the enemy altogether. The battle ended with no Japanese ships sunk. Both Bali and the adjacent island of Lombok easily fell into Japanese hands; the airfield on Bali was captured intact and Japanese planes began arriving the very next day.[23]

A ring of Japanese airfields now surrounded Java on three sides – Sumatra to the west, southern Borneo in the north, and Bali to the east. All the key port cities, including Tjilatjap and approaches to the south, were under attack from the air. A large air battle over Surabaya on February 19 saw ABDA fighters, many obsolete, mauled by Japanese Zeroes. About forty Dutch and American fighter planes were shot down against the loss of only one Japanese airplane.[24]

The isolation of Java allowed Japanese naval leaders to unleash a new menace in the waters south of the island – large aircraft carriers. A force of four carriers, all Pearl Harbor veterans, under the command of Admiral Chuichi Nagumo had recently left Staring Bay in Celebes for a voyage south. A group of 188 planes launched from the carriers on the morning of February 19 under the command of Mitsuo Fuchida – famous for leading the Pearl Harbor attack. The target was Darwin, which was serving as a logistics base for ABDA forces further north. The Japanese hoped the raid would interdict plane reinforcements to Java.[25]

Waves of Japanese planes descended on Darwin beginning just before 10.00 am attacking shipping, storage facilities, and airfields. A second group of fifty-four land-based bombers arrived around 11.45 am to continue the rain of destruction.[26] The damage was severe, including thirty planes destroyed and eleven ships sunk. The town was temporarily abandoned over fears of additional attacks.[27] The Japanese naval units operating south of Java in the coming weeks were to wreak havoc on vessels trying to escape to Australia, and put a stranglehold on supplies trying to reach the embattled Dutch island.

The loss of Singapore and Sumatra, coupled with the unrelenting air attacks on Java, was enough to cause the ABDA command to start falling apart. General Wavell favored abandoning the island and sending the remaining forces elsewhere. He was overruled by officials in London. Wavell departed Java on February 25 to organize the defense of India. The Crown Colony was threatened by the Japanese thrust into adjacent Burma. The ABDA command was all but finished and largely existed in name only. Control of the naval forces, air remnants, and local forces around Java now fell to the Dutch. Admiral Helfrich cabled London asking for help in the form of planes, ships, and soldiers. He still believed Java could hold out with reinforcements.[28]

PART V

THE LONG JOURNEY HOME

Chapter 23

Wounded officer William Goggins passed the crisis stage and started a long slow recovery from his wounds less than two weeks after his arrival at Petronella Hospital.[1] The improvement could not have come sooner. Goggins and the other sailors would soon be on the move. Also moving was P.W. Wears; the British airman's time at the hospital came to an end with his stay having lasted only about a week. Before his departure the American sailors gave him a picture of a ship which he believed was *Marblehead*, pasted onto the cover of a folder. The folder was filled with autographs of the men from *Houston* and *Marblehead*.[2] The airman rejoined his unit and eventually became a prisoner of war when Java fell to the Japanese.

Doctor Wassell knew he had to somehow find a way to get his wounded men out of Java and to the safety of Australia. His effort was later described as 'almost like a Christlike shepherd devoted to his flock'.[3] Wassell continued to make rounds in the hospital and spend time with his patients, even as he desperately tried to find a way out.

A general state of confusion existed on Java as the Japanese were moving ever closer. Wassell made several attempts to schedule a departure on a warship or auxiliary by calling the U.S. Navy office in Tjilatjap. He was unsuccessful in all attempts, and only on one occasion was he able to speak to someone; unfortunately, he was yelled at for asking questions to which no one knew the answer.[4]

The doctor was not about to give up trying. A potential breakthrough happened when Wassell spoke directly with the senior American naval officer in Tjilatjap. He may have spoken with Captain Lester Hudson, an administrative officer who moved to the southern port from Surabaya. Hudson oversaw a recently opened U.S. Naval Port Office. Wassell was told to bring the wounded sailors – at least those who were ambulatory and could withstand a rough passage – to the port for evacuation.

Wassell instead decided to take all his men. The journey was to take place by train on the morning of February 25.[5]

Ambulances came to the hospital to transport the men to the local train station. However, there were hospital rules that still needed to be followed. Each sailor was formally released by the Dutch doctor. The hospital staff waved goodbye as the head doctor wished the group luck. Doctor Wassell in turn sincerely thanked the staff for their help and kindness. 'There were ten of us that could not walk,' Goggins recalled. 'They occupied bunks in the hospital car, the others rode in a sort of coach.'[6]

The train ride proved to be a hot and slow journey with frequent stops, including a delay for an air raid alert. Wassell rushed off the train at some of the stops to buy food and drinks for the men. Goggins explained:

> We got down to Tjilatjap along in the afternoon and were taken over to the large house which was being used by the men of the admiral's staff. There were no hospital facilities whatever for us and the doctor was forced to get cots and put us on the porch of this house for the night.

The city was swarming with people – both military and civilians. Everyone seemed to be moving around in a hurry wanting to get away as the enemy was closing in on what was increasingly looking like a doomed island. American Lieutenant Commander J.S. Mosher was an eyewitness to the conditions at Tjilatjap. Having previously served as the Assistant Naval observer in Singapore, he escaped the fortress island before the fall and joined the American naval staff on Java and was now waiting for a ride to Australia.

The American naval personnel in the port city took up quarters in the only hotel. According to Mosher:

> Tjilatjap, by no means a popular resort even in peacetime, was not equipped to deal with the flood of transients that descended on it now. At the time the writer arrived, two or three hundred persons of all sorts and persuasions seemed to be quartered in the hotel, sleeping on veranda floors, in the lounge chairs, or even in parked cars. Meals became strictly

cafeteria affairs, in that impatient diners helped themselves
in crowds from the kitchen range while the Javanese waiters
ran confusedly about with empty beer bottles or dirty plates.[7]

He remembered many dinners eaten in pitch dark during air raid alarms. Mosher declined a spot aboard *Pecos* because the tanker was not going to his destination of Perth. He instead escaped on a British plane with three American aviators.

A series of narrow city streets led to the port area. There were warehouses close to the docks and anti-aircraft gun emplacements spread about. The conditions at the port area have been variously described as 'complete bedlam' and 'indescribable confusion'.[8] About fifteen or twenty ships were anchored in the crowded harbor area. Numerous small boats were continuously ferrying people out from the shore. Two wooden-planked wharfs were positioned on the waterfront; one was able to accommodate three ships, and the other only one. Abandoned supplies of all types were strewn nearby.

The sailors were not earmarked for departure aboard any ship. Wassell searched in vain for ships willing to take aboard his passengers. The doctor was far from alone. There were servicemen of all nationalities and branches looking to find a ship to board. The fact that his men were wounded put him at a disadvantage; there were so many able-bodied people wanting to leave that required ships' captains less worry and maintenance. Wassell spoke with an American naval officer and just about anyone else who would listen.

The ambulatory sailors were split among several departing vessels. The chaotic situation at the docks, with hundreds of people cramming aboard ships, prevented accurate record keeping. The usual formalities of checking orders and authorizations of individuals boarding ships did not take place; the drafting lists from various sources over time are not in total agreement. The exact disposition of how Doctor Wassell's walking wounded escaped Java may never be known with complete certainty.

Perhaps the best information comes from an article about the evacuation written later in the war, appearing in *Our Navy* magazine, based on interviews with several of the wounded sailors. The story mentions men departing on three different vessels – two ships and a submarine. According to the author of the article, 'He [Wassell] found a submarine commander who would take ten or twelve men who needed little or no medical treatment. He found places for five more on a navy oiler and found a Dutch freighter that would take the other men who could walk.'[9]

One of Wassell's successes occurred when he came across Lieutenant Commander Paul Abernethy, the skipper of the American tanker *Pecos*. He likely lobbied to get all his men aboard. The available space, however, was likely limited. Abernethy later wrote:

> With daily air raid alarms and intelligence that enemy warships were en route to the southern coast of Java, I knew that the *Pecos*, as the only fleet tanker in the area, was a ship especially marked for destruction. I explained this to Dr Wassell and declined to accept any men except those who were ambulatory and could take care of themselves.[10]

Ensign Charles Coburn was among the small group of Wassell's men to go aboard the tanker. One account put the following four additional ambulatory sailors aboard: Chief Watertender Frank Brown, Baker Third Class LaMoine Marsh, Mess Attendant Second Class Billie Tsu, all from *Marblehead*, and Marine Corporal George Kelton of *Houston*.[11] The tanker was scheduled to leave for Australia on February 27.

The American submarine *Sturgeon* was diverted from war patrol duties to participate in the evacuation of United States personnel from Java. She arrived at Surabaya on February 13. With the northern port under increasing Japanese air attacks, the submarine was sent south to Tjilatjap. She took aboard members of the Asiatic Fleet Submarine Force staff.

An officer then told other sailors waiting dockside there was only room for ten more passengers on the submarine. Fireman Second Class Robert H. Clark of *Marblehead* was among those in the crowd. He was part of an ammunition supply chain sending shells up to the 3-inch guns during the action in the Flores Sea when he was seriously wounded, suffering burns on his face, arms, and body.[12] Clark remembered how the submarine officer resolved the situation. 'And he said, now I don't know who's going to go, so he put a bunch of paper chips in his hat, there were ten goes and the rest were no's,' he later recalled.[13] He was one of the lucky ten to be allowed on board. Another *Marblehead* veteran later recalled Fireman Second Class Walter Joyner also among those aboard *Sturgeon*.[14] The submarine sailed for Freemantle, Australia, arriving on March 3.[15]

The third group of wounded men found space aboard a merchant ship. There were two ships tied up next to the smaller wharf, one moored outboard of the other, with a single narrow stairway serving as the boarding point for both vessels. The arrangement resulted in a long line of people waiting to get up the stairs. The 7,900-ton Dutch Freighter *Abbekerk* was moored closest to the dock. She began the war in Europe, sustaining bomb damage during the Battle of Britain in 1940. The ship had made her way to the Pacific as part of a heavily guarded convoy bound for Singapore. Her stay at the fortress island was brief, having arrived just before the fall. She eventually sailed for Tjilatjap, via Sumatra, to assist in the Java evacuation effort.[16] Her holds still contained some of the unloaded ammunition earmarked for Singapore.

With a crew of about fifty sailors and accommodation for only twelve passengers, *Abbekerk* was hardly set up to function as a transport. Yet streaming aboard were hundreds of people. Young engineer Adriaan Kik later recalled the assortment of passengers. 'A more diverse lot I have never seen,' he wrote. 'Aircraft crews still wearing their thick woolen jackets, a few high and a lot more lower officers, soldiers, and sailors, both with and without weapons, and then some civilians, many with worried and tired faces.'[17] The passengers included American oilmen and about fifty Dutch flying cadets.

Also coming aboard was a contingent of American airmen who arrived dockside in a convoy of trucks and cars after traveling from another part of the island. All the vehicles – numbering seventy-two in total – were abandoned since the ship had no side hatches.[18] Any semblance of order broke down during the boarding process resulting in an 'every man for himself' type of situation. Passengers crammed aboard as best they could under the difficult circumstances.

The ship was likely carrying all of Doctor Wassell's remaining ambulatory sailors who were not aboard *Pecos* and *Sturgeon*. Australian records can only confirm the following two *Marblehead* men: Harold Hunter and Oscar Rudie.[19] Both sailors held the rank of machinist's mate second class. One source reported the wounded sailors endured 'a long and trying wait on the docks' before an American Army Air Corps doctor could get them aboard.[20] The doctor could have been Captain James Crane, who arrived at the docks with some wounded airmen.

He came across a few other medical men after initially being told by a Dutch crewman he would be the only medical person aboard for the voyage.[21] The wounded passengers – presumably including Doctor Wassell's men – were placed in the few available cabins.

Occasional air raid alerts added additional confusion to the boarding process. The possibility of the ship sinking was never far from the passengers' minds and extra preparations were made for the contingency. Local Javanese natives hastily constructed life rafts by lashing bamboo to empty fifty-gallon drums. The makeshift rafts were brought aboard for added safety.[22]

The freighter was underway at about 5.00 pm on February 27 bound for Australia. More than 1,500 passengers were crammed aboard.[23] She was initially part of a slow convoy with three other ships, hurriedly formed when all the vessels departed from the harbor at about the same time. With *Abbekerk* capable of making eighteen knots – faster than the other vessels – her captain later pulled away under the cover of darkness and set an independent course at full speed. There would be no accompanying ships to rescue survivors if *Abbekerk* went down.

Feelings of bleakness and impending doom swept through the vessel when rumors circulated of the three other ships from the convoy having been sunk by bombers, and of multiple Japanese submarines operating in the immediate area. Passengers were quickly recruited as lookouts. Many sets of eyes continuously scanned the horizon looking for any sign of a periscope or airplane.

The main weapon on *Abbekerk* was a single 4-inch deck gun. Some of the servicemen brought aboard rifles, submachine guns, and other assorted small arms. The weapons were set up at the rails and loaded for action. She was one day out of Tjilatjap when, at about 4.30 pm, a lookout cried 'plane sighted'.[24] The *Abbekerk* had been found by a single-engine Japanese reconnaissance plane.

The aircraft was heading directly at the ship flying at an altitude of about 2,000ft. It circled for several minutes before diving from the direction of the sun for a strafing run. A heavy volley of small arms fire caused the pilot to turn off. The plane made three more passes, appearing to drop two small bombs far off the stern, during one of the runs. Bullets were seen hitting the fuselage on the final pass. The plane dipped erratically a couple of times, but stayed in the air. A radio operator on the freighter heard Japanese radio chatter as the plane disappeared off into the distance. Although *Abbekerk* sustained no damage in the attack, it was clear her position was now known by the enemy.

Many on board worried it was only a matter of time before more planes returned to sink their ship. However, no trace of the enemy was seen again during the remainder of the voyage. The weather turned cold as *Abbekerk* neared Australia and some passengers were forced to sleep on deck with only thin blankets. The freighter safely arrived in Fremantle on March 5.[25]

No vessel at Tjilatjap was willing to take aboard the ten stretcher cases. Wassell's pleas were regularly denied due to the lack of facilities aboard to adequately care for the patients. He had no choice but to tell the remaining sailors the demoralizing news that they were not departing Java. Instead, with no available hospital space in Tjilatjap, they would have to return to the hospital in Jogjakarta. The men spent the night at the house before departing by train the next day.

The morning of February 26 found no hospital car available for the train going to Jogjakarta and the wounded men were unable to ride in a coach car. The sailors were loaded, still on their cots, into a freight car added to the back of the train. Goggins recalled:

> It doesn't sound as bad as you might think, as the side doors of the cars were open and one could get a fairly good view of the countryside which is very beautiful, but it was hot and it was quite dirty. We arrived in Jogjakarta that afternoon at about 3.30 [pm] and were met by the staff of the hospital as well as a number of Dutch ladies who were waiting for us with cold drinks and hot coffee, etc. We were transferred to stretchers and rested about fifteen minutes in the station while we received refreshments.

During this time, Goggins noticed a group of British soldiers also at the train station. There was no officer among the men and they did not seem to know where they were going. 'They were on their way apparently to Tjilatjap if they could get a train,' Goggins added. He did not stay at the station for very long. 'We returned to the hospital, the ten of us and Dr Wassell, and were scrubbed up that night and made comfortable again in the same bunks that we had before.' The return to the hospital ward marked the end of a long, disappointing, and fruitless journey for the wounded sailors.

Chapter 24

The final acts in the naval defense of Java were playing out during the last week of February in the waters north of the island. A powerful array of Japanese naval forces was heading towards Java, including two large invasion groups – each moving towards an opposite end of the island. The enemy invasion plan was to engulf the island in the form of a large pincer movement.

The Western Attack Group departed Camranh Bay on February 18 with fifty-six transports and cargo ships steaming under a strong escort of cruisers and destroyers. The transports contained a full Japanese infantry division, supplemented by one additional infantry regiment. The small aircraft carrier *Ryujo* provided additional air support beyond what was available from the various land bases in the area.

The Eastern Attack Group left Jolo, an island in the southwestern corner of the Philippines, one day later with six destroyers escorting forty-one transports. The ships made a brief stopover at Balikpapan before proceeding south towards Java. The ships transported a full infantry division and a regimental combat group. Additional covering forces, including a powerful group of heavy cruisers and destroyers, moved into the area to protect the invasion convoys from any interference by ABDA naval forces. The operation amounted to the largest Japanese amphibious undertaking to date in the war.

The invasion groups approaching from the north were supplemented by more Japanese naval forces converging on the southern part of Java. A powerful mobile force of aircraft carriers and surface warships was assembled at Celebes. Admiral Nagumo's carrier force returned to Staring Bay after delivering the punishing air raid on Darwin. He was joined by Admiral Nobutake Kondo's Southern Force of two battleships, three heavy cruisers, and three destroyers to provide distant cover. The ships departed Celebes on the morning of February 25 and were roaming the waters south of Java a day later.[1] The forces were to patrol about 200 miles south of the island, a good position to interdict any reinforcements moving up from Australia. Admiral Nagumo was under orders to attack any warships or merchant vessels trying to slip out from the southern part of the island.[2]

The Japanese commanders may have had few concerns about ABDA airpower as they closed in on Java. An earlier intelligence estimate considered most of the Dutch planes to be second rate.[3] Subsequent battles heavily favored the Japanese and reduced ABDA air power to ineffectiveness. The ADBA naval forces were their likely adversary.

Sighting reports from planes and submarines alerted Admiral Helfrich to the approaching enemy fleets. He ordered his remaining warships to congregate at Surabaya. Admiral Doorman's Combined Striking Force put to sea in various sweeps to search for the enemy, only to find nothing. The ships were passing the outer entrance of Surabaya for a refueling stop during the early afternoon of February 27 when a new sighting report arrived providing the location of three groups of approaching Japanese ships, all members of the Eastern Attack Group. Doorman had little choice but to reverse course. He signaled the other vessels via semaphore: 'Am proceeding to intercept enemy unit, follow me, details later.'[4] The upcoming battle was to be the last desperate chance for ABDA naval forces to forestall the Japanese advance on Java.

Doorman's group included five cruisers – *De Ruyter*, *Java*, *Perth*, *Houston*, and *Exeter* – and eleven destroyers. The Combined Striking Force was a formidable force on paper. However, as with past operations, it was hobbled by a host of disadvantages. The force was without suitable air cover, no ships were equipped with radar, and no spotter planes were available to assist in locating the enemy and directing gunfire during battle. The cruiser seaplanes had been left ashore as Doorman was anticipating a night battle. The ABDA ships were to be plagued by having no set of common communication codes and tactics among the four nationalities represented.

The quick turnaround from Surabaya did not give Admiral Doorman time to prepare and distribute an operational plan. His orders would have to be translated by an American liaison officer stationed aboard the flagship, sent to *Houston* by signal lamp, and then radioed to the other ships – all having to be done in the heat of battle.[5] The difficult arrangement amounted to a tremendous disadvantage for the force.

Japanese reconnaissance planes quickly located and began tracking the ABDA ships. Having to rely on visual sightings from his lookouts, Doorman likely did not initially know he was up against three groups of enemy ships. The first was composed of a light cruiser and eight destroyers under the command of Admiral Raizo Tanaka, the second was a light cruiser and six destroyers, and the third force was Admiral Takeo Takagi's two heavy cruisers and four destroyers.

The Battle of Java Sea was to be the largest naval engagement during the entire Malay Barrier campaign. The battle began shortly after 4.00 pm on February 27 in the waters north of Java with the opposing ships moving roughly parallel to each other. The Japanese heavy cruisers *Nachi* and *Haguro* opened fire with their 8-inch guns at extreme range with spotter planes patrolling overhead to radio adjustments. The *Houston* and *Exeter* began to return fire a short time later. Admiral Doorman tried to close the range to allow the smaller guns of his light cruisers to be brought in range of the enemy. Admiral Takagi ordered his destroyers to close for a torpedo attack.

No serious damage was sustained on either side during the first hour of fighting. Then, at 5.08 pm, the battle then took a disastrous turn for Doorman. An 8-inch shell from *Haguro* slammed into *Exeter*, starting a fierce fire amidships. The badly damaged cruisier swung out of formation throwing the ships behind her into temporary confusion.

Japanese torpedoes, deadly in range and explosive power, converged on the Combined Striking Force during the first phase of the battle. Two destroyers fell victim to the underwater missiles – a Dutch destroyer was sliced in half a short time after *Exeter* was hit and a British destroyer later succumbed to a direct hit. A torpedo attack staged by four American destroyers was unsuccessful.

Admiral Doorman was desperate to find the transports after the warships on both sides disengaged. He led his ships in various directions in a futile attempt to find the invasion force, even unknowingly steaming directly towards it at one point. With nothing more than visual lookouts to gather information on the location of enemy ships, Doorman had no way of knowing the convoy had already been diverted away from the area and was now about thirty miles north. He eventually settled into a westward course roughly parallel to the Java coast. His position was about 100 miles north-west of Surabaya and the new direction brought the ABDA ships dangerously close to a Dutch minefield. At the same time, Japanese floatplanes were keeping a careful watch on Doorman's movements, occasionally setting off flares after daylight faded.

Misfortune again struck the Combined Striking Force when the night erupted in a fiery explosion at 9.25 pm, followed by a brief radio message from the British destroyer *Jupiter*: 'I am torpedoed.'[6] The ship most likely hit a friendly mine from a newly laid defensive field in the area as Japanese sources reported no destroyers in the immediate area at the time of the sinking.[7] The American destroyers diverted to Surabaya at about this time for fuel and the last remaining Dutch destroyer was later directed to rescue survivors from a ship sunk earlier, temporarily leaving the cruisers without escort.

The battle resumed after nightfall, with Admiral Doorman's cruisers steaming alone and Japanese forces advancing to block his route to the transports. Admiral Tanaka moved his destroyers into position for a torpedo attack, while Admiral Takagi's heavy cruisers resumed fire with 8-inch guns.

A torpedo suddenly slammed into the after part of *Java*, causing the back part of the light cruiser to burst in flames. The raging fire ignited the after magazine causing a tremendous explosion that severed the after part of the ship. Her captain gave the abandon ship order a short time later. The Dutch ship rolled to starboard and sank about fifteen minutes after the torpedo hit.[8]

A torpedo also hit the after engine room on the starboard side of *De Ruyter* just after she began steadying her course after a completing a turn. She lost power and began taking on a slight list. A fierce fire developed from leaking fuel and exploding anti-aircraft ammunition. An immense internal explosion then rocked *De Ruyter* causing her to lose power and trapping many sailors below deck. A mass of flames soon engulfed about half of the ship, from amidships back to the stern. The Dutch flagship was in her death throes.

The *Perth* made a hard turn to avoid colliding with *De Ruyter*, while *Houston* similarly had to avoid the Australian light cruiser. One historian later called Captain Rook's ship handling 'a masterpiece of seamanship and quick thinking'.[9] The evasive maneuvers may have saved both ships from Japanese torpedoes.[10]

Admiral Doorman knew the Japanese cruisers were close by. He ordered *Houston* and *Perth*, to retire to Batavia and not to stay in the area to rescue survivors. The brave Dutch admiral choose to stay aboard the sinking *De Ruyter* and went to a watery grave with his flagship.

***

The return to Jogjakarta put Doctor Wassell and his sailors in the path of Japanese planes. The regular visits from enemy aircraft were a constant reminder of how vulnerable the area was to attack. Goggins remembered:

> Every day we were having air raid alerts – the sirens would go and we would be put under the beds, then all clear and out we came. At this time I knew that unless I could get up on my feet and walk that I had no chance of ever getting away, so I managed after some effort to get on my feet and walk around the room.[11]

Doctor Wassell did not give up hope that things would turn out alright for his wounded flock, even as the situation was becoming increasingly grim. He was discouraged, but did not let it show to his sailors. One possibility for escape was evacuation by air. American planes were still operating from Java at the time.

Colonel Eugene Eubank of the Army Air Force was originally in command of the Nineteenth Bomb Group based in the Philippines. The unit operated B-17 bombers. After initially moving south to Australia after the early setbacks in the Philippines, the planes returned north to participate in the defense of Java. The unit operated from the Singosari Airbase in Malang, south of Surabaya. Eubank moved his remaining planes and support personnel to the Jogjakarta Airfield as the situation on Java began to deteriorate. Goggins remembered seeing the American airmen in the hospital during his stay and recalled, 'the army pilots, doctors, and chaplains came around frequently to see us'.

The situation looked promising after Wassell was in contact with Colonel Eubank. The doctor came to the wounded sailors with some good news – the airmen thought they would have enough room on a plane that very evening for the navy men to be taken out. The American planes generally either stayed away from the airfield or remained high in the air during the day coming down at night for the loading of passengers and a quick departure under the cover of darkness. The prowling Zero fighters made it too dangerous for the bombers to fly over Java in daylight hours.[12] The Japanese bombed and strafed the airfield during the afternoon, destroying a B-24 Liberator bomber on the ground. 'I think that that plane was our ride,' Goggins later said. 'We heard about that shortly after the attack.'

Wassel was not yet ready to give up of the possibility of evacuation by air. 'That night the doctor told me that if he would wait on the telephone and they had room, they would call him up – he sat on the phone all that afternoon and all that evening,' Goggins recalled. The sailors knew American planes were in the immediate area due to the thundering noise made by the four engines. 'During the night, we could hear the planes come in and eventually take off one by one, but no word came so we did not get our ride to Australia.'

By late February, Eubank was under orders to withdraw his planes and personnel to Australia. The scope of the departure expanded after he was given permission to commandeer non-military planes for the evacuation of civilian employees.[13] The departing planes were traveling just over 1,000 miles to Broome on the northwestern coast of Australia. In the scramble to get their own airmen out, there apparently was no room for the stranded sailors. The last American planes took off from the Jogjakarta Airfield loaded with passengers bound for Australia on March 2, effectively ending American air operations on the island.[14]

Chapter 25

The damaged *Marblehead* set out on a lengthy journey after departing Tjilatjap on February 13. The ship needed to get out of the war zone to an area affording a greater amount of safety. The extended voyage involved multiple ports of call and was to ultimately end with her arrival in New York City, where permanent repairs could be made. From Java, a ship could travel east or west to return to the United States. Both directions were lengthy voyages, fraught with danger, and involved sailing through active war zones.

The easterly route required the damaged ship to travel across much of the Pacific, a dangerous undertaking given the ongoing Japanese military operations throughout the theater, before passing through the Panama Canal and into waters on the Atlantic side infested with German submarines. Captain Robinson's orders were to sail west through the Indian Ocean. The first stop was to be the British Crown Colony of Ceylon. The island territory, located off the south-eastern coast of India, was more than 2,000 miles from Java.

Adding to the difficulty of the voyage was *Marblehead*'s jammed rudder, resulting in the continuing need for the ship to be steered by her engines. Her four propellers were positioned two per side. The combination of increasing and lowering the speed of the propellers on each side slowly changed the heading of the ship. Wind speed, ocean currents, and the vessel's damaged magnetic compass (her automatic gyro compass was knocked out) added an additional level of complexity to the operation.[1] The best the crew of *Marblehead* could do was to keep their ship on a general heading, as opposed to a precise course.

The light cruiser initially traveled south from Java at a slow speed with the destroyer *Pillsbury* positioned off her port quarter. Her destroyer escort departed late in the evening on the first night out, leaving *Marblehead* in company of *Otus* for the remainder of the voyage.[2]

Officers aboard the warship believed the submarine tender could serve as a visual navigation marker to aid their steering in keeping on course. However, the two ships lost sight of each other during a rain squall on the first night and remained out of contact for almost the entire voyage.[3]

A variety of risks shrouded the long excursion. The warship would first have to avoid Japanese air and surface forces in the immediate waters south of the Malay Barrier. The threat of enemy submarines was to be present during much of the voyage – initially by Japanese boats operating in the Indian Ocean and later by German U-boats prowling the waters of the Atlantic. Perhaps the greatest danger was the possibility that *Marblehead* could sink from her battle damage during one of the long stretches between ports. An internal explosion also could not be ruled out. 'Steaming in waters of probable action, it was necessary to exercise great care in accomplishing vital work below decks,' Captain Robinson explained. 'With fuel oil spread throughout the hold and both platform levels, the danger of fire and gas was ever present.'

The heading of Robinson's ship changed to the southeast during the early afternoon hours of February 14, and then to a more westerly direction the following day. An officer equipped with sound powered phone connected to the engine room was poised on the bridge ready to relay instructions every time a change of direction was ordered. No sign of the enemy was seen during the first full day of sailing from Tjilatjap. It appeared *Marblehead* had successfully eluded any Japanese forces south of Java.

An unidentified ship was sighted by lookouts on two separate occasions during February 15. The sighting prompted a general quarters alarm, sending sailors rushing to their battle stations during the early evening. No action was taken when the vessel disappeared off the starboard quarter shortly after 7.00 pm.[4]

Keeping *Marblehead* afloat required a constant vigilance by her crew throughout the entire time at sea. Robinson wrote at the time:

> Special watches were set on water-tight integrity, and submersible pumps were in constant operation. It was necessary to maintain continuous pumping. The repair force was constantly on the alert for leaks within the damaged area, and many leaks were stopped to prevent the spread of water.[5]

Although the inflow of water in the forward part of the ship was initially contained, the leaking never actually stopped. Problems developed during the voyage when the level of water began to increase. The electrical submersible pumps could no longer control the water.

A group of sailors under the direction of damage control officer Martin Drury and Harvey Anderson improvised a solution by moving a large steam powered pump from the forward engine room to a location on the first platform deck above the flooded areas. They connected it to the steam heating system to provide power. Next came the rigging of hoses – 6-inch diameter hose used for fueling. One was put down into the water in the flooded compartments below. 'A special port with hose fitting connection was manufactured to permit the pump discharge through the port hole,' Robinson explained. 'With this pump in operation, it was possible to keep the water level below the second platform deck.' The arrangement worked with great results. 'This pump operated constantly from the time it was installed until the ship was docked, to control the leakage of water.'

The repair work aboard *Marblehead* never really stopped. Her sailors continued toiling above and below deck during the voyage. 'While at sea, work toward ridding the ship of oil soaked wreckage and debris continued,' Robinson wrote. 'Vent systems and trunks were repaired where possible. Useable lockers and bunks from uninhabitable areas were reinstalled on and above the main deck.'

An improvised galley was rigged up for the cooks to keep the men fed. Food supplies were mainly limited to cans with unknown contents, the labels having been washed off during the flooding, and some potatoes. Seating areas and utensils were in short supply. Many sailors ate their meals sitting down on deck. The officers' galley was converted into a makeshift dishwashing room. Machinists and electricians pieced together an improvised ice box made from parts from several wrecked or broken boxes.[6]

Sailors sorted through ammunition in the storage areas far below deck. 'More powder cans from the magazines, now only partially flooded, were removed and inspected,' Robinson wrote. 'Damaged powder was thrown overboard, and good powder stowed in dry spaces. Small arms, ammunition, impulse charges, etc., were removed, inspected and disposed of.'

Electrical power was restored to many parts of the ship. The list of projects to be done – large and small – seemed endless. 'Minor but essential repairs too numerous to list were being accomplished each day,' Robinson added. In one of the larger undertakings, engineers managed to save about 45,000 gallons of contaminated fuel oil by settling out saltwater that had leaked into the tank.

The captain was added to the sick list for two days during the voyage on orders from the medical officer. The deck log offers no clues as to his ailment. Perhaps he was suffering from exhaustion resulting from the ordeal of keeping the ship afloat. Like many of the sailors, the captain likely needed some rest.

The remainder of the passage across the Indian Ocean was uneventful, with *Marblehead* remaining largely out of contact. A British steamer was spotted on February 19, followed by a Greek merchantman the very next day. Both vessels passed on opposite courses. Lookouts aboard the light cruiser sighted *Otus* during the early morning hours of February 21.[7] It was the first time of seeing the submarine tender since losing her in a rain squall shortly after departing Java.

Lookouts sighted land, about twenty-five miles distance, a short time after regaining contact with *Otus*. A variety of ships and a plane – all British – were seen as the morning progressed. The damaged *Marblehead* was nearing the first stop on her extended journey. Her initial port of call was Trincomalee, Ceylon.

Captain Robinson's initial orders were to take his ship to Columbo, the capital of the colony on the south-western side of the island. The destination was changed to Trincomalee while en route. The city sits on the north-east coast Ceylon, with two peninsulas extending out from the mainland creating an enclosed bay that served as a harbor area. Trincomalee was the long-time home of a Royal Navy base. The naval facilities took on greater importance for the British Far Eastern Fleet after the fall of Singapore. With Hong Kong, Singapore, and Malaya all in Japanese hands, no other Royal Navy bases existed in the Pacific, short of Australia and New Zealand. Almost all the British ships fleeing Java went to Ceylon.[8]

The British tug *Sampson* nestled alongside *Marblehead* as she slowly moved into Trincomalee Bay at 9.26 am, and a harbor pilot came aboard a few minutes later. The tug took the light cruiser under tow, while *Otus* took up a position astern and caught up to the other ships a short time later.[9] Captain Robinson ordered the anchor dropped in the inner harbor area at 11.27 am.[10] Various British warships and small craft were in the area, including the venerable old battleship *Royal Sovereign* and aged Dutch light cruiser *Sumatra*. A group of officers from the battleship came aboard the visiting American ship a short time later for an official welcoming.

Various ships entered the harbor during *Marblehead*'s stay, including the aircraft carrier *Hermes* and heavy cruiser *Dorsetshire*. Two damaged vessels, a submarine and destroyer, each arrived separately under tow by a merchant ship. Nicholas Van Bergen noted 'it was rather depressing to notice the ships that were limping in, or being towed in, from Singapore. Destroyers and submarines on the ends of tow lines, merchant ships that were shot up, and we realized that Trinco was going to be a rather crowded harbor.'[11] Commanding officers from various warships made visits to *Marblehead*.

Routine port activities took place aboard *Marblehead* during her stay in the harbor, including taking aboard supplies for the remainder of the voyage to New York. Shore patrols and sailors went ashore for liberty. A limited number of men faced punishment for activities ashore or late arrivals back aboard. 'When we got inside we found that there were no repair facilities, just simply some very hospitable Britishers, some fuel oil, and some more stores which we needed,' Van Bergen explained of the visit.

The repair and cleanup work continued throughout the port stay, mostly done by *Marblehead* sailors. A dredge was placed alongside the ship for the removal of oil, sludge, and debris from a ruptured fuel oil tank close to the area of the forward bomb hit. A patch was installed on the tank after the cleanup was completed. 'Where stanchions had been torn from decks, due to buckling overhead, extension pieces were inserted and welded between the dangling stanchion and deck,' Robinson explained. 'Bent stations were straightened and braced.'

Repairs were made to the damage done to the bow by the collision with the tug boat back in Tjilatjap. The flooded compartment was fully pumped out. Sailors welded and patched all noticeable ruptures and a cement box was put in place for reinforcement. Divers from the small net layer ship *Guardian* toiled for three days inserting plugs and caulking to help shore up the underwater damage. 'The effect of this work was to reduce the leakage considerably,' Captain Robinson wrote. 'This last was the only work done on the ship by outside forces at Trincomalee.'

Captain Robinson needed to determine the availability of facilities in the immediate area to further help his ship. Robinson and Engineering Officer Lieutenant Commander F.C. Camp met with British naval officials. The captain learned 'there were no facilities available for improving the temporary repairs already accomplished at Tjilatjap, and it was soon determined that no work could be undertaken in any Indian port for many weeks.' The ship would have to go elsewhere and it was decided that South Africa was the best place. 'Orders were issued to proceed when ready,' Robinson noted.

The harbor pilot came aboard *Marblehead* on the morning of March 1 to help guide the ship to the fuel dock.[12] A small lighter came alongside later in the day to transfer drums of aviation gasoline. The vessel took aboard 384,092 gallons of fuel oil by the end of the day. Captain Robinson's ship started moving out of the Trincomalee harbor area during the late afternoon hours of March 2 with the help of a tug boat and harbor pilot. She soon left the assistance behind and was heading on her own for the open sea.

Chapter 26

While ABDA and Japanese naval forces were clashing in the Java Sea during the last days of February, a last-minute effort was underway further south at about the same time to bring air reinforcements up to the beleaguered Dutch island from Australia. A convoy of ships left Fremantle on February 22 bound for India, with some of the vessels diverted to Tjilatjap five days later. Those heading for Java included the American ships *Langley* and *Sea Witch*. Once the only aircraft carrier of the United States Navy, *Langley* was now serving as an aircraft transport ship. She was loaded with thirty-two P-40 fighter planes in ready-to-fly condition, and thirty-three pilots. Accompanying her was the new cargo ship *Sea Witch*, with twenty-seven additional P-40 planes disassembled in crates. The destroyers *Edsall* and *Whipple* were serving as escorts for the transports.

The poorly conceived reinforcement mission ended in utter failure. Japanese land-based bombers found the convoy on the morning of February 2,7 about seventy-five miles south of Java. The old *Langley* was hit by three bombs during a series of high-level bombing runs. She quickly caught fire and lost speed while taking a heavy list to port. The ship was eventually abandoned so her sailors could be rescued by the two destroyers. She later sank after taking gunfire and torpedoes from the rescue ships.[1] The two destroyers and *Sea Witch* managed to escape unharmed.

The cargo ship continued north to dock at Tjilatjap on February 28 after a message diverting her to India arrived too late. The crated planes were unloaded and sent inland. The much-needed fighters arrived too late to help in the defense of Java.[2] Historians have roundly criticized the mission, rightly speculating the fifty-nine fighter planes aboard the two ships would have not made any difference in the outcome of the battle for the island, especially given the time needed for some to be assembled.[3] The battle of the Malay Barrier was all but lost by this time; the valuable fighters could have been used elsewhere, and *Langley* and sailors saved.

***

The Battle of Java Sea was a resounding defeat for ABDA naval forces. Half of the Combined Striking Force was destroyed in exchange for just one Japanese destroyer damaged. The invasion convoy was untouched and amphibious operations were delayed only a couple of days. The surviving ABDA ships were left in a precarious position. No warships were now safe in the Java Sea, or in any port on the north side of Java. Some vessels in the region had already fled to Ceylon or Australia. Those who remained were trying to find a way to escape the area before the Japanese noose around Java closed for good. Three groups of ABDA ships lingered in this dangerous area – a group of American destroyers at Surabaya, the damaged *Exeter* and her escorts, and the cruisers *Houston* and *Perth*. The options for an escape to the south were few and dangerous – either sail east through Japanese-held waters around Bali, or travel west to attempt passage through the Sunda Strait between Sumatra and Java.

The days of Dutch control in Java were clearly numbered. Admirals Glassford and Palliser knew the end of organized naval operations was close at hand, but Admiral Helfrich was determined to continue the fight, over the objections of his subordinates. The Dutch admiral wanted to reassemble the remaining naval forces at Tjilatjap.[4] However, Helfrich eventually gave in to the requests of the American and British admirals to withdraw some of their warships.

Helfrich ordered *Houston* and *Perth* to pass through the Sunda Strait off western Java for the voyage south. He authorized Glassford to allow a group of American destroyers at Surabaya to proceed to Australia for rearming via the eastern route. The ships were nearly depleted of torpedoes and no replacements were available on Java. The destroyers returned to port during the Battle of Java Sea for refueling, missing the final stages of the action.

Commander Thomas Binford was under no illusion the passage around Bali would be easy. He departed late in the day on February 28 and guided his destroyers into the narrowest part of the Bali Strait shortly after midnight, staying as close to the shore as possible in the hope his ships would blend into the darkness of the land behind. The ships encountered some Japanese destroyers about two hours later. 'My idea was to fight off the enemy and to retire to the south as quickly as possible, because I expected other enemy forces in the immediate vicinity,' Binford wrote.[5] The plan was successful. After exchanging some long-range gunfire with the Japanese pursers, the American ships disappeared into the darkness to Australia.

The damaged *Exeter* limped into Surabaya after the Java Sea battle for a short stay to undergo emergency repairs. Admiral Glassford wanted the ship to make a run through Lombok Strait. Admiral Palliser, however, directed for the force to go through the Sunda Strait, believing the former was heavily defended.[6] The cruiser left port in the company of destroyers *Encounter* (British) and *Pope* (American), intending to pass south of Java for a run to Ceylon. The ships steered around a small group of Japanese ships sighted shortly after their departure, though the force was unable to escape detection.

The ABDA ships later encountered the Japanese heavy cruisers *Ashigara* and *Myoko*, along with two destroyers. The situation only worsened as the day of March 1 continued. An additional force of enemy cruisers and destroyers arrived in the area to ensure the fleeing ships did not escape. A fierce naval battle developed and *Exeter* was quickly overwhelmed. She became a burning wreck after sustaining hits by 8-inch gunfire. Her crew abandoned ship, setting scuttling charges to ensure the heavy cruiser sank. The Japanese were not going to let the destroyers escape – both were sunk by the end of the day. The action has sometimes been referred to as the Second Battle of the Java Sea.

The undamaged *Perth* and *Houston* successfully reached Tandjong Priok, the port area of Batavia, during the middle of the day of February 28. Both ships evaded the torpedoes that sank *De Ruyter* and *Java* during the last phase of the Battle of the Java Sea. The warships quickly refueled and departed for a night voyage through Sunda Strait.

The cruisers subsequently happened on a large group of anchored Japanese transports at 10.15 pm near Bantam Bay on the western end of Java – members of the Western Attack Group conducting an amphibious landing. The warships opened fire to begin a series of fatal events. The Japanese transports were guarded by a large group of powerful escorts in the immediate area. About a dozen enemy warships quickly closed from all directions to surround the attackers, including the large heavy cruisers *Mogami* and *Mikuma*.

A confusing mêlée quickly developed in the moonlit night as Japanese ships poured gunfire and torpedoes at the two cruisers. Unsurprisingly, due to the confined area, friendly fire hit five Japanese ships. A transport and minesweeper were sunk.[7] The ABDA ships bravely fought back as their ammunition supplies began to dwindle. The Australian ship sustained a direct hit from an 8-inch shell near the water line. A torpedo crashed into her engineering spaces a short time later. The hits sent *Perth* to a watery grave around midnight.

The *Houston* followed less than an hour later. She was initially hit by a torpedo directly under the bridge on the starboard side. The heavy cruiser was then on the receiving end of a deluge of shells and torpedoes. The enemy fire seemed to come from all sides. The hits were so numerous that an exact count has never been established.[8] A column of flame shot high into the air when one of the forward main battery turrets exploded with a roar.[9] The ship lost speed and took a heavy list to starboard.

Aviator Walter Winslow was on the bridge when it was clear the end had arrived. 'The time had come for Captain Rooks to give his last command,' he later wrote. 'Bugler, sound abandon ship,' the captain directed a nearby Marine bugler.[10] The gallant *Houston* rolled over a short time later. About half of her crew survived only to spend the rest of the war in Japanese prison camps. Among those killed were Captain Rooks and Chaplain George Rentz – the chaplain who had officiated the burial of *Marblehead*'s dead on Java only a few weeks earlier.

***

Following the disastrous actions at sea, ABDA naval power was decimated and Java lay wide open to a Japanese invasion. With only 25,000 Dutch soldiers, supplemented with a limited number of British, Australian, and American troops, there was no possible way to adequately defend the nearly 500-mile coastline.[11] The lone American ground unit was the 2nd Battalion of the 131st Field Artillery. The federalized National Guard unit was comprised of soldiers from the north central part of Texas.

Dutch General Hein ter Poorten commanded all ground units on Java. He divided the island into four combat areas for defensive purposes.

Most of the meager forces available were divided up, with only one region having the equivalent of two full-strength regiments. The remaining forces were assembled into a mobile strike force known as the Black Force, after the Australian commander. The ad hoc unit included assorted infantrymen, medics, administrative staff, pilots with no planes, and the American artillery unit. The Black Force was given the mission of reinforcing command areas needing help after the Japanese attacked. The Dutch general planned a fighting withdraw to protect the capital of Batavia and other important political centers such as Bandung. The concept put most of the ground forces on the western side of Java.[12]

Enemy amphibious forces appeared at three locations off the northern Java coast during the early hours of March 1 to begin landings on both the eastern and western sides of the island. The western landings took place near Merak, about sixty-five miles west of Batavia and at Eretenwetan, more than eighty miles east of the capital. Japanese soldiers also came ashore at Kragan, west of Surabaya, on the opposite end of the island. Japanese troops quickly pushed inland on both fronts.

The exodus from Java was already well underway, ahead of the advancing enemy. The ABDA headquarters ordered the departure of all merchant ships at Tjilatjap not assigned special duties in the days after the Java Sea defeat. The orders came to Commander Schokking. The Dutch officer was serving as the port's Commanding Officer of Maritime Resources. 'All merchant ships, seaworthy and with sufficient radius of action to reach Australia or Colombo to leave the port immediately and await radio orders in position 200 miles south of Tjilatjap.'[13] The harbor area was filled with ships of all types of many nationalities.

The fleeing vessels were forced to run a dangerous gauntlet south of the island. A powerful armada of Japanese naval forces was now prowling the waters south of Java. Admiral Kondo's Southern Force and Admiral Nagumo's carrier force parted company after moving south from Celebes. The groups were positioned some 70 and 320 miles south-southwest of Tjilatjap on the morning of March 1.[14]

The female voice of Tokyo Rose, emanating in near perfect English over the airwaves of Radio Tokyo, taunted the Americans still on Java. 'Your ships are swiftly being sunk. You haven't a chance. Why defend foreign soil which never belonged to the Dutch or British in the first place?'[15]

The thirty ambulatory patients brought to Tjilatjap by Doctor Wassell were among the Americans escaping the island. The group was spread among several vessels. The tanker *Pecos* was the ticket out for some. The service vessel had been in Tjilatjap since early February providing fuel for American, British, and Dutch warships. She left on the morning of February 27 bound for Australia, with her normal crew augmented by many additional sailors. Her crewmen made extra preparations, knowing the odds of survival were slim, including lashing large bamboo poles to the upper decks for use as extra life rafts.[16]

The tanker picked up the last radio transmissions from *Langley* about three hours out from Tjilatjap. The aircraft transport was then under attack by Japanese bombers. Subsequent reports of her survivors being rescued by the escorting destroyers were also heard.[17] Instead of escaping directly to Australia, the orders for *Pecos* were changed to rendezvous with *Whipple* and *Edsall* near Christmas Island about 225 miles south of the west end of Java. The *Langley* survivors were to be transferred to the tanker for her voyage to Australia, thus freeing up the destroyers for other duties.

The three ships arrived off Christmas Island on the morning of February 28. The trio escaped damage when three Japanese bombers attacked the island shortly after their arrival in the area. The destroyers successfully transferred a large group of *Langley* survivors to the crowded *Pecos* before parting ways. The tanker pointed her bow southward for Freemantle.

The ship was still within range of prowling Japanese forces. A lone high-level reconnaissance plane was sighted by lookouts aboard *Pecos* as she steamed towards Australia on March 1. Many sailors aboard, especially those from *Langley*, knew it was an ominous foretelling of impending doom. She was attacked twice by dive bombers from Japanese aircraft carriers starting at noon. Gunners did their best in trying to fight off the attackers with the tanker's light guns, but were ultimately unsuccessful. A third wave later in the day sank the veteran tanker.[18]

Masses of sailors were trying to get off the sinking ship. The wounded *Marblehead* officer Ensign Charles Coburn watched as whaleboats, life rafts, and mattresses were put over the side to be followed by 'nearly a hundred men'.[19] He then jumped off the sinking tanker.

The destroyer *Whipple* sped to the scene to rescue survivors after picking up a distress call. She plucked 232 *Pecos* survivors out of the water, including Ensign Coburn. The *Marblehead* man was among the lucky sailors who were delivered to Australia.

Only *Whipple* survived the poorly orchestrated rendezvous off Christmas Island. The surviving fighter pilots, who were passengers on *Langley*, were transferred aboard *Edsall*. They no longer had any planes to fly, the P-40 fighters having been lost with *Langley*. The destroyer was then inexplicably ordered to deliver the pilots back to Java at a time when other Allied servicemen were all trying to leave.[20] The lonely *Edsall* apparently sailed into the enemy task force operating south of Java. She was attacked by Japanese heavy cruisers and was eventually sunk by additional warships and aircraft.[21]

Chapter 27

Doctor Wassell never gave up trying find a way for his remaining wounded sailors to escape, even as the fall of Java was imminent. He heard plenty of bad news after returning to the hospital in Jogjakarta, including a rumor of Tjilatjap having been bombed by enemy planes. The men knew the alternatives to escape were not good – stay and possibly be slaughtered by the Japanese, or become their prisoners. Many sailors heard stories of the brutal Japanese treatment of prisoners during the war in China and dreaded the possibility of capture.[1] Trying to escape seemed a far better alternative, if they could only find a way out.

The Jogjakarta airfield was abandoned after the last of the American airmen departed. Dutch soldiers began blowing up the runway to keep the enemy from capturing the airfield in operational condition. They then proceeded to start destroying ammunition. The airfield was bombed the next morning by a large formation of enemy planes that flew right over the hospital. 'It made a tremendous racket and of course it was largely a waste of bombs because the work had all been done beforehand,' William Goggins recalled. 'They were just one day late.'

The transportation options for those interested in leaving Jogjakarta appeared to be almost nonexistent. The only option was the south coast of Java. The trains stopped running due to the prowling Japanese planes. 'It began to look pretty dismal at this time because there was no way of getting transportation to Tjilatjap, the only port now open,' Goggins remembered. 'The trains weren't running and trucks and so forth were not procurable.'[2]

There were seven *Marblehead* men, including Goggins, among the desperate group – William Anderson, Melvin Francis, Pao San Ho, Benjamin Hopkins, Joseph Leinweber, and William McCurdy. Three additional sailors were from *Houston* – Fire Controlman First Class Thomas Borghetti, Coxswain Robert Kraus, and Electrician's Mate Second Class Robert Whaley.[3]

It did not take long for the situation to become desperate. Wassell was awake in his room when he heard a tap on his door during the night-time hours. The head Dutch doctor was waiting to tell him some bad news – the Japanese amphibious landing operations were underway on Java. If the Americans' predicament was not already serious enough, it was now urgent. Wassell went back to trying to reach authorities in Tjilatjap by phone. He waited a long time, ultimately to be unsuccessful in trying to arrange passage out.

The two doctors probably did not know how bad the battle for Java was going for the Dutch. Japanese forces had made substantial gains in only two short days since landing on the island. On the western side of Java, columns of enemy soldiers led by light tanks were moving along Dutch-built roads and railways to surround the Batavia-Bandung area in a double envelope.[4] An important airfield quickly fell into enemy hands. Further east Japanese forces pushed aside weak resistance and pushed inland.

Doctor Wassell's patients were all sound asleep in the hospital ward. Seemingly out of available options, he decided to take a walk into town. News of the Japanese landings was apparently traveling fast. Crowds were gathering on some of the streets and in the lobby of the hotel in which he entered. A level of tension, though short of panic, seemed to be in the air. It was now the early morning hours of March 2.

A noisy convoy of trucks led by some dusty staff cars rolled to a stop in front of the hotel just before dawn. The group was the advanced echelon of a retreating British Army anti-aircraft unit. Wassell immediately knew it was the lucky break he needed … and most likely the last possible chance of escape for his sailors. The British commanding officer walked into the hotel to inquire about the availability of food and supplies. He was clad in khaki colored pants with a sun helmet perched on top of his head and looked to be somewhat aloof. Wassell started a conversation and found the convoy was going to Tjilatjap. The British officer agreed to take along the wounded men as long as they could fit into trucks. There was no time to delay – the convoy was moving out in about two hours.

The doctor rushed through the crowded lobby back to the hospital. He was about to put to good use an inherited Ford sedan left behind by the departed American airmen. 'Just when our hopes had almost gone, Dr Wassell walked in and told us to get ready as quickly as we could,'

Bob Whaley explained. 'We've another chance to get out of here and it's our last chance,' Wassell told the wounded men.[5] There was no time for an explanation. 'I threw the stuff I needed and a few small souvenirs into a zipper bag and limped out of the hospital,' Whaley continued. Goggins remembered Wassell 'came rushing into my room and told me to get onto the dolly that they wheel you around and not to ask any questions, we had no time to lose.'

There was only time for a quick goodbye to the nurses. Bob Whaley remembered another sailor jokingly yelling to the ladies on the way out. 'Don't worry, we'll be back. We're just taking an excursion to the beach.' Two trips with the sedan were required to get all the men to the hotel. 'He assembled one carload of us and put us in the Ford in front of the hospital and took us over to the hotel,' Goggins explained. 'None of us had any clothes – we were wearing pajamas that belonged to the hospital. I managed to grab my bag up on my way and save that.' Some of the men did not even have shoes.

Once all the sailors were at the hotel, it was just a matter of finding space in the convoy before it pulled out. Those in the best condition were loaded aboard two large British Army trucks. The three patients considered to be in the worst shape – William Anderson, Robert Whaley, and William McCurdy – were put into the back seat of the Ford. The seats and springs in the car offered a more comfortable ride than the trucks. William Goggins joined Wassell in the front, with the doctor serving as the driver.

The trucks began moving out at about 1.00 pm going at the slow speed of about twelve miles per hour.[6] The long convoy included about 200 vehicles representing everything needed for a mechanized unit – trucks, staff cars, mobile anti-aircraft guns, repair shops, and field kitchens.[7] The Ford took up a position at the end of the line. The position in the rear gave Wassell a clear view of what was happening up ahead. He wanted to be sure all his sailors made it out. The temperature was hot as the convoy lumbered along on narrow roads that were rutted and rough.

There was no assurance they would make it to Tjilatjap. Goggins recalled,

> On the way now and then a truck would fail and the British would wheel it off the side of the road and throw gasoline on

it and set it on fire so the Japs couldn't get it. We took roads which were well grown over with trees so that we would not be easily sighted by the Japs who were then flying all over the island. All day long we continued to Tjilatjap.'

Dutch soldiers, ambulances, and locals with oxcarts made up a variety of traffic moving along the road in the opposite direction, with the numbers increasing throughout the day.

The car ride mostly took place in silence with little in the way of conversation taking place among the passengers. All the passengers fell asleep at one point and Doctor Wassell struggled to keep awake at times. 'One of the men had had a shrapnel wound in his bladder and had to have a catheter in it, and it was necessary to lift him around and look out for this thing also,' Goggins said of William McCurdy riding in the back seat.[8] 'He was in some pain and was always miserable.'

The ride was much rougher for the men ahead in the trucks, including Melvin Francis. The *Marblehead* sailor had been injured in his left eye, in addition to burns suffered on his arms and back. He stared discontentedly at the mangrove trees and lush brush on the side of the road during the bumpy ride. The convoy was occasionally stopped by Dutch sentries. During these times, the sailors in the trucks could overhear snippets of conversations about the number of ships still in port at Tjilatjap. The numbers given by various Dutch soldiers often contradicted each other. It did little to bolster the spirits of the wounded passengers.

The convoy rumbled to a stop for a rest break after traveling for hours in an area where tall trees were near the road and rice fields not far beyond. 'At about 5.00 in the afternoon we stopped and the British made tea and had something to eat,' Goggins later said. The soldiers ate corned beef and chocolate bars, sharing both with the sailors along with some tea.[9] Some small Javanese boys, who looked to have appeared out of nowhere, climbed up a few nearby coconut trees. They cut down coconuts that fell to the ground for the soldiers, who in turn gave them some small coins.[10]

Wassell did not stay long at the stop. Goggins's account continued:

We went along the convoy, we had been at the rear of it, and our people waved to us that they were alright. The doctor decided that the best thing to do was to go to Tjilatjap and try to make arrangements to go. So we went on ahead and got to Tjilatjap, not having anything to eat.

The amount of traffic on the road increased as the car came closer to Tjilatjap.

The convoy restarted and continued forward, passing over bridges getting ready to be demolished ahead of the advancing enemy. Trucks and vehicles were spaced far apart as a precaution against air attacks. Japanese planes were largely free to roam across the island attacking at will.

Doctor Wassell and William Goggins arrived in the port ahead of the convoy in their car, and Goggins explained:

> We got to Tjilatjap at about 10.30 that night. We drove up in front of the Grand Hotel, where our staff had been staying and the Dutch liaison officer, Lieutenant Schmidt came out in his bathrobe and said that we were too late, that they had all gone. Our navy had all shoved off.

The sailors would have to find their own transportation out of the port.

***

The information from Lieutenant Schmidt was correct – the American sailors and their ships had already departed Tjilatjap. The ABDA Command was gone, having been hastily dissolved on February 25 after General Wavell departed for India with Admiral Helfrich assuming command of all remaining naval forces in the Dutch East Indies.[11] Admiral Glassford also remained on Java in a subordinate position to the Dutch naval leader. However, he was under standing orders from American naval leaders to withdraw from Java when necessary.[12] The admiral was making plans for the eventual departure of his remaining forces after the dissolution of ABDA. He had no illusions about the future of Java as his last lingering ships gathered in Tjilatjap.

American servicemen of all branches were streaming out of the southern port by plane, ship, and submarine during the last days of February. By March 1 it was clear Tjilatjap was no longer tenable. Admiral Helfrich dissolved the Allied naval command on Java and accepted requests from Glassford and British Admiral Palliser to withdraw their remaining ships. 'Very well then, Admiral Pallister, you may give any orders you wish to His Majesty's ships,' Helfrich told his commanders. 'Admiral Glassford, you will order your ships to Australia.'[13] Helfrich reportedly thanked Glassford for the loyal support the American Navy gave in Dutch in the defense of Java.[14]

The American admiral promptly notified all U.S. Navy vessels to 'clear the [Java] region'.[15] The few remaining PBYs available in the area were flown in to aid the evacuation. A large submarine arrived and then quickly departed full of passengers. Old gunboats and British corvettes escorted merchant ships chartered as transports for citizens and diplomatic staffers.[16] The port was to be abandoned.

All the remaining American ships departed Tjilatjap on March 1.[17] Admirals Glassford and Palliser left for Australia in two American PBYs around midnight of the same night, arriving safely during the morning hours on March 2.[18] Admiral Helfrich ordered all remaining Dutch ships on the south side of the island at Tjilatjap to attempt escape. He left by plane soon thereafter for Colombo, Ceylon.

The escaping American ships faced a new threat, beyond the Japanese naval forces already prowling the area below Java. A newly operational Japanese airfield near the southern tip of Bali allowed enemy planes to range far out into the waters south of Java. We know some American vessels, including *Pecos* and *Edsall*, were already sunk. Other U.S. ships fleeing during the last days of Java faced a variety of fates. The destroyer *Pillsbury* and gunboat *Ashville* met cruel endings at the hands of Japanese forces. Both vessels slipped out of Tjilatjap on March 1 bound for Australia and subsequently disappeared. The true details of their fates were not known until after the war.

The commanding officer of the old destroyer *Pillsbury* hoped to use the evening darkness to aid his getaway. She was spotted by a Japanese reconnaissance plane almost a day later and misidentified as a light cruiser. Admiral Kondo ordered two heavy cruisers to make for the sighting. The giants *Atago* and *Takao* found *Pillsbury* during the night. The little destroyer was blasted with gunfire and sunk after being taken by surprise. The heavy cruisers turned away making no attempt to pick up survivors, leaving the details of *Pillsbury*'s fate to be a mystery for decades. The Japanese ships reported sinking an 'enemy light cruiser of *Marblehead* class'.[19]

The small *Ashville* radioed she was 'being attacked' about 300 miles south of Java on the afternoon of March 3. A second message clarified the attackers were surface vessels. She was overwhelmed by the Japanese destroyers *Arashi* and *Nowaki*. The details of her last battle remained unknown until after the war when sailors from *Houston* reported meeting someone from *Ashville* in a Japanese prison camp. The lone survivor of the gunboat perished in a camp only months before the end of the war.[20]

The gunboat *Tulsa*, patrol ship *Isabel*, destroyer *Parrott*, two small minesweepers, and the converted yacht *Lanikai* all managed to escape to Australia. Some of the voyages were aided by inclement weather.[21] The submarine tender *Otus*, on her way back to Java from Ceylon after escorting *Marblehead*, was safely diverted to Australia. The only American vessels still operating in the Dutch East Indies were submarines. The underwater boats were based in Fremantle, Australia.

Admiral Glassford's departure left Captain Lester Hudson as one of a few American naval staffers still in Tjilatjap. He worked effortlessly during the next couple of days to help any remaining American personnel escape.[22] Glassford later wrote that Hudson 'subsequently did fine work in evacuating our wounded and our numerous civilian refugees, the latter not only from Java, but from Singapore via Java.'[23] Doctor Wassell and his small group of wounded sailors were among those still looking for a way to get out.

Chapter 28

The arrival of Doctor Wassell and William Goggins in Tjilatjap on March 2 put the two navy men in the middle of a mass of humanity. Allied personnel – American, British, Australian, and Dutch – from all around Java were converging on the city in the hope of getting away from the advancing Japanese. The port was now the scene of a great evacuation. The throngs of people included sailors from lost ships, shore personnel, airmen, soldiers, and civilian workers, not to mention an overabundance of refugees. Many of the servicemen were confused and looking for leadership from someone.[1]

Java was literally the last bastion of freedom in the Dutch East Indies. Included in the crowds were people lucky enough to have escaped from Singapore and Sumatra ahead of the Japanese advances. They now faced the real possibility of capture on Java unless they could get to Australia.

The Dutch port officer, Commander B.J.C. Schokking, had received no written orders or instructions for how to handle the evacuation.[2] Unchecked rumors of Japanese warships and submarines roaming in nearby waters were circulating throughout the city. The stories were supplemented by the true reports of sunken ships, such as *Langley* and *Pecos*. Ships in port heard a steady stream of frantic radio calls for help in recent days from merchant vessels under attack to the south.[3] The combination of the various sources of information, along with the reported landings and movements of the Japanese on Java, brought about dropping morale and near panic conditions.

Many facilities in the city were overloaded with people crammed into every conceivable area. The hotel and a nearby Dutch club were overflowing with humanity. Ships in the river awaiting orders became temporary floating hotels.

Doctor Wassell delivered the three wounded men in the back seat of his Ford to a small hospital for the night, before going back to the

Grand Hotel with Goggins. The hotel featured a variety of architectural trimmings and a porch. The building was crowded with people, many of whom were sound asleep in almost every conceivable location. The two Americans were able to get a small room, through the help of the Dutch liaison officer they spoke with after arriving in town, with a bed to spend the night. Goggins remembered the hotel facilities as 'primitive' and that there was 'much activity' in the area. 'The Dutch had hoped to hold Tjilatjap as long as possible in order to evacuate as many people, as they even thought they might be able to hold it for some time,' he continued.[4]

Wassell learned he was not the only early arrival from the British convoy. The commanding officer of the English unit also drove ahead arriving hours before with one of the wounded sailors. The man departed for Australia aboard a ship that had already left. An enduring question, however, surrounds the identity of the lucky sailor.

Several men from Wassell's group interviewed for a 1945 magazine article about their time on Java put the individual as *Houston* sailor Thomas Borghetti. They reported he left 'for Australia a day before the other sailors arrived,' but no mention was made of his departure ship.[5] Borghetti suffered serious injuries aboard the heavy cruiser, including a shattered elbow and leg. Goggins recalled hearing of 'one of our men who had a shattered elbow' arriving ahead of the convoy with the British officer and departing 'on a destroyer that had left that night'.[6]

The destroyer *Pillsbury* was among the American ships departing Tjilatjap during the time in question only to be sunk south of Java with no survivors recovered.[7] However, Borghetti was not a prisoner and was known to have survived the war. He spoke with President Roosevelt during a short visit made by the president to the Mare Island Naval Hospital near San Francisco in September 1942.[8]

Another account comes from Lodwick Alford, formerly of the destroyer *Stewart*. His former ship was not leaving Tjilatjap – she previously capsized in the drydock while undergoing repairs. Sailors set off a demolition charge and believed she was damaged beyond use. The Japanese later repaired the old destroyer, putting her into service in the Imperial Navy.[9]

Alford was among the many American sailors departing Tjilatjap during the first days of March. His escape occurred aboard *Isabel*, an old yacht converted into a patrol boat. The vessel had been anchored close to shore covered with palm leaves and brush as camouflage. She was earmarked to provide transportation for Admiral Glassford. He ended up flying out on a PBY, although some of the headquarters staff came aboard. Good luck and bad weather contributed to her successful escape to Australia.

Alford later wrote of one of Doctor Wassell's sailors delivered dockside by the British commander. 'He delivered the patient alongside *Isabel* just as we were taking in our docklines,' he recalled. Other historians conclude the man leaving on *Isabel* was *Houston* sailor Donald Boucher.[10] While he was on Java, Boucher does not seem to have been part of Wassell's group. The sailor was reported to have transferred from the heavy cruiser to the gunboat *Tulsa* in Tjilatjap before ending up aboard *Isabel* and surviving the war.[11] The exact details of the sailor who departed early may never be known for certain.

***

The morning of March 3 began with a cloudy sky over Tjilatjap. A fine mist was coming in from the ocean and later turned into a light rain. The day also began with the droning whine of the air raid siren accompanied by a flurry of activity outside of the hotel. According to Goggins:

> The next morning when we got up there was an air raid and considerable scurrying around out in the courtyard, a couple of Dutchmen came running up and ask[ed] if we had any weapons, which, of course we did not have. They said that parachute troopers were landing and that everyone would have to fight.

The paratrooper story turned out to be false alarm. The planes may have been Japanese aircraft passing nearby on the way to a bombing mission. The all clear was sounded about an hour later.

Doctor Wassell spent the morning trying to find a ship to take aboard his men. The prospects did not look promising between the previous departure of the American vessels, the limited number of ships remaining in port, and the Japanese naval forces operating south of Java. 'We learned at this time that two ships that had gone out with refugees the night before had been sunk off the entrance and that some survivors had been brought in that morning,' Goggins recalled. 'This did not look like a very cheerful prospect to us at least.'

The British convoy pulled into town around noon after traveling through the night. Wassell drove down to the dock area, where the convoy had arrived, to ferry his men back to the hotel in his car. However, he learned from the British soldiers one of his patients did not make it.

The missing sailor was Benjamin Hopkins. He told others that the first trip down to Tjilatjap and back nearly killed him. Now ill and weak, he did not think he could bear the pain finishing the truck ride through the jungle.[12] He insisted on being left at an aid station about thirty-five miles back with a British soldier in a similar situation. Goggins explained:

> The doctor was much disappointed about this, but there was nothing he could do about it, except get a promise from the British that they would go back and get our man if they could. They said that they would get him and their own. They had left one man who had broken both legs on a motorcycle accident about the middle of the previous afternoon.

Wassell really had no choice other than to continue working with the men with him.

All the remaining wounded sailors – now numbering eight – were together at the Grand Hotel by early afternoon. The sailors were tired and hungry – some fell asleep in chairs. Wassell found the men some food. Goggins remembered '… we all sat around and had some kind of rice and stew. This was about 1.00 o'clock.'

The doctor continued his frantic effort to find a ship shortly after lunch. He left the hotel with a Dutch sailor by the name of Gelarins serving as the assistant to the local liaison officer. Perhaps unknown to the doctor, Commander Schokking was working diligently on trying to get as many people transportation out of Tjilatjap as possible. Before his own departure, Admiral Helfrich had designated six ships as evacuation transports. Some of the vessels were at sea and were recalled from locations south of Java.[13] The small Dutch steamer *Janssens*, already in port, was to remain there to take aboard any late arrivals who missed the larger ships.

Some of the evacuation vessels had already departed after loading up with people. Doctor Wassell arrived at the docks to find two ships.

One likely was the Dutch cargo ship *Kota Baroe*. She arrived from the United States on February 27 carrying Dutch planes and personnel.[14] The unloading process in Tjilatjap proved to be a painfully slow process, delaying her departure. The other ship possibility was *Janssens*.

Doctor Wassell boarded *Janssens* to talk with her skipper, Lieutenant Commander Gerrit Prass, about taking aboard his sailors. Prass was tall, somewhat gaunt, and composed. He was not keen about having wounded men aboard his ship. Prass initially refused on the grounds his vessel was already overcrowded and he had no sick-bay or medical supplies.[15] The American doctor, however, eventually convinced the officer to let his men aboard. Prass sternly warned Wassell that he would be wholly responsible for his men.[16]

Wassell rushed back to the hotel with the good news, arriving at about 3.00 pm. The voyage would no doubt be risky and fraught with peril, but it was their only chance of escape. 'Then we were all put in a sort of bus our navy had had there,' Goggins continued. 'Gelarins got ahold of about three mattresses which, I remember he remarked, that if they were thrown overboard they would float and I think Gelarins thought we would probably need them.' All Doctor Wassell and his men could now do was to get back to the docks as fast as possible.

***

As Doctor Wassell was frantically trying to arrange passage of his wounded men out of Java, *Marblehead* was on the second leg of her long cruise home. The voyage was taking her from Trincomalee, Ceylon, off the southeast coast of India, deep into the Indian Ocean. By now it had become plainly evident to many of her sailors that the warship escaped Java just ahead of disaster. A steady stream of bad news reached her men during the latter part of the stay in Ceylon. The news began with the disastrous Battle of the Java Sea and the following Japanese invasion of Java. Then came the demoralizing reports of the sinking of *Houston*, *Langley*, and *Pecos*, among other ships in the region. The lives of many American sailors – including numerous friends from the Asiatic Fleet days – had surely been lost. The men had no way of knowing some of their wounded shipmates were aboard *Pecos* trying to escape Java ahead of the Japanese.

The early days of March saw the light cruiser steaming in a southwesterly direction across a long stretch of the Indian Ocean towards her next destination of South Africa. She was traveling alone without escort and zig-zagging. The distance between ports, somewhere around 4,500 miles, was more than double the distance covered during the first leg of the voyage.

The warship was in better sailing condition during the current leg of her voyage owing to the long list of repairs accomplished by her crew during the stay in Ceylon. Captain Robinson wrote of great progress 'toward the improvement of water-tight integrity, preparations and readiness for handling any unforeseen flooding, and in steps taken to improve the living conditions of the officers and men. Damage control equipment and facilities had been overhauled and redistributed, ready for further action.'

The work effort was spread among all the damaged areas. 'Bomb holes in all decks were patched or covered with plate,' Robinson continued. Steps were taken to prevent additional flooding in the after part of the ship. 'To reduce the possibility of flooding the steering gear room, a cement box was installed on the newly fitted deck and along the forward side of the ruptured armored bulkhead, thereby segregating the steering gear room from the demolished compartments forward of the armored bulkhead,' he explained. A large pump was moved from an engine room and remounted in the after part of the ship to pump out any water as needed.

Some compartments deep in the forward part of the ship, close to the near miss, were still flooded and inaccessible. 'There being no drydocking facilities at Trincomalee, it was accepted that leakage would continue into the ship in the area of the underwater explosion,' Robinson wrote. 'Efforts were concentrated on repairs to prevent the spread of this leakage through the damaged structure throughout the forward part of the ship.' The focus was to prevent the water from spreading to decks directly above, where it could then easily move into adjoining areas. A special watch was maintained in the forward area during the entire voyage to South Africa, including an inspection of all damaged compartments once per hour.

Limited improvements were made to the steering arrangements just before leaving port, although the equipment was not entirely repaired. 'Using parts of both disabled steering motors, the electrical force had succeeded in putting one steering motor and panel back in commission, and the ship cleared the harbor using the rudder, operated by the trick wheel in the steering gear room and controlled by sound powered telephone from the bridge,' Robinson explained. 'The rudder angle and speed of movement were, however, reduced.'

Electrician Walter Jarvis personally delivered the news to Robinson on the bridge shortly before *Marblehead* departed Trincomalee. The warrant officer was among the sailors who worked diligently to find a solution to the steering problem. He had spent most of his recent time laboring in the steering engine room – even eating and sleeping in the compartment.[17]

Nicholas Van Bergen had nothing but astonishment and praise for the work completed by Jarvis and his men. 'It seemed impossible that they could ever be put back into commission again due to the blow they'd taken from the armored bulkhead, the bend in the shafts, and the fact that they had been so long submerged in oil and salt water,' he later said. He noted Jarvis and his electricians 'never ceased working in exercising their ingenuity in new ways of drying out the coils, reinsulating them, building new end bells for motors, new bearings, and in lining up the system. Their work was really excellent.'[18]

The *Marblehead* sailors again heard a Radio Tokyo report during the voyage proclaiming the sinking of their ship. The March 11 broadcast reported *Marblehead* was sunk by a Japanese naval squadron operating in the Indian Ocean as she was 'fleeing to Australia'.[19] The sunken ship was likely one of the four-stack American destroyers lost south of Java, or the story was a complete fabrication. The same news agency previously reported the light cruiser was sunk by aircraft. 'The United States warship *Marblehead* and all on board have been sunk to the bottom of the ocean by our brave bombers,' the previous report read, the announcer adding the 'sinking cruiser flamed until the sea had closed over her'.[20] The light cruiser was very much alive and well.

The Colony of South Africa was positioned in the east-west middle of the British Empire at the very southern tip of the continent of Africa. The strategic location, touching both the Atlantic and Indian Oceans, made it important for naval operations. The Royal Navy maintained bases at four coastal cities – Durban, Simon's Town, Cape Town, and Port Elizabeth. Captain Robinson's initial orders were to take *Marblehead* to Simon's Town on the southwestern side of the colony. While at sea it determined she should first stop at Durban for fuel.

A new threat faced the sailors as *Marblehead* steamed towards South Africa. The waters of the Indian Ocean contained critical trade routes between England, her colonial possessions, and even the United States. The sea lanes facilitated the movement of troops and supplies, oil from the Middle East, and other types of raw materials. Captain Robinson was now largely clear of Japanese surface and air operations, but not necessarily of submarines.

The Axis powers sought to disrupt the Indian Ocean supply lines from the onset of the conflict. German commerce raiders, often disguised as merchant ships and armed with guns and torpedoes, were known to have been operating in the area since the early days of the war.[21] The small German battleship *Admiral Sheer* made a successful raiding foray into the Indian ocean in early 1941. She eluded Royal Navy searchers before slipping back to Europe via the South Atlantic. The large island of Madagascar, lying off the southeast coast of Africa, was under Vichy French rule, a nominal French government who collaborated with the Germans after the fall of France in 1940.

The dangerous situation was at the forefront of Captain Robinson's mind after he was reported to have received a warning message sent out by British Admiral Campbell Tait. 'Enemy raiders and blockade runners are eluding our patrols. All men of war, including those taking passage, will be held responsible for positively identifying all merchant ships before allowing them to proceed.'[22] Tait was serving as Royal Navy commander of the South Atlantic area.

The German raiders posed a serious threat. The modern Australian light cruiser *Sydney* was lost with all hands after battling the raider *Kormoran* off western Australia on November 19, 1941.[23] While *Marblehead* could likely outgun a German commerce raider, she was in no position to sustain any additional battle damage.

A tense situation developed when an unidentified vessel was sighted approaching just after 8.00 am on March 4. What looked to be a large freighter initially headed directly towards *Marblehead* before beginning to turn away.[24] The light cruiser maneuvered closer to investigate after a request for identification went unanswered. Captain Robinson ordered general quarters. He sent a single 6-inch shot across the bow of the unknown ship after orders to stop were ignored. The ship then properly identified herself as the British cargo ship *Silverlarch*.[25]

The route to Durban required *Marblehead* to sail through the Mozambique Channel, a wide body of water separating Madagascar from mainland Africa. She entered the channel during the early morning hours of March 11. A careful watch was kept on any ships encountered along the way with the 6-inch guns manned as a precaution when a ship approached.

Lookouts aboard *Marblehead* sighted the city of Durban on the distant horizon just before 7.00 am on March 15. She was moving into the harbor, with the help of a tug and pilot, during the mid-morning hours. The city features an enclosed harbor area, almost fully surrounded by land except for a narrow entrance channel. The white buildings were glistening in the sunlight.

The warship began taking on fuel shortly after mooring dockside. The anti-aircraft guns were secured, but were to be manned on five minutes' notice. A large load of fresh produce was brought aboard, including potatoes, onions, cabbage, and carrots. Doctor Wildebush was on hand to inspected the goods for quality. The light cruiser filled her tanks with 143,783 gallons of fuel oil before shifting to a nearby berth.[26] Sailors were able to take liberty ashore, with more than one getting into some trouble on land. Additional large quantities of food were brought aboard along with some additional supplies, including some cases of Lucky Strike cigarettes.

Captain Robinson and his men had once again skirted disaster with their timely departure from Ceylon. As Imperial forces finished up operations in the Dutch East Indies, Japanese troops staging in Thailand pushed west into the neighboring British Colony of Burma. The advance soon captured the capital and important port city of Rangoon. The loss severed the beginning of the Burma Road, an important overland supply route to China. India was threatened as Japanese forces advanced north and west.

Two Japanese naval task forces subsequently forayed into the Indian Ocean to attack the British Far Eastern Fleet. One was Admiral Nagumo's powerful carrier force; the other was a smaller group of cruisers and destroyers with the carrier *Ryujo*. Nagumo's ships retired to Kendari on Celebes after completing operations south of Java before departing on March 26 for the voyage west. Both major British naval bases on Ceylon – Colombo and Trincomalee – fell victim to air attacks. The most damage, however, was done to ships at sea, where the victims included the aircraft carrier *Hermes*, heavy cruisers *Dorsetshire* and *Cornwall*, destroyer *Vampire*, and twenty-three merchant ships.[27] The crippled British Far Eastern Fleet withdrew west to bases along the African coast.

The stay at Durban was little more than a short refueling stop. The ship was underway on the morning of March 17 for the voyage south to Simon's Town, a port with a drydock large enough and available to make repairs to *Marblehead*'s damaged hull. However, like many of the South African ports, Simon's Town was full of ships. The light cruiser would have to make a stop at Port Elizabeth until the dockyard at Simon's Town was ready. Captain Robinson steered a zig-zag course as a precaution against submarines. The damaged warship was slowly making her way back to the United States.

Chapter 29

The vessel Doctor Wassell hoped would carry his men to the safety of Australia was neither a large transport nor an ocean-going liner or merchantman. The Dutch ship *Janssens* was constructed at the Smit P Jr. Shipyard located in Rotterdam, Holland in 1935. She was built for the Dutch KPM Shipping Line, a company largely engaged in the shipment of goods and people between the various islands of the Netherlands East Indies. The vessel displaced 2,071 tones with her hull measuring 265ft long and 43ft wide.[1] She was operated by a crew of sixty.

As an inter-island steamer, *Janssens* was not built with long ocean voyages in mind or to accommodate large numbers of passengers. She was requisitioned by the Dutch Navy for use as a supply ship and submarine tender on December 1, 1941.[2] Her role in the latter capacity was rushed into service to fill a void until the larger tender *Columbia* arrived from Europe.[3]

The American sailors were lucky *Janssens* was still in port. The vessel had been operating as a supply ship in Tjilatjap since February 4 and was later pressed into service as part of the mass evacuation. Commander Schokking directed Lieutenant Commander Prass to be able to get underway on thirty minutes' notice if necessary.[4] The skipper was originally ordered to depart during the evening hours of March 2 with a large load of evacuees. Had the departure taken place as scheduled, the ship would probably have been gone by the time Wassell and Goggins arrived in town.

Prass was used to undertaking dangerous voyages by this time. His *Janssens* supported a small group of Dutch warships that sailed to the southern coast of Borneo in response to a reported Japanese convoy in the South China Sea in May 1941.[5] The operation was in response to one of many invasion scares during the tense months leading up to the start of the conflict.

She sailed into Singapore on December 19, 1941, while Malaya was under Japanese attack. The ship departed three days later bound for Surabaya with a contingent of British seaman who were to assist with the manning of a Dutch torpedo boat squadron and the light cruiser *Java*.[6] She transported the dangerous cargos of torpedoes and aircraft bombs in her role as a supply ship.[7]

The fluid situation at Tjilatjap resulted in a delay of the pending voyage with the orders changed to a departure during late afternoon of March 3. The passengers, numbering somewhere close to 600, were transferred to another ship. Prass was to wait for a different load of evacuees. The new group was to include crewmen from a submarine, assorted Dutch sailors from various ships, civilian workers, and a variety of senior officers.

Lieutenant Herman Jorissen was among the many Dutch sailors to come aboard *Janssens*. The young officer was a member of a torpedo boat squadron. The boats deployed off eastern Java in a futile attempt to delay the Japanese invasion. The small craft were scuttled at Surabaya on March 2, with crews firing off the remaining torpedoes into the harbor before using axes to break holes in the bottom of each boat.[8] 'It was one of these very old government ships and was not built for any naval action,' Jorissen later said of the steamer.[9] He remembered some of the senior Dutch military officers aboard, most likely army, thought they could take command of the ship. Prass would have nothing of it. The skipper made it known from the start it was his ship and he was in charge.

A continual stream of people came aboard the small vessel as the day progressed. Prass was told to expect about 750 passengers. The departure was rescheduled for 6.00 pm on March 3.[10]

***

A steady rain was falling when Doctor Wassell and his sailors arrived at the dock late in the afternoon. Most came in the bus from the hotel, while a few of the more seriously wounded rode in a car. They brought along the mattresses given to them by the officer back at the hotel. Wassell gave his Ford sedan to the Dutch sailor who assisted in arranging the transportation.[11] A small launch ferried the men out to *Janssens* in the harbor. A burly Dutch sailor helped the wounded get aboard.

The sailors quickly took stock of their new ship. The vessel was much smaller than the larger warships they came from. Two masts protruded high into the air from the forward and after decks of *Janssens*. A superstructure with a single smoke stack dominated the middle part of the vessel. Awnings covered some of the open deck space.

She was powered by a single diesel engine allowing for a maximum speed of eleven knots.[12] However, the engine had not been overhauled since the start of the war, causing her actual speed to be much less – possibly as slow as only seven knots.[13] The speed was probably not fast enough to out run any type of threat waiting for her in the waters south of Java. The vessel had little in the way of weaponry, with her armament consisting of two light machine guns rumored to have been salvaged from a wrecked PBY.[14]

William Goggins estimated the vessel to be about 3,000 tons, slightly larger than actual. 'It was already overcrowded with refugees,' he remembered upon his arrival. He noted the crew was mostly Javanese and the wide variety of passengers. 'There were the Dutch officers who had blown up the naval base at Surabaya, torpedoed British seamen, Australian soldiers, fliers, women and children, Dutch Navy ratings, and our own wounded.'[15] Pratt protested at having to accept the women and children, citing the dangerousness of the voyage in trying to deny their boarding. He was overruled by Commander Schokking and the civilians were brought aboard.[16]

According to Goggins, the Americans quickly settled into their new surroundings:

> We had no place to sleep except on the deck. All they would promise was deck space, so we got the mattresses set out on one of the decks, put our wounded on them, and the rest of us were helped into the place where we were to live. They had the officers up in a little sort of smoking room and dining room and that's where I was assigned.

***

Wassell's sailors were not the only Americans on the ship. Several war correspondents, including Bill Dunn and George Weller, were also aboard *Janssens* trying to escape from Java. Dunn was a CBS radio reporter who had been covering events in the Pacific for nearly a year before the attack on Pearl Harbor.[17] Newspaper reporter George Weller arrived on Java after barely escaping from Singapore just ahead of the Japanese. He traveled all over the island before finally ending up with Dunn and American radio correspondent Frank Cuhel at Bandoeng.

The newsmen knew it was time to get out of Java, even though they hated the thought of leaving their Dutch friends behind. They were in contact with several American Air Corps officers about getting transportation off the island. However, most of the American planes had already left for Australia and only ground personnel remained. A rumored promise by Colonel Eubank to send a B-17 back for them never materialized.

The correspondents decided to make the difficult drive to Tjilatjap – more than 150 miles away – after attempts to leave by plane failed. The southern city was thought to be the only safe port still open. The group set out in Frank Cuhel's car after dismissing rumors Tjilatjap had already fallen to the Japanese. They searched for other newsmen to take along, only finding Australian reporter Winston Turner of the Australian Associated Press.

Leaving late in the afternoon resulted in much of the drive taking place during the night hours. Many vehicles were going the opposite way towards Bandoeng – few were traveling in their direction. The reporters occasionally stopped to ask directions. The answer was always the same, with locals saying they were fleeing just ahead of the Japanese. However, no one said they actually saw the enemy.[18]

The reporters arrived in Tjilatjap on March 2 after driving about 180 miles. They found the docks empty of ships and the adjacent area deserted. A guard told them the last ship had already left and provided directions to the residence of the port officer. 'We found the commandant very much awake and quite sympathetic,' Dunn later wrote.[19] The Dutch officer told them to come back in the morning as he was expecting another ship to make the run to Australia. They stayed part of the night at the local hotel, sleeping on billiard tables and apparently not having any contact with the wounded American sailors.

Winston Turner remembered approaching the commandant the next morning and being given passes to board *Janssens*.[20] Frank Cuhel dumped their car into water off a jetty, to keep it from falling into Japanese hands, before the men waited their turn to get aboard. 'All that day the tenders shuttled back and forth between ship and shore, bringing more and more naval personnel to compete with us for the limited deck space,' Dunn later wrote.[21]

The reporters made it aboard before the other Americans. They patiently waited for departure and worried. 'All day we waited in the tiny harbor expecting raids, but Jap fighters, based on Bali, were harassing the defenses around Rembang and only one alarm sounded and no bombs were dropped,' Weller later wrote.[22] He estimated there were about 600 people crammed aboard the small ship. 'About ninety per cent of the passengers were Dutch Navy people.'

The loading of several stretcher cases caught their attention later in the day. Weller went to investigate and found them to be American sailors. 'We went below to greet them,' Dunn continued. 'Some of the seamen were also ambulatory, but all were assigned cots on a lower deck protected from the elements.' He remembered Wassell and Goggins sharing a room. 'These men, with Cuhel, Weller, and me, were the only Americans on board,' Dunn wrote. George Weller spent some time talking with Doctor Wassell. 'One topic of conversation was our chances of piercing the Japanese submarine blockade,' Weller recalled. The chances of the ship successfully making it all the way to Australia was probably the top thought on everyone's mind.

***

A final count of the number of people crammed aboard *Janssens* may never be known for certain. The small vessel was clearly overcrowded. A Dutch patrol ship was under orders to escort her all the way to Australia. However, the Javanese crew disappeared before departure, forcing *Janssens* to sail alone. Prass faced a similar problem just as his steamer was getting underway during the late afternoon. Fourteen Javanese sailors jumped overboard and swam ashore before disappearing on land.[23] The Dutch skipper decided to continue his departure as planned. There was no harbor pilot aboard as Prass navigated *Janssens* through the channel near dangerous minefields on the way to open sea.

Favorable weather conditions helped conceal the small ship after dark. 'We were very fortunate in that off the entrance we encountered very severe tropical thunderstorms,' Goggins recalled. 'With a reduced visibility and heavy rains, lightning etc., we managed to get through and

I believe that this storm saved us from being sighted by submarines off the entrance.' The little vessel pitched and rolled as she made it through the protective cloak of darkness. The storm did little to ease the jitters among some of the passengers. 'That night no one slept much,' Goggins continued. 'There were not enough life boats for everyone, but they did get everybody a life preserver and most wore them all night long – as a matter of fact some of them wore them all the rest of the voyage.'

William Dunn settled into a small space of empty deck behind the bridge and quickly fell asleep in his makeshift bed. A small bath rug was among his limited possessions. The carpet was serving him well as he tried to get some sleep. The newsman also took aboard an atlas he had 'purchased in Batavia, an ordinary volume possibly a little more comprehensive than a high school geography book'. The book quickly became in high demand with other sailors and passengers studying it in detail. The atlas eventually caught the attention of Prass. 'As soon as the skipper spotted the atlas, he commandeered it and took [it] to the bridge where he used it to draw up his own charts,' Dunn later wrote. The inter-island steamer apparently did not have maps of the Indian Ocean area south of Java.

Chapter 30

A meager breakfast and better weather awaited passengers aboard *Janssens* the morning after her departure from Tjilatjap. 'The weather had cleared and it promised to be a beautiful day, although personally I would have welcomed rain and fog all the way to Australia,' William Dunn later wrote. Passengers expecting to see nothing but open waters were sorely disheartened. 'The next morning when we looked out we thought we would be well to the south of Java, but were disappointed and rather alarmed to find that we were steaming to the eastward from the south coast of Java,' Goggins said.[1] Prass was sailing east about ten miles off the coast before a planned turn to the south. The course likely was to avoid the expected concentration of enemy naval vessels directly south of Tjilatjap and may have been ordered by Dutch authorities.[2]

Both Wassell and Goggins were uneasy with the arrangement, knowing it put them dangerously close to the Japanese air base on Bali. Goggins had already lived though one air attack and perhaps knew better than anyone else aboard the dangers of having a ship caught in the open sea. He glumly concluded 'we would be very lucky if we got through'. Their worries came true later in the morning when a large formation of Japanese bombers was spotted.

The very sight was enough to strike a jolt of terror through many aboard *Janssens*. 'We thought our number was up, but they didn't bother us,' Goggins remembered. 'They were after bigger game.' George Weller looked to the sky counting the enemy planes. 'First came nine, then seven, then nine again,' he later wrote. 'They were directly overhead, their motors humming incessantly.' Winston Turner saw the planes and thought it was the beginning of the end. He then noticed the enemy was 'flying fast and in perfect formation' as the planes passed to the west.[3] The enemy was on the way to bomb Tjilatjap.

Robert Whaley remembered 'everyone but the three of us who couldn't walk scrambled below deck' after the planes were sighted.[4] He was referring to the three stretcher cases – himself, along with William Anderson and William McCurdy. 'They went over,' a relieved Whaley later said. 'They didn't bother about our small tramp steamer.' The encounter left many aboard with an uneasy feeling.[5] 'We felt rather unhappy about our prospects now that the Japs had definitely seen us,' Goggins explained, certain the bombers radioed a sighting report back to base.

The worst fears for everyone aboard *Janssens* came true about an hour later when a small group of Japanese planes suddenly appeared without warning. Two or three Zero fighters (accounts differ as to the number) dove towards the ship for a strafing run. Although the planes were not bombers, their guns nonetheless packed a powerful punch – enough to seriously damage or even sink the unarmored steamer while causing scores of casualties among the crowds of passengers. Each Zero was equipped with two 7.7-millimeter machine guns and two 20-millimeter cannons.[6] Unlike machine guns, the latter weapons fire a small exploding shell capable of causing damage and spreading deadly shrapnel.

Doctor Wassell and Goggins were talking in a small dining room full of people when there was a sudden commotion. Everyone immediately dove to the floor. People all over the ship were rapidly scrambling for cover. 'Everyone who could move dashed down the ladder to the deck below where some protection would be had from the steel hull of the ship,' Goggins remembered. The protection offered by *Janssens* thin metal skin was minimal. The men knew it was better than nothing. Sailors Whaley, Anderson, and McCurdy were on deck. They initially rolled next to a hatch for cover – the best they could immediately find in their near helpless condition.

William Dunn had just started eating a snack while gazing out at the Java coastline when he suddenly heard approaching planes. The dreaded drone of the engines alone was enough to strike panic in many of the passengers. The rattling sound of gunfire quickly followed. He ran into a nearby cabin, with steel walls, and dove under a bunk. Others quickly piled on top of him. 'It really never occurred to me that the *Janssens* might survive,' he later wrote. 'I lay there measuring the distance to shore and wondering if I could clear the ship when she sank.' Skipper Prass stayed on the bridge throughout the attack carefully watching the movements of the planes.

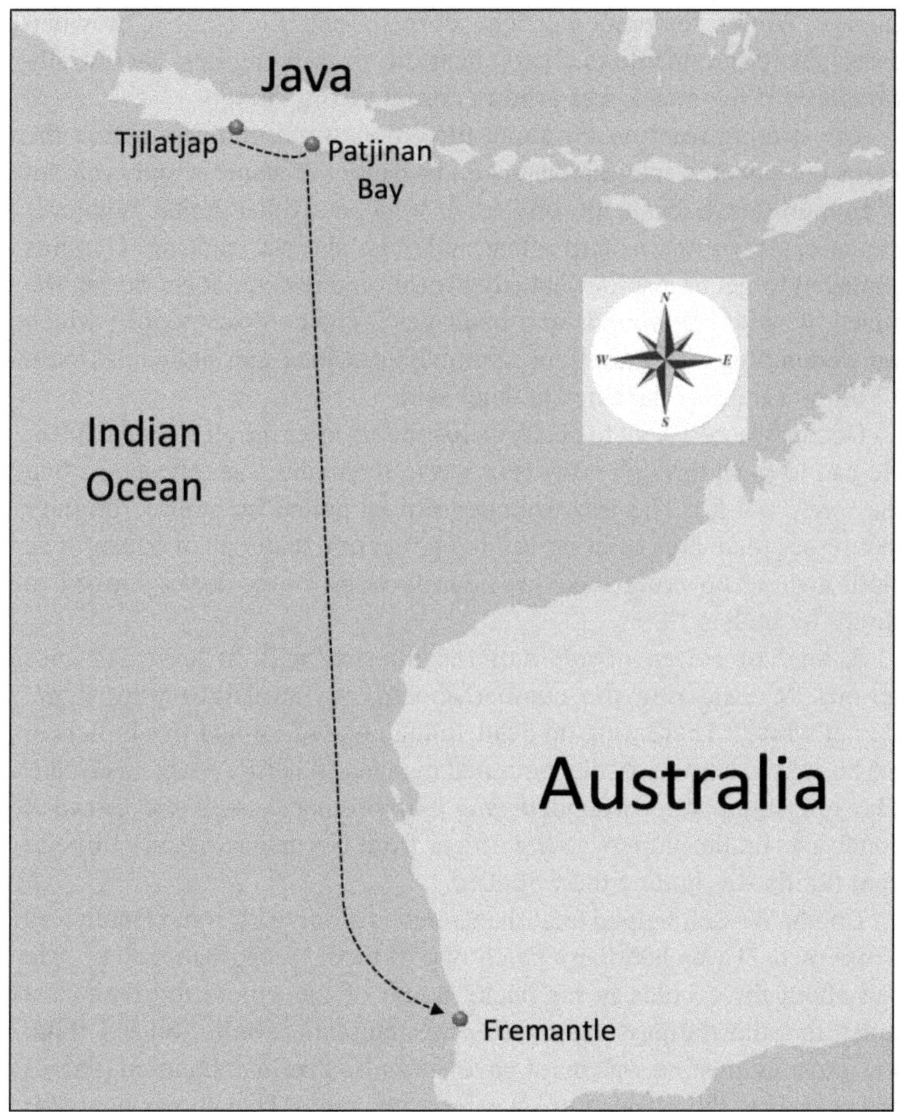

Escape of *Janssens* March 1942.

The terrifying sound of gunfire filled the air when the Zeros passed. Their blazing guns sent bullets streaming through the small vessel. A group of Dutch sailors bravely manned the machine guns to return fire. Many passengers stayed down as the planes looped around for another pass. 'Then came again the terrible hammering and tearing of wood, running like a xylophone the full length of the ship,'

George Weller remembered. The correspondent was in a crowded passageway and unable to clearly hear the aircraft engines. He initially wondered if the attack was gunfire coming from land.

The strafing went on for about fifteen or twenty minutes before the Zeros disappeared into the distance.[7] Possibly the planes simply ran out of ammunition, became low on fuel, or went on to other duties. Whatever the case, *Janssens* was still afloat, although she was shot up. Goggins managed to get to a somewhat safer location one deck down during the attack, despite his wounds and bandages. 'The compartment in which we were sitting was literally riddled with machine gun bullets, as were all of the cabins of the ship.' he later said.

Doctor Wassell went to check on his sailors after the all clear sounded. He had to push through crowds to get to them and was relieved to find they were not hit. The less wounded sailors pulled the injured on their mattresses to an area offering limited protection under an overhang. The cloth awning covering their previous location on deck was ripped to shreds by bullets.[8]

A total of eleven people suffered injuries, with at least one case serious. 'Considering the number aboard, our casualties were light,' Turner wrote. 'There were no dead, though one sailor had five bullets in his body, and another badly wounded man could hardly have survived.'[9] The low number of wounded was extraordinary given the crowded conditions on the ship. A young officer from Herman Jorisson's torpedo boat flotilla was among the wounded.

Doctor Wassell helped treat the wounded along with some Dutch Red Cross men. 'I watched them patch one of them,' Goggins recalled. 'He had about three holes in his back.' Some of the sailors did their best to try to calm the passengers after the traumatic event. 'What I think was most interesting was that I gave out more than five hundred glasses of water after the planes left,' Wassell later said. 'That shows how fear makes human bodies exude perspiration.'[10]

The episode left some of the passengers nearly hysterical and wanting to get off the ship to dry land – and fast. Those included an angry Dutch army officer who was pounding his fists on the deck in frustration. He brought his demands directly to Prass.[11]

The skipper initially kept the ship on an easterly course after the attack. However, the sun was still high in the afternoon sky and the weather conditions good. The enemy knew their location and there was no telling if more planes would return, perhaps even bombers. 'Everybody expected that these Japanese Zeros fighters would come back or that other units of the [Japanese] navy might intercept us,' Jorissen later recalled. Several of the lifeboats were damaged and unusable, presenting even greater problems for survivors if the ship were to sink.

One possibility was for *Janssens* to divert to Patjinan Bay. Prass was against the idea, fearing more of his Javanese crew would desert. The angry army officer, who was the most senior ranking Dutch military officer aboard, gave Prass a direct order to go to the bay. The skipper felt he was obligated to obey.[12] Prass turned *Janssens* north towards Patjinan Bay. The small inlet on the Java coast was about an hour away.

Anchoring close to shore allowed Prass to hide his small ship, as inconspicuously as possible, for the remaining daylight hours. The move also offered a chance for any passengers who did not want to continue the voyage to get off. There were no people on the shoreline when *Janssens* moved into the bay. 'The skipper mustered all hands and told them the ship would try to make Australia, but that those who wished to go ashore could do so,' Winston Turner recalled. Goggins remembered the ship dropping anchor 'very close to the beach' and an announcement made telling any passengers wanting to leave to do so. The undamaged life boats served as small ferries to transport people ashore.

All the American sailors decided to stay aboard, although accounts differ as to how the decision was made. Goggins later recalled:

> Dr Wassell went down and saw our own wounded and came back and said he had asked them all if they wanted to stay with the ship or land, the idea being that if they did not want to make the attempt to get to Australia that he would stay with them and I would too.

George Weller also wrote of Wassell allowing his men to decide.

William Dunn wrote of Wassell initially wanting to go ashore. 'I'm going to take my men ashore,' he apparently told the reporter. 'My orders are to stay in Java with my wounded, and that's what I am going to do.' Dunn wrote of Goggins, technically the senior American officer of the group, intervening in the decision-making process. 'Wait a minute, Doc, I think we should give the men the right to make their own decisions. Let's take a vote,' he reported Goggins as saying.[13]

During a speech in Canada more the two years after the event, Wassell spoke of giving the men a vote. 'Stick with the ship, Doc,' he remembered as the decision. Regardless of how the events played out, the American sailors were staying aboard. Wassell also recounted going up to the bridge and finding Prass in a solemn mood with some Dutch officers. 'Captain, I want to report to you that the American Navy boys want to stick with the ship and take a chance.'[14]

The American reporters also decided against going ashore. 'It was by far the hardest decision I have ever had to make,' Dunn later wrote. 'I was still scared as hell from the attack, and the lovely green slopes of Java looked very inviting. Still, I knew that leaving the ship would mean automatic internment at best.' He also knew that staying aboard could mean enduring another air attack and possibly a sinking at sea. All the correspondents decided to stay aboard.

Prass pleaded for his crewmembers to stay, but to no avail. About 250 people were thought to have left *Janssens,* including most of the civilian passengers and much of her remaining crew.[15] The angry senior Dutch army officer was among the first to depart. Numerous other Dutch army men left, especially those with families on the island. Those wounded in the air attack were taken ashore, along with a Dutch medical person, after it was learned a small hospital was nearby. Wassell then took over duties as the ship's doctor.[16]

Herman Jorissen remembered a 'road ending near the bay' with a small jetty sticking out into the water making the process of getting the wounded ashore easier. He later said the skipper 'knew his country well,' marveling at Prass for finding such a good bay for shelter. 'We all stayed aboard,' Jorissen said of the nearly twenty Dutch naval officers on the ship. He recalled only a few of his fellow navy men getting off.

Winston Turner remembered those going ashore being given strict instructions not to leave the area around the bay for two days.[17] The Japanese ground forces were thought to have advanced into the town of Solo, almost directly north of Patjinan, and only a few hours away. The last thing Prass wanted was for word of his departure to reach the enemy before he had a chance to get far away from Java.

The remaining afternoon hours were spent at anchor. Those departing were slowly ferried ashore. Others, who were staying aboard, worked on fixing the damaged life boats. Worried eyes were probably scanning the sky for any sign of approaching planes.

Although the Americans were staying aboard, Goggins was not overly optimistic about the chances of making a successful escape. 'Well, the doctor and I were both rather doubtful about our chances because it looked as though the bombers would certainly be back that afternoon and get us,' he later said. He speculated the ships yellow and green paint may have helped her blend into the surrounding area. 'Then about two hours later there was another alarm, and we all dove down below again, but whether it was a false alarm or whether the planes didn't see us, I don't know.' The episode was likely a false alarm.

Doctor Wassell was forced to confront his worst fears.

> That was my one horror, that the bombers would come over and drop bombs on that ship. I never worried about being killed. The only thought that came up in my mind was how in the world would I take care of all the sick and wounded on the ship.[18]

Even Prass may have harbored doubts about the ability of his ship to complete the voyage. George Weller remembered the skipper saying they had a 'slight to perhaps fifty-fifty chance' of successfully making Australia. As the late afternoon sun slowly began to get lower on the horizon, the future of the small *Janssens* and her remaining passengers was very much in question.

Chapter 31

Daylight was starting to fade along the southern coast of Java during the early evening hours of March 4; the small *Janssens* weighed anchor at 6.45 pm before slowly disappearing in developing darkness.[1]

Prass turned his ship south with her bow pointed directly towards the western part of Australia. No one aboard knew if the vessel might encounter Japanese planes, ships, or submarines along the path to safety. American reporter William Dunn remembered 'tension was still high' as the ship plodded through the waters of the Indian Ocean, 'intent on putting as much distance as possible between ourselves and the Java coast before sun up'.[2]

William Goggins knew the single diesel engine could not provide the ship with much speed. 'It was, therefore, not necessary to even attempt to zig zag, so we steamed on a steady course,' he recalled. 'We had bright moonlight and didn't feel very cheerful about evading the Japs outside.'[3]

The ship became more spacious after the departure of numerous passengers. Doctor Wassell moved into a small cabin with a Dutch priest. The wounded men chose to stay out on deck where they could enjoy the cool evening breezes. Many aboard helped with the routine duties. Only one Javanese cook remained to prepare the food. Wassell helped serve the limited meals and did cleaning work. Dutch sailors stood extended watches, with two officers always on the bridge with the helmsman.[4] Others manned the machine guns. Lookouts continuously scanned the horizon for any sign of the enemy. Dunn unsuccessfully tried to notice if Prass ever took some time off to sleep. The skipper always seemed to be on duty – either on the bridge or somewhere else around the ship.

Many aboard *Janssens* had an uptight feeling all through the coming days, worried about the possibility of being found by the enemy. The air raid alarm sounded on one occasion after a lookout mistook a large bird gliding through the air for an approaching plane. The ringing alarm was the last thing the remaining passengers wanted to hear. Wounded *Marblehead* sailor Pao San Ho took no chances – he kept his life vest on for the rest of the voyage.[5] Correspondent George Weller was of similar mind. He slept on the open deck each night with his life belt securely snuggled under his arm.

Dutch First Machinist J. van Klaveren labored endlessly below deck to keep the diesel engine running.[6] The loss of the only engine would have been a catastrophic event. It would have left *Janssens* dead in the water, far from land, and an easy target for the Japanese.

There were no contacts of any type for a few days. A setback occurred when the ship was about 500 miles south of Java – a comfortable distance traveled, although not far enough to necessarily be considered safe from the enemy.[7] The steamer suddenly started turning. Doctor Wassell assumed the small ship was maneuvering to dodge a torpedo. 'Everybody was trying to see what was up,' he later said. 'Nobody could see a submarine, nobody could see an aeroplane. We soon found out what was wrong.'[8]

Goggins later explained what happened. 'About the third day out, the steering gear broke down and we ran in circles for about two hours while attempt was made to repair it,' he related. 'This failing, we steered by hand all the rest of the way.' A small bit of normalcy returned when *Janssens* sailed south on a straight course, even with the strenuous work the steering by hand created for some of the crewmen. 'We continued on our way, eating and sleeping the best we could and the Dutch doing everything possible for our wounded, for their comfort, etc.,' Goggins continued.

A much-needed dose of good news came on March 11 while *Janssens* was sailing far down the west coast of Australia. Her location far to the south of Java most likely put her away from all potential enemy hazards except submarines. A big lumbering plane was suddenly spotted approaching the ship.

William Goggins assured Wassell it was friendly. 'Didn't you see him dip to the right, staying well away from the ship, and then circling?' he told the doctor.[9] A loud cheer rang out when she was identified as an American PBY seaplane. It was the first friendly aircraft many aboard had seen in weeks.

The last scare of the long voyage came the very next day when *Janssens* was in her final approach to Australia. William Dunn was awakened from a midday nap and told to go quickly to the stern. At about the same time, Goggins was sitting in the dining room when a disturbance out on deck attracted his attention. Doctor Wassell awoke from a nap to what he later recalled as a 'terrible commotion' on deck.

Everyone was surprised to find a submarine on the surface astern of *Janssens*. The boat appeared to be a couple of miles away. 'We did all kinds of evasive action – all at the speed of seven knots,' remembered Dutch navy passenger Herman Jorisson.[10]

Dunn remembered seeing skipper Prass and several officers studying the submarine with binoculars. Goggins recalled, 'We didn't know if it was friendly or not, and the consequences if it were enemy were obvious'. The long perilous voyage would have come to a heartbreaking end if the ship had successfully escaped from Java only to be sunk by a submarine so close to friendly shores. Goggins assured Wassell, just as with the plane sighting, she was a friendly boat. 'Well, that submarine can make ten to twelve [knots], we can't make over five and a half to six knots,' Goggins said. 'We could have been sunk a long time ago.'

The tension broke when an Australian plane abruptly appeared from the southeast, exchanging recognition signals with the steamer, before heading over the submarine. The wounded sailors on deck noticed the plane did not attack the craft, causing even the grim-faced Pao San Ho to smile. A short time later the plane signaled *Janssens* that the boat was a Dutch submarine heading to port.[11]

A day with unlucky implications for so many in history, Friday March 13 could not have been better for the men aboard *Janssens* as they watched her drop anchor outside of Fremantle, Australia. The sailors aboard the steamer later saw the submarine, previously sighted off the stern while out at sea, now flying the Dutch flag. 'Why in God's world didn't they put the flag up out there when we could see it?' Wassel later said. Herman Jorisson subsequently heard that the boat was full of evacuees, sailing from Surabaya directly to Freemantle and feared *Janssens* was a Japanese destroyer. Winston Turner later added the Dutch submarine, like *Janssens*, was trying to get to Australia without adequate maps.

The small *Janssens* sailed more than the straight-line distance of over 1,700 miles between Tjilatjap and the southwestern Australian city. 'The following morning, we pulled in alongside the dock in Freemantle Harbor and the wounded were taken off to the Hollywood Hospital where our wounds were dressed again for the first time since we left,' Goggins remembered.

Robert Whaley shaved before slipping into a pair of white trousers and a sport shirt. His face was covered with a big smile as he was carried off the ship. He remarked how the harbor looked to be the next best thing to being home.[12] Wassell and Goggins later went for lunch at the house of a local officer. The wounded American sailors were eternally grateful to Doctor Wassell for staying with them on Java and to the determined skipper Prass for piloting his little ship through such a treacherous voyage. 'As it proved to be, we were extremely lucky,' Herman Jorisson said. His statement likely summarized the feelings of everyone aboard.

***

The Japanese were swiftly overtaking Java while Doctor Wassell and his sailors were making their escape to Australia. The Dutch ground units on Java were unable to mount a serious defense against the multi-pronged attack.[13] Members of the Black Force, the ad hoc collection formed into a mobile unit, were deployed on the western side of the island. Japanese soldiers advanced faster than expected, causing ABDA troops to fall back in retreat. A fierce battle raged along the Tjianten River near Batavia. The effort to keep the Japanese from crossing the critical body of water failed. Batteries of the American 131st Field Artillery were in action near the town of Leuwiliang south of Batavia, but were soon in retreat with other Black Force members. Both Batavia and Bandoeng fell into enemy hands on March 5. Black Force units moved east and eventually scattered into the hills south of Bandung.

The port of Surabaya was overrun in the east. Japanese forces rapidly moved inland, racing nearly 150 miles in a week while moving diagonally across the island towards Tjilatjap. The garrison at Jogjakarta, numbering about Dutch 700 soldiers, surrendered after a short skirmish with advancing Japanese troops. The enemy ground units left Jogjakarta during the early morning hours of March 6 to begin advancing along the beaches towards Tjilatjap.[14] The port city was still jammed full of the servicemen and refugees trying to get out. Tjilatjap was occupied on March 8.[15]

The enemy now controlled most of the important cities on Java – there was little else to defend. Dutch General Hein Ter Poorten unconditionally surrendered to the Japanese on March 9.[16] A total of 541 Americans on Java, mostly the Texas artillerymen, became prisoners and were marched to a camp near Batavia.[17] The men were eventually sent to Burma to spend the rest of the war in brutal captivity enduring forced labor. The unit became known as the Lost Battalion.

The Allied defense of the Malay Barrier was essentially over. The defeat on Java left the Japanese able to threaten Australia to the south and India to the west. Only scattered pockets of resistance remained, most notably the American and Filipino defenders trapped at Bataan and Corregidor in the Philippines.

***

The light cruiser *Marblehead* was continuing her long voyage back to the United States as the events were playing out on Java and at sea towards Australia. Tragedy struck the warship while she was at sea during the first hours of March 18. She was sailing from Durban to Port Elizabeth, South Africa. Regular inspections were made of the damaged forward compartments, same as was done in previous legs of the journey, to keep a careful watch on potential additional flooding. 'On the way down we found that fuel oil, salt water, and cordage would generate methane gas,' Nicholas Van Bergen explained. The highly flammable gas is generally nontoxic, unless it is very concentrated – then it can cause asphyxiation. The gas buildup took place in a storage compartment at the very bottom of the ship near the bow. The room was one of many to incur flooding following the damage sustained in the air attack.

The problems started around midnight when a member of the night watch, Carpenter's Mate Third Class Bernard Wardzinski, went into the compartment to make a routine check. He was quickly overcome by fumes and lost consciousness. Shipfitter Third Class Laurence Oldham, who had been waiting at the top of a hatch for Wardzinski to return, noticed something was amiss and ran for help. Oldham quickly returned with Shipfitter Second Class Clarence Aschenbrenner. He immediately left to report the incident to the bridge and obtain a rescue breather, a medical device used to force air into the lungs of a patient needing artificial respiration. Aschenbrenner then entered the compartment alone, only to be overcome by the fumes himself.

Officer of the deck John Bracken, on duty at the bridge, sent additional sailors to help after learning of the situation. Suspecting it could be explosive gas, he later ordered the smoking lamp turned off, prohibiting sailors from lighting cigarettes aboard the ship.[18] A doctor was put on standby. Sailors notified Captain Robinson and Van Bergen. Both officers were asleep in their respective cabins.

The executive officer, only half dressed, rushed down to the compartment upon receipt of the news. He found neither of the trapped men answered when other sailors shouted into the compartment. Van Bergen tied a rope around his waist before entering the compartment on his own with a light. He saw Aschenbrenner slumped over near Wardzinski. Before Van Bergen could do much more he was also overcome and his legs gave out from under him.[19] Sailors quickly pulled him out by the rope.

By this time some rescue equipment arrived on the scene. A sailor with a mask went in and put a rope around the other two unconscious men. Sailors waiting outside hurriedly pulled them out. All three rescued sailors were taken to the wardroom and laid out on tables. The medical staff jumped into action to work on the stricken men. Other steps were taken on the ship to keep the accident isolated, including increasing the ventilation in the forward part of the ship.

The executive officer, who was in the compartment for the least amount of time, was successfully revived. He was placed on the sick list on orders from Captain Robinson. Van Bergen eventually made a full recovery. The other two sailors, who had been in the compartment for much longer, were not as fortunate. Both succumbed to asphyxiation after an exhaustive effort by the medial staff to keep them alive failed. A popular sailor with the nickname of 'Bull', Clarence Aschenbrenner was pronounced dead at 4.15 am. Bernard Wardzinski clung to life before passing away later in the day.[20]

The light cruiser was a sad ship when she moored in Port Elizabeth during the late morning of March 19. South African soldiers joined with Royal Navy sailors and marines in gathering dockside to form an honor guard. The bodies of Aschenbrenner and Wardzinski were carried off *Marblehead* in flag-draped coffins by some of their closest friends. Planning began for funerals to take place the next morning.

The colors on *Marblehead* were lowered to half-mast when a funeral party left the ship on the morning of March 20. A simple graveside service, conducted by Father Edward J. Wynne, was held at a local cemetery. Captain Robinson was in full dress uniform and was among the many to shed tears as the coffins were lowered into the ground as a bugler was playing somber notes.[21]

A subsequent investigation confirmed gas buildup was the culprit of the accident. 'During the evening and night prior to the time of the casualties, the sea had become moderately rough, causing considerable motion of the ship,' Captain Robinson later reported. 'It is probable that the ship's motion agitated the water in the hold enough to release the noxious gas.'[22]

The warship moved out of Port Elizabeth on the afternoon of March 22. Her next stop was a drydock waiting for her in Simon's Town. The short trip took *Marblehead* around the southern tip of Africa where she passed from the Indian Ocean into the Atlantic.

The sea turned choppy and the wind had a bit of a chill once the ship rounded the bottom of Africa. The destination city was positioned on a finger of land jutting out into the water. The land ended with the Cape of Good Hope, the generally recognized boundary between the Indian and Atlantic Oceans. The much larger city of Cape Town was close by to the north. The peninsula and surrounding mainland created a large inlet known as False Bay. The area had long been home to an important base for the Royal Navy.

The light cruiser dropped anchor off Simon's Town at 2.18 pm on March 24.[23] Captain Robinson left *Marblehead* to visit Admiral Douglas Budgen, the senior British naval officer in the area. She went into a drydock within a few hours of her arrival in port. The ship was finally, for the first time since suffering the battle damage on February 4, able to have some proper repairs completed.

Yard workers began working on the ship immediately. Their focus was to repair the underwater hole in the hull from the near miss and rebuild the steering gear. The extended port stay was the first time since the start of the war that the *Marblehead* sailors could relax from the state of readiness required by the wartime conditions. Many of the crew went ashore on liberty during the time in drydock. The American visitors found the local people to be friendly – and the girls plentiful. More than a dozen were married. However, some honeymoons were cut short when the ship eventually departed.[24]

The war had been almost nonstop for the *Marblehead* sailors. Her lookouts had spent months constantly scanning the horizon for any sign of the enemy. Anti-aircraft batteries were partially or fully manned during most daylight hours. The crew was called to general quarters every day just before dawn. The standard practice took place whenever at sea to have the ship ready in case of a surprise attack. The port stay was greatly appreciated by all aboard.

There was still some work for the crew to do aboard ship. 'With the hold of the ship dry, the ship's force concentrated in cleaning up debris and dirt, and removing oil and water from the bilges and pockets,' Captain Robinson explained. 'The forward hold was thoroughly washed out and vented.'[25]

The stay at Simon's Town ended for the *Marblehead* men on April 15. She departed for Brazil after spending more than three weeks in the South African port. The repair work was completed on her hull. The steering gear allowed for a stability and maneuverability not experienced since before the air attack back on February 4.

The *Marblehead* sailors went to sea with a new level of confidence about their vessel. 'When we left there our principal worries had been taken care of,' Van Bergen recalled. While the repairs were not permanent fixes, it was enough for the warship to complete her trip back to the United Sates without great fear of sinking from her battle damage. 'Strength was built into our ship at Simon's Town. Our stern was covered permanently, the leaks forward were stopped … a fairly sound ship, but not one quite ready for action.'[26]

The month of April is winter in the southern hemisphere. The ship was plodding through the cold and choppy waters of the South Atlantic – far different from the tropical climate her crew had grown accustomed to. Lookouts again scanned the horizon for enemy vessels – the main threat was now German submarines. The underwater raiders were prowling all over the Atlantic in search of merchant ships to sink.

The voyage to Brazil was uneventful. She arrived at Recife on April 23. The port city was in the State of Pernambuco, an area of Brazil jutting eastward into the Atlantic. Among the American ships present in the harbor area was *Marblehead*'s sister ship *Milwaukee*. Sailors aboard the latter ship initially challenged her approaching sister, fearing an enemy ruse amid the various Japanese reports of *Marblehead*'s sinking.[27] The commanding officer of *Milwaukee* and the American consul came aboard for a visit shortly after her arrival.[28]

The visit was nothing more than a short fuel stop. However, some time was also spent rigging an improvised depth charge rack for the ship at the insistence of Captain Robinson.[29] The final leg of *Marblehead*'s voyage to New York was to take the ship through North Atlantic waters considered extremely dangerous due to German U-boats. The submarines were taking the war to the very edge of United States East Coast. Although Captain Robinson likely had no way of knowing the count, U-boats had sunk more than 100 ships in the waters between Brazil and New York since the start of the year.[30]

The light cruiser was sailing without escort and she was not equipped with any type of sonar or underwater sound gear. Locating submarines not on the surface would be difficult to near impossible. The depth charges may have provided piece of mind for the *Marblehead* sailors, but the weapons offered no real protection without a way to find the underwater boats. Robinson sailed his ship out of Recife knowing his path north was filled with reported locations of U-boats.

The light cruiser zig-zagged at regular intervals as she plodded north. The voyage to New York passed without incident. The morning hours of May 4 found *Marblehead* approaching the Lower Bay with lookouts sighting the entrance buoy at 8.05 am.[31] The body of water wedges into the mainland of the United States, separating New Jersey and New York. The area served as the entrance channel for large port facilities in both states. It was heavily patrolled by ships of all types and airplanes. She passed through the submarines net entrance and dropped anchor in Gravesend Bay about an hour later. The small indentation of water separates the southern part of Brooklyn from adjacent Staten Island.

The warship remained anchored for much of the day while awaiting the short final voyage to the Brooklyn Navy Yard. Looking out at the United States mainland was something the *Marblehead* sailors could only have dreamed of while on the front lines of the Pacific. What only a few short months ago seemed like an impossible dream became a reality.

Chapter 32

The New York City skyline loomed in the distance across the East River as *Marblehead* eased next to a dock in the Brooklyn Navy Yard during the late afternoon of May 4, 1942. By 5.31 pm she was firmly tied to the port side of Pier B-2 with a variety of wires and ropes holding her firmly in place.[1] The yard was rich with American naval history since its formal establishment in 1801. The location was the building site of some of America's most famous warships, including the Civil War Ironclad *Monitor* and sunken battleship *Arizona*.[2]

The yard was a hub of activity with piers, drydocks, and buildings of all shapes and sizes. Workers were busy building new ships and repairing or refitting older ones. Captain Robinson could see a variety of warships from his position on the bridge, including the heavy cruiser *Quincy*, light cruiser *Philadelphia*, and various modern destroyers. The massive 45,000-ton battleships *Iowa* and *Missouri* were under construction nearby.

The battered *Marblehead* had sailed across the world – nearly 13,000 miles – to arrive there. The yard would become her home for the next five months. An old friend in the form of Admiral Hart came aboard the ship for a visit on the afternoon of May 5. He stayed on *Marblehead* for almost an hour.[3] The admiral was not yet retired and still on active duty.

Boatswain's mate Second Class Robert Wesley was among the many happy sailors who could not wait to set foot on American soil. He called home to Chicago after arriving in Brooklyn. 'I'm fine, Dad,' Wesley said on the phone. 'Never felt better. I'm hoping to get a furlough so that I can come home for a visit.'[4] Plenty of *Marblehead* crewmen eventually went home on leave or transferred to other assignments during the long stretch of time at the yard.

Much of the warship's time at the Brooklyn Navy Yard was spent in drydock. She underwent an extensive refit, with an array of new armaments and equipment added, in addition to repairing battle damage. Among the structural changes made was the construction of a new deck house built between the forward and after pairs of funnels and the addition of splinter shields around the three-guns to provide a layer of protection for the gun crews. Extensive upgrades were made to anti-aircraft weaponry with the addition of 20- and 40-millimeter guns; the latter were given a separate fire control system.[5] Radar was added for the first time. The additions could not change the top-heavy design of the light cruiser. The seldom-used torpedo tubes were removed to save on weight.

***

The struggle to save *Marblehead* from sinking and her subsequent long voyage home had all but consumed the sailors aboard the stricken ship during the recent months. However, other than scant pieces of information, such as Japanese radio broadcasts claiming her sinking, the American public knew very little about what happened to the warship or of the miraculous escape made by Doctor Wassell and his wounded men from Java. That all changed during a radio address by President Roosevelt on April 28, 1942.

Roosevelt began a series of periodic evening radio addresses early in his administration. These 'fireside chats', as the broadcasts became known, continued through the depths of the Great Depression and into World War II. His voice was familiar to millions of Americans.

Much of the April 28 radio address was an update on the war effort and a review of domestic economic policies related to the conflict. 'I should like to tell you one or two stories about the men we have in our armed forces,' Roosevelt said in changing topics. He introduced Dr Corydon Wassell, a name likely unknown to most Americans, and told of his mission to oversee the wounded sailors of *Marblehead* and *Houston* on Java. 'When the Japanese advanced across the island, it was decided to evacuate as many as possible of the wounded to Australia,' Roosevelt continued. 'But about twelve of the men were so badly wounded that they couldn't be moved. Dr Wassell remained with them, knowing that he would be captured by the enemy. But he decided to make a last desperate attempt to get the men out of Java.'[6]

The remaining part of story was explained on a high level. Although somewhat embellished and not wholly accurate, it was the first time the American public heard about the daring escape led by Wassell. The short passage provided a small bit of good news from the otherwise bleak Pacific front. With *Marblehead* still at sea, approaching the East Coast from Brazil, her sailors likely had no idea of what became of their wounded shipmates left behind on Java. It is unclear if her sailors heard the broadcast live.

Naval authorities released information about what happened to *Marblehead* once she was safely back in the United States. A navy press release for the first time told the complete story of the damaged warship and her miraculous return to New York. The navy provided a short history of *Marblehead*'s war activities, involvement in the Balikpapan Raid, the air attack in the Flores Sea, heroic effort to keep her from sinking, and voyage back to the United States. Major newspapers around the country carried the story, often on the front page, using direct quotes from the navy as an important feature of the article. Some included a file picture of the ship and map of her travels.[7] The stories often ended with some praise for the men aboard. 'These hits turned this once sleek fighting ship into a shambles of wreckage – a wreck, nevertheless, which the hard-headed seamen of the *Marblehead* persisted in navigating over half of the world's ocean ways,' noted the *New York Times*.[8]

Captain Robinson met with reporters in a *Marblehead* cabin on May 8 in the aftermath of the navy press release. Other crew members stood in the background as he spoke candidly about the events of the previous three months. The talk took place with the backdrop of construction noises from the yard workers busy laboring on the ship. 'I was on the bridge when the attack came. We were on an offensive mission,' he explained in starting the story with the air attack.[9] He then told of the bomb hits, losing control of steering, the desperate struggle to keep *Marblehead* from sinking, and of limping into Tjilatjap. The captain also recounted the highlights of the long voyage home.

Robinson spoke of several sailors by name, including Nicholas Van Bergen, Martin Drury, and Harvey Anderson, and how they helped save the boat. 'Van Bergen was everywhere, down aft pulling men out of the oil and water; helping me on the bridge; reporting on the condition of the ship – without regard for his personal safety,' Robinson said. He spoke of damage control officer Drury as 'a tower of strength'. The talk continued with the captain naming a long list of sailors whose action helped save the ship. However, time did not allow for their individual stories to be told. 'All reacted perfectly, they were marvelous; they had things to do and did them,' Robinson stated.

His final comments were aimed towards the public. 'The safe return of the *Marblehead* is a tribute to the courage, stamina, and resourcefulness of the American officer and bluejacket, and to the rigid technical training which prepared him for the demands of war,' Robinson said. 'The people of this country can well be proud as I am of the courage and accomplishments of the *Marblehead*'s crew.'

The *Marblehead* saga was the topic of two books, each covering a different aspect of the story, published during the next two years. Shortly after Doctor Wassell's return to the United States in the summer of 1942, popular American filmmaker Cecil B. DeMille commissioned an author to write the story in the form of a book.[10] The writer was none other than acclaimed British novelist James Hilton. Now a resident of the United States, Hilton was famous the world over for numerous books, including the international best seller *Lost Horizon*.

Hilton completed the project in an astounding eleven weeks after spending several days with Wassell, talking to his friends and family, and interviewing some of the other *Marblehead* sailors.[11] *The Story of Dr Wassell* was released by Little, Brown & Company in 1943. Although the names of the sailors were changed, it was based on the true events and reads somewhat like an action story of fiction. The book was well received by the public and sales were strong.

The movie maker DeMille, who was captivated about the Wassell story after hearing President Roosevelt's radio address, turned the book into a movie of the same name. Popular actor Gary Cooper was tapped to play the role of Doctor Wassell. The movie was filmed, in color and utilizing great special effects, over a ninety-five day schedule with much of the location work done in Mexico.

The goal of bringing *The Story of Dr Wassell* to the big screen, as with any motion picture, was to sell tickets. A fictional romantic sub-plot was added to the story to make it more inviting. The film was heavily promoted by Hollywood publicity people. 'The reason the story is great and different [is that] while it is war, it isn't a question of killing; it's a story of life saving rather than life taking,' DeMille said at the time.[12] Doctor Wassell felt the overall story line was largely kept true to actual events. 'I will shock you when I tell you that the picture is ninety-eight per cent true,' he said in a 1944 speech.[13]

The movie premiered with high acclaim in New York City on June 6, 1944, the same day Allied forces were landing in France. The nationwide release took place on July 4. However, film critics gave the movie mixed reviews.[14] The movie earned an Oscar nomination for best special effects.[15]

Wassell was heavily involved in the movie project while stationed in California and was paid for his work. 'The most trying period in my life was the thirty-one months I spent with Cecil B. DeMille,' he later recalled of the period of making and promoting the film.[16] Wassell did not keep the money he earned while working on the movie. He instead donated the funds to various institutions helping the deaf and blind in Arkansas.[17]

The second book about the *Marblehead* saga focused on the ship's war career in the Pacific, including the air attack in the Flores Sea, struggle to save the ship, and long voyage back to the United States. Released in 1944, *Where Away: A Modern Odyssey* was a collaboration between authors George Sessions Perry and Isabel Leighton. Perry was a popular magazine contributor and war correspondent, while Leighton was an actress turned author.

Based on a variety of first-hand accounts from *Marblehead* sailors, *Where Away* is told largely from the perspective of her sailors. The story is filled with vivid first-person accounts of events and gives readers insights into some of the sailors aboard the ship. However, as with many wartime books, some of the overall battle and background details are inaccurate. Coast Guard artist John J. Floherty contributed sketches of the officers and enlisted men to illustrate various scenes throughout the story. War correspondent Foster Hailey, in a review published in the *New York Times*, wrote 'it is a record of a gallant ship's company raggedly but often times brilliantly told'.[18]

***

A variety of medals were awarded, related to the *Marblehead* saga, by the navy during the months the warship spent under repair in the Brooklyn Navy Yard. Military awards are given at the unit and individual level. The warship was awarded the Navy Unit Commendation for her activities in the Dutch East Indies. Every sailor who was aboard during the span of time received the commendation in the form of a ribbon.

The Navy Cross represents the second highest military decoration that can be awarded to an individual member of the United States Navy – only the Medal of Honor ranks higher – for extraordinary heroism during action.[19] Numerous officers and enlisted men were given the award for their actions aboard *Marblehead*. Secretary of the Navy Frank Knox gave the Navy Cross to Captain Robinson during a ceremony held in Washington on May 14, 1942. 'The excellent seamanship displayed by Captain Robinson, combined with the highest actions of his well-trained officers and crew, resulted in saving his badly damaged and crippled ship,' the citation read in part.[20] Three other officers later received the same award – Nicholas Van Bergen, Martin Drury, and Harvey Anderson.

Doctor Cordon Wassell received the Navy Cross for his actions 'in caring for and evacuating the wounded of the U.S. Navy under his charge in Java'.[21] Always known to be a modest person, he later deflected the credit to his men. 'I was given a Navy Cross for bringing those boys out, but I want to tell you that Navy Cross belongs to those boys and I will wear it for them,' Wassell later told an audience during a speech.[22]

A total of eight Navy Crosses were awarded at a ceremony held at the Brooklyn Navy Yard on August 8, 1942. The recipients included two officers – Drury and Anderson – and six enlisted men. The medals were presented by Rear Admiral E.J. Marquart, commandant of the yard and commander of the Third Naval District. An assortment of naval officers, enlisted men, and several thousand shipyard workers were on hand for the event.

Claude Becker was among the enlisted sailors to have previously received the award from the admiral. He was 24 years old and came from Ogden, Utah. Marquart read the citation aloud recounting how Becker pried open a burning hot hatch, allowing trapped men to escape and assisted in removing gunpowder bags from a burning compartment. 'Your brave deed gives inspiration to us all. My heartfelt congratulations,' Marquart added. 'I wouldn't mind being out there again,' Becker commented to reporters. 'I'm getting tired out of it here.'[23] The six other enlisted men were: Chief Boatswain's mate Herman Hook, Chief Shipfitter Hale McCully, Metalsmith First Class Martin Moran, Machinist's Mate First Class Dale Johnson, Quartermaster Second Class Lester Barre, and Chief Electrician's Mate Frederic Ritter.[24] Each played an important role in saving the ship.

Nicholas Van Bergen was the last to receive the Navy Cross. He was decorated by Frank Knox in late October. The ceremony was held at the Navy Department in Washington.[25] William Goggins was the recipient of the Purple Heart. The medal is awarded by the president to service members wounded in battle.

***

Members of the engineering crew started lighting fires under *Marblehead*'s boilers at the early hour of 6.00 am on October 15, 1942. About an hour later she was underway for the open ocean.[26] The voyage off New York marked the beginning of the end to the warship's long stay in the Brooklyn Navy Yard. Among the first actions undertaken at sea was to test her new anti-aircraft guns – one round from each gun was fired. A variety of drills and training was conducted throughout the day, including a fire drill, loading ammunition, and a collision drill.

The newly repaired *Marblehead* was ready for a return to the war. She would, however, never again venture to the Pacific front. Although greatly modernized, she was still smaller and much less powerful then the new light cruisers rolling out of shipyards across the United States. The modern warships, with advanced radar-controlled gunnery, were largely handling the frontline duties where much of the fierce fighting was taking place. The older ships were delegated to commands of lesser prominence.

Her first assignment was to the South Atlantic area. Although the threat of German naval activity was much lower than earlier in the war, Allied warships and aircraft maintained regular patrols to protect the vital trade routes between North America, Europe, and Asia. The light cruiser operated out of ports in Brazil, undertaking routine and sometimes monotonous patrols, until February 1944.

The warship returned to New York on February 20, 1944.[27] She subsequently patrolled the North Atlantic convoy routes between North America and Europe. The next assignment took *Marblehead* to the Mediterranean. She arrived in Palermo, Italy, on July 29 and joined in preparations for the Allied invasion of southern France. The light cruiser provided gunfire support for troops landing near Saint Raphael on August 16 and 17 before retiring to Corsica.

The war for *Marblehead* was largely over. She returned to the United States after the completion of the operations off France. The warship's final duty was to conduct a summer training cruise for midshipmen at the Naval Academy. The annual event gave young men studying to be future naval officers some practical shipboard experience.

The final voyage for the gallant warship was to the Philadelphia Naval Shipyard. She was decommissioned on November 1, 1945 and struck from the Navy Register later in the month. The venerable old *Marblehead,* caught on the front lines during the opening days of World War II in the Pacific, badly damaged by Japanese bombs, and whose crew fought courageously to keep her afloat and ultimately bring her back to the United States, was scrapped on February 27, 1946.

Chapter 33

Many of the officers and enlisted men who played critical roles in the *Marblehead* story went separate ways after the warship returned to the United States. When the newly repaired and modernized *Marblehead* returned to the war in late 1942, she was heavily staffed by new sailors. The navy experienced a great influx of men in the months after the attack on Pearl Harbor. Many of the new crewmembers aboard *Marblehead* had entered the service after the light cruiser made her return to New York.[1]

A trio of *Marblehead*'s top officers, starting with Captain Robinson, went on to other duties. His time aboard the ship came to an end while the repair work at the Brooklyn Navy Yard was still in progress. He was appointed the commander of all forces in the Aruba-Curacao area of the Caribbean in June 1942.[2] As with many parts of the Atlantic, the region was under fierce attack by German U-boats. No less than seventy-two merchant ships had been sunk in the general area since the start of the year.[3] Robinson's command was expanded to include adjacent ocean areas in April 1943. He was promoted to the rank of rear admiral.

Robinson transferred back to the United States to serve as the president of the Board of Inspection and Survey when his duty in the Caribbean ended in the Spring of 1944. He traveled across the Atlantic in March of 1945 to assume command of U.S. Naval Ports and Bases, Germany, also known as Task Force 126. The war in Europe was in its final months with Allied ground forces closing in on Berlin from the east and west. At the end of the war Robinson accepted the surrender of the German naval commander in the Wesermude area of Germany. He was involved in the operation to clear heavily mined channels and rivers that were needed to supply American occupation troops.[4] He later directed the disarmament of the German Navy in the Bremen area; the northern German city was not far from the North Sea.

Robinson returned to the United States in November 1945. Post-war duties included time in the Pacific, with involvement in the trials of Japanese war criminals, and administrative positions back in Washington. He retired from the navy with the rank of vice admiral on June 30, 1951.[5] The admiral amassed a lengthy list of medals and commendations for service in both world wars. He spent his later years in Pacific Palisades, California. Arthur Robinson passed away in September of 1967.

Commander William Goggins did not stay long in Freemantle after his arrival in March 1942. Doctor Wassell's unwavering efforts to find a way out of Java ahead of the invading Japanese put the *Marblehead* officer and a small group of wounded sailors aboard the inter-island steam *Janssens* for the daring voyage to Australia. 'I remained there for about ten days and was put on the *West Point* with a number of other officers who were returning to the States, and arrived in San Francisco without further incident on the 24th of April and went to the Mare Island Hospital,' he later said.[6]

The wounded officer later went to Coronado, near San Diego, for further recuperation. He spoke to a newspaper reporter about his experiences in the Pacific during his stay. 'It is a very helpless feeling to be on a surface ship with the sky full of enemy aircraft on a clear day when there are no helping airplanes to be seen,' he explained about the attack endured by *Marblehead*. Goggins spoke with great praise about Doctor Wassell's activities on Java. 'No matter what new or unforeseen difficulties would arise, Comm. Wassell always seemed to have something in reserve.'[7]

Goggins eventually recovered from his wounds. He spent a brief amount of time aboard the oiler *Ramapo*, before a shore assignment in intelligence. Goggins was the officer in charge of a radio intelligence unit in the Pacific area from October 1942 to January 1945. After completing the long stretch of land duty, and now holding the rank of captain, Goggins assumed command of the battleship *Alabama* on January 18, 1945, while she was undergoing an overhaul at the Puget Sound Navy Yard near Seattle.[8] The veteran ship held a long battle record, serving throughout the Pacific and participating in naval operations around the Marianas and Philippines.

The battleship returned to the war zone in May after the completion of the refit work and training exercises. The final months of the war were spent supporting operations around Okinawa and the Japanese home islands. The operations in Japanese home waters included a devastating bombardment, delivered by her massive 16-inch guns, of industrial facilities north of Tokyo where the battleship delivered more than 500 tones worth of explosives to demolish the assigned targets.[9]

Goggins returned to the United States after the war in January 1946. His post-war assignments were all administrative in nature, including time as the commanding officer of the Naval Administrative Command of the Central Intelligence Group in Washington. The unit was a forerunner of the modern day Central Intelligence Agency.[10] He retired as a rear admiral on June 30, 1949. His long list of medals included the Purple Heart, Navy Unit Commendation, Legion of Merit, and the Gold Star.

In addition to spending time with his family, the officer's retirement years included research at John Hopkins University and time at the Army Research Center. Goggins also operated his own computer and communications company, General Kinetics Institute. William Goggin died on December 27, 1985. He was a resident of Arlington, Virginia, at the time of his passing.

Nicholas Van Bergen was awarded the Navy Cross for his actions during the struggle to save the warship in the Pacific after *Marblehead*'s return to the United States. 'His tireless energy in performing these duties coupled with his complete disregard for his own safety were outstanding factors in saving of the ship for further war service and in saving the lives of many of those on board,' the citation read in part.[11] Like Captain Robinson, his time aboard *Marblehead* came to an end while she was at the Brooklyn Navy Yard.

Van Bergen reported to the Bureau of Naval Personnel in Washington on June 23, 1942 to begin a series of shore appointments. He was promoted to the rank of captain less than a year later and spent time at the Amphibious Fleet Training Command in California. The officer returned to sea duty when he assumed command of *Clay* on August 9, 1944. The navy transport departed Pearl Harbor loaded with soldiers for a long voyage across the Pacific. She participated in the invasion of Leyte, Philippines, several months later. Van Bergen remained in the Pacific for almost a full year as *Clay* shuttled between moving troops to the front lines and transporting the wounded to rear areas.

The captain was relieved of his duties aboard *Clay* on July 15, 1945 and sent for treatment to the Naval Hospital in Oakland, California.

Van Bergen was suffering from a chronic lung disease, possibly from the injuries he sustained when inhaling noxious gas while aboard *Marblehead*.[12] He assumed a teaching position at the Naval Reserve Officers Training program at the University of Colorado in September 1945. He was advanced to the rank of rear admiral upon his retirement from the navy on January 1, 1947. Nicholas Van Bergen died on May 3, 1947 at the Naval Hospital in Oakland.[13] He was less than a month away from turning 48 years old.

***

Admiral Thomas Hart's orders sent *Marblehead* on the long journey back to the United States, saving the ship from certain destruction had she stayed on the front lines. His removal from the ABDA naval command was bittersweet. He headed back to the United Sates knowing he did the best he possibly could under the difficult circumstances of trying to stop the Japanese onslaught with mostly old and outdated warships. 'It's all on the laps of the gods and, whatever happens, I don't now see any forks over the long road back there [where] I feel that I took the wrong turn,' he philosophically wrote in his diary.[14]

Admiral Hart was in full dress uniform when he visited the White House on May 22 to receive a Gold Star medal from President Roosevelt. Navy Secretary Frank Knox and Chief of Naval Operations Admiral Ernest King looked on as Roosevelt spoke of the admiral's 'unfailing judgement and sound decision making' during his time in the Pacific. The President noted Hart's 'marked moral courage in the face of discouraging surroundings and complex associations'.[15]

Although transferred to the retired list in July 1942, Hart remained on active duty serving on the Navy General Board into 1944. The advisory body was typically staffed by senior officers, many near retirement. The admiral spent much of 1944 conducting a one-man inquiry on the Pearl Harbor attack. The Navy Department ordered the 'Hart Inquiry' to secure important testimony from participants who might perish in the war.[16] The project took him across the Pacific.

Hart officially retired from the Navy on February 9, 1945. He was appointed to the United States Senate to fill the remaining term of an open seat in his home state of Connecticut. He served in the capacity until January 3 1947, did not seek re-election, and moved to his family home in Sharon, Connecticut. Thomas Hart died on 4 July 1971 at the age of 94.[17]

***

Doctor Corydon Wassell spent some time in Australia after arriving in Freemantle with his wounded men aboard *Janssens*. He later recalled the lack of defenses in the area, saying 'one cruiser and two transports of soldiers could have come in and taken the whole of West Australia in no time. We had nothing there.'[18]

The doctor encountered Admiral Glassford shortly after arriving in Freemantle. The pair had not seen each other since their brief encounter back in Surabaya. The admiral was profoundly struck when he heard the story of Wassell's escape from Java. He later wrote:

> A war epic it seemed to me of magnificent conduct throughout by an apparently insignificant but deeply religious man, who rose to the height of courage, self-effacement, and devotion to duty and to his fellow man in emulation of the Christ himself. I recall being deeply moved by his simple story; it all seemed so incredibly fine, it was difficult to grasp that such decency and goodness was in any man – he apparently was completely unaware that he had done anything out of the ordinary.[19]

Glassford's stay in Australia was short. He returned stateside, but the vivid memory of the story remained with him. 'Later in Washington soon after coming home, the Secretary to the President called me by telephone asking for illuminating stories or episodes which might be included in the President's fireside talk, scheduled to be broadcast that same evening.' The admiral's passing along the story ultimately led to the world knowing about Doctor Wassell's great escape.

Wassell was still stationed in Freemantle at the time of President Roosevelt's radio talk and did not hear the broadcast. He said later:

> We had a nice party that night, but we always had a rule that we were to break up between 12.30 and 1.00 because we

had to work the next day. My first trip in the morning from the home was to the Hollywood Hospital and my next was the medical storehouse. I had the only naval storehouse in Australia at that time for the United States Navy.

An enlisted man approached Wassell upon his arrival at the hospital asking if he had heard the president talk about him the night before. He dismissed it as a joke. Wassell arrived at the storehouse later in the day to find many people staring at him. He only began to believe it was true when a trusted subordinate, a woman named Grace, came running to him asking about the president's speech. She was holding a copy of the local newspaper – the *Perth Gazette*. 'That is the way I got the news that the president talked about me.'

Wassell was assigned to the Naval Operating base in San Pedro, California, after his return to the United States in June of 1942. He remained there until June 26, 1944 when he transferred to nearby Los Angeles as Assistant Director of Public relations – West Coast.[20] His time in Los Angeles included work on the movie production about his escape from Java. His final duty was at the Naval Training center in Miami before retiring at the rank of rear admiral. Corydon Wassell died in Little Rock, Arkansas on May 12, 1958 at the age of 74 and is buried in Arlington National Cemetery.

***

Thousands of Allied soldiers, sailors, and airmen became Japanese prisoners after the fall of Java. Among the Americans was *Marblehead* sailor Benjamin Hopkins, part of Doctor Wassell's small group of wounded men making the trek to Tjilatjap with the convoy of British soldiers. His injuries were just too painful to endure the bumpy truck ride and he decided to stay behind at a tea break. 'I just couldn't make it,' he later said in summing up the situation.[21]

The British sent Hopkins back to the hospital in Jogjakarta. The Japanese were approaching fast. A doctor put Hopkins and a Dutch officer – the only military patients left at the hospital – into the sidecar of his motorcycle and sped away. However, they found a car – a better form of transportation – and returned to get another doctor and a nurse named Teramina. The group soon upgraded to an even better car. The explosion from a mortar shell killed Teramina and damaged the vehicle on March 9. Hopkins surrendered at Tasikmalaya, in western Java, during the middle of the month.

Like many of the servicemen taken prisoner on Java, Hopkins was eventually moved off the island. He was initially sent to Singapore in early November, before departing in a 'hell ship' for Japan arriving on December 7, 1942. He labored for the rest of the war under brutal conditions. Hopkins was initially assigned to a shipyard in Nagasaki and later sent to a coal mine in Orio.

His parents back in Plattsmouth, Nebraska, initially knew little about his whereabouts or fate. Then in late December of 1942 his voice was heard over the radio in a broadcast emanating from a prisoner camp somewhere in the Pacific. More than a year later he was heard again. The second time his family received a transcript from officials in Washington. 'Hello, mother and dad. I'm in very good health and living comfortably,' the message began.[22] It was clearly a Japanese propaganda ruse, as Hopkins and the other prisoners in Japan were enduring ruthless treatment at the hands of their captors. The isolated prisoners knew little about the progress of the war. They grasped the United States was winning when the American B-29 bombers began appearing overhead.

Benjamin Hopkins was liberated from Fukuoka PoW Camp #1 – Kashii (Pine Tree Camp) on Kyushu Island shortly after the end of the war.[23] He boarded the aircraft carrier *Lunga Point* at Nagasaki for the short trip south to Okinawa. The former prisoner subsequently joined hundreds of other servicemen aboard the hospital ship *Rixey* for a voyage to Guam. His eventual return to the United States perhaps marked the last *Marblehead* sailor to make it home from the Pacific front.

Epilogue

An Enduring Mystery – Who Helped Doctor Wassell?

Doctor Corydon Wassell's intrepid escape from Java in early March 1942 remains a little-known story from World War II in the Pacific. He was steadfast in his determination to find a way to get his wounded sailors off the doomed island ahead of the advancing Japanese. Ultimately, the biggest reason for the successful escape came down to one key individual and that was Corydon Wassell. The doctor, however, could not have accomplished such a feat alone.

The supporting cast was large and included many people whose roles were well established. The parts played by others were less well-known, and in some cases, remain somewhat unclear. The escape clearly could not have been possible had it not been for the Dutch medical staff at the Petronella Hospital. The dedicated effort of the doctors and nurses allowed the patients to become well enough to be moved, even if some could not walk.

The importance of the decision by Lieutenant Commander Gerrit Prass to allow Doctor Wassell's wounded sailors aboard his ship *Janssens*, when the captains of numerous other vessels refused, cannot be understated. The departure of the small steamer from Tjilatjap on March 3 was not a day too soon. She was one of the last vessels to escape and left behind a harbor crowded with ships and thousands of desperate people waiting ashore, trying to get away. Japanese planes delivered a devastating attack on Tjilatjap one day later. Eighteen Betty bombers escorted by ten Zero fighters attacked ships and harbor facilities, causing extensive damage to the latter and hitting at least five ships.[1]

A larger attack took place on March 5 from carrier and land-based planes, followed by a heavy bombardment from two Japanese battleships. The port area suffered extensive damage. The result was a long list of ships lost at Tjilatjap after the Dutch surrender. The list represented all types of vessels, including tankers, cargo ships, and tugs. Some were sunk outright, while others were heavily damaged or scuttled. The losses totaled 21,639 tons of shipping.[2]

Doctor Wassell likely received some help from Captain Lester Hudson in Tjilatjap. The American naval officer remained at the small port office even after Admiral Glassford, his immediate staff, and most other U.S. Navy personnel departed. Historian Samuel Eliot Morison noted Hudson 'did wonders evacuating the wounded and able-bodied by submarine or small Dutch merchantman'.[3] Hudson may have directed Wassell to *Janssens*, but the actual extent of his help remains largely unknown. The officer was among the last Americans to leave Java and successfully escaped to Australia.

The details of the final departure from Tjilatjap aside, Wassell and his remaining wounded sailors would not likely have made it to the port city had it not been for the help of the British soldiers who facilitated the transportation. It was nothing more than a chance encounter. Doctor Wassell ventured out to a local hotel in Jogjakarta in the middle of the night after hearing of the Japanese landings on Java. He came across a convoy of British soldiers heading for Tjilatjap. In *The Story of Doctor Wassell*, James Hilton writes of Wassell encountering 'the foremost vehicles of an apparently endless British convoy'.[4] Wassell spoke to a British Army officer who was thereafter referred to as a captain. The officer agreed to let Wassell's sailors join the convoy and the men were soon on the way to Tjilatjap.

Both *Marblehead* officer William Goggins, in his interview about time aboard the light cruiser and the events of Java, and the sailors interviewed for the 1945 article in *Our Navy*, identify the British soldiers as members of a mobile anti-aircraft unit. Goggins recalled Dr Wassell having 'persuaded the captain of this battery to take us with him down to Tjilatjap', and identifies March 2 as the date the American sailors joined the British convoy.[5] The American sailors subsequently traveled with the soldiers to the port city. Enduring questions remain about the encounter – who was the British officer and what unit did he represent?

About 5,500 British servicemen were on Java during the last days of Dutch rule. The men were under the command of British Major General Hervey Sitwell.[6] The majority were army soldiers, including various anti-aircraft units and a light tank regiment. A limited number of Royal

Air Force personnel were also on the island. The British servicemen were a mix of some stragglers who came from Singapore via Sumatra, and others who arrived directly to the island as reinforcements. The soldiers who assisted Doctor Wassell were most likely in the latter group.

After departing the United Kingdom on December 6, 1942 bound for the Middle East, the British soldiers crammed aboard Convoy WS14 likely did not expect their destination to be Java. The departure corresponded – almost to the day – with the Pacific erupting into war and Japanese troops landings in Malaya. The large convoy was heavily escorted as it sailed south through waters infested with German submarines. Ground forces of the British Empire were locked in desperate combat with Germans and Italians in North Africa. It was common for reinforcements to be sent the long way around the bottom of Africa and up through the Suez Canal rather than traversing the dangerous waters of the Mediterranean Sea.

Among the servicemen packed aboard the ships were a large contingent of Royal Air Force personnel and some anti-aircraft units. British anti-aircraft artillery underwent a great expansion in the late 1930s as World War II in Europe drew near. New weapons were introduced to better combat the perceived threat from German aircraft. All units were classified as heavy (HAA) or light (LAA) units, given a regimental number, and put under the command of a brigadier general.[7] The anti-aircraft soldiers were commonly referred to as 'gunners' among the British military establishment. The typical British Army regiment spanned 500 to 1,000 men.[8]

Each regiment was comprised of a series of batteries or groups of anti-aircraft guns, along with trucks and equipment for support and transportation. A troop consisted of four to six individual guns and the associated crew and support personnel. Two or more troops together with a headquarters group (under the command of a major) combined to make a battery.[9] Two of the anti-aircraft units making the long voyage from England would end up on the island of Java.

The 77th HAA originated in Wales, a member nation of the United Kingdom, bordered on the east by England, and by the Irish Sea to the north and west. By late 1941 the unit was comprised of 239, 240 men, and 241 batteries under the leadership of Lieutenant Colonel H.R. Humphries. As a heavy anti-aircraft unit, the regiment was equipped with twenty-four 3.7-inch guns.[10]

The 21st LAA came from the city of Chester in the north-west of England, and close to the Welsh border. The outfit included the 48, 69, and 79 batteries equipped with 40-millimeter Bofors guns.[11] The unit was under the command of Lieutenant-Colonel M.D.S. Saunders. Both regiments were combat veterans, having participated in the defense of England during the relentless German air attacks of the Battle of Britain.

The convoy made stops at Freetown, on the West Coast of Africa, and in Durban, South Africa. The changing war situation caused a portion of the convoy to be redirected to the Far East in late January. Some ships were sent to Singapore, then under Japanese attack. The 77th HAA and 21st LAA regiments were headed to Java. The long voyage across the Indian Ocean ended at Batavia when the troop ships *Empress of Australia*, *Warwick Castle*, and other merchantmen arrived on February 4.[12]

No formal British Army unit war dairies survived the Java campaign. Exact dates, operational details, and precise movements are difficult to ascertain with a high degree of certainty. Reports written from memory after the war, and soldiers' recollections fill the narrative of the little-known, and somewhat forgotten, episode in British military history.

The fortress Singapore surrendered just two weeks after the anti-aircraft units arrived in Batavia. The Japanese quickly invaded Sumatra while simultaneously closing in on Java. The role of the anti-aircraft units took on great importance with the enemy having almost complete control of the sky. The British soldiers ventured inland shortly after their arrival on the island. Additional anti-aircraft units later arrived from Singapore and Sumatra without their guns and equipment. Depleted in numbers, many of these soldiers were employed in an infantry role to help defend airfields.[13]

Most of the 77th HAA Regiment was sent east to Surabaya by road and rail. Disaster struck the part of the unit was moving by rail when a train carrying the British soldiers collided with an ammunition train while crossing a ravine during the early hours of February 6; the trains were both traveling on a single track. The accident occurred less than sixty miles from Surabaya, killing about thirty soldiers and injuring nearly a hundred others.[14] Two batteries of the 21st LAA Regiment deployed to eastern Java. The third, the 70th Battery, was sent east to the island of Timor to defend an airfield with local Dutch and Australian troops.[15]

The situation for the British soldiers drastically changed by the end of February. The ABDA Command was dissolved and General Wavell departed for India. General Sitwell became commander of all British troops on Java. The island was now isolated and under attack by air. Two batteries (240th and 241st) of the 77th HAA Regiment were in Surabaya and elements of the 21st LAA Regiment were defending airfields at Singosari, Moaspati, and Malang in eastern Java.

With the Japanese invasion pending, General Sitwell ordered some of the anti-aircraft units to move south to Tjilatjap on the night of February 28 – March 1.[16] The orders covered the 240th and 241st batteries (and regimental headquarters) of the 77th HAA Regiment and a smaller group of men (three troops) of the 21st LAA Regiment. The remainder of the latter unit was initially sent to Jogjakarta and later west to Tasikmalaya.

Multiple groups of British anti-aircraft soldiers were moving to Tjilatjap as Doctor Wassell was desperately trying to find a way for his small group of remaining wounded sailors to escape. More than 300 miles separates Surabaya from Tjilatjap. The best roads on Java during Dutch rule ran along coastal areas in the north and south. However, a period map of island reveals an interior road traversing the geography between the two port cities, passing either close, or through, Jogjakarta.[17] The route was almost certainly the one employed by the two batteries of 77th HAA Regiment.

The convoy joined by the American sailors was without a doubt (from the various descriptions) very large. William Goggins described it as 'a long train of trucks'. Hilton's writings, undoubtedly from information provided by Wassell, went further in describing it as 'some two hundred trucks, containing ack-ack guns, field kitchens, traveling repair shops – the whole outfit of a modern mechanized force'.[18] No mention is made of the types of anti-aircraft guns.

The information appears to correspond with the movements of a force the size of the two batteries of 77th HAA Regiment – even with depletions due to casualties. By the end of February, the two batteries and regimental headquarters numbered twenty-eight officers and 659 enlisted men operating sixteen guns.[19] Lieutenant Colonel Humphries was the senior officer of the unit making the move south.

Some insights on the road trip from Surabaya to Tjilatjap come from the diary of British soldier Les Spence. A member of the 77th HAA

Regiment on Java, Spence survived the train crash outside of Surabaya shortly after his arrival on the island. He kept a diary and his secret writings survived his time on Java and later as a Japanese prisoner. The materials were first published in 2012.

After enduring heavy Japanese bombing in the north, Spence departed for Tjilatjap on February 27. He noted only half of his battery started the journey, due to the rush evacuation, with the remainder moving out the next day. The soldiers likely had no illusions about being able to hold Java and were thinking they were going to be leaving the island. 'It looks as if we are making a dash for a boat to Australia,' he wrote at the time. 'I think the Japanese will soon take this island.'[20]

Spence clearly encountered Americans on the way south. 'A lot of Americans pass us on their way to Tjilatjap,' he recorded on February 28. The soldier's diary has his arrival in the port city taking place on March 1, making it too early to have been joined by Wassell's group as per the information contained in the Goggins interview. Could one of the two have recorded the wrong date? It is certainly possible, given the Goggins interview took place after the events and Spence was writing during the difficult conditions of moving across the island. Or were the Americans written about by Spence airmen making their way south for evacuation? His assertion of other British soldiers leaving for Tjilatjap after his group would have put those men in a better position to have crossed paths with Wassell.

The British soldiers did not board ships for Australia after arriving in Tjilatjap as Les Spence had hoped. They instead set up their anti-aircraft guns and defended the port against Japanese planes in the subsequent series of air attacks. The defense of Java rapidly fell apart as enemy troops advanced across the island, culminating with the Dutch surrender about a week after Spence arrived in Tjilatjap.

General Sitwell pondered over assembling the remaining British forces in the hills to continue fighting. However, he came to realize the situation was hopeless. The general did not want to risk potentially severe repercussions if his men were caught fighting after the formal Dutch surrender and reluctantly ordered all his men to lay down their arms.[21] As Doctor Wassell and those aboard *Janssens* slowly steamed towards Australia, the British anti-aircraft gunners back in Tjilatjap joined tens of thousands of Allied servicemen across the Malay Barrier as prisoners of the Japanese.

Many Allied prisoners were sent to camps near Batavia. Some of the British prisoners may have been taken to what became known as the 'Bicycle Camp' in the city. The prison camp was located at the former quarters of the Tenth Battalion Bicycle Force of the Netherlands East Indies Army. The conditions there were reasonably good for a Japanese prison – possibly the best the British PoWs would have for the remainder of the war – with running water, showers, and barracks with cement floors.[22]

Many of the men were later transferred to other locations and endured the most brutal conditions for the remainder of the war. Some were forced into slave labor working in Japan or building the infamous Burma-Thailand Railway (made famous in the book and movie *Bridge on the River Kwai*).[23] Les Spence was among those sent to Japan. He survived the war.

What British unit helped Doctor Wassell? I looked through various accounts about the British soldiers on Java, including books, diaries, webpages, and oral histories, searching for a smoking gun statement or a recollection. I did not find any account such as 'we helped some wounded American sailors get to Tjilatjap', or anything similar. Could it have been Lieutenant Colonel Humphries, who made the decision to let the American join his convoy? The answer may be out there somewhere, but I was not able to find anything definitive. My best guess is it was soldiers of the 77th HAA.

Bibliography

Books

Adcock, Al, *U.S. Light Cruisers in Action.* Carrollton, TX: Squadron Signal Publications, 1999.

Adcock, Al, *U.S. Navy Float Planes of World War II in Action* Carrollton, TX: Squadron Signal Publications, 2006.

Alford, Lodwick H., *Playing for Time: War on an Asiatic Fleet Destroyer* Bennington, VT: Merriam Press, 2008.

Anderson, Charles Robert, *East Indies* Washington, DC: U.S. Army Center of Military History, 1991.

Anderson, Irvine Henry, *The Standard-Vacuum Oil Company and United States East Asian Policy, 1933-1941* Princeton, NJ: Princeton University Press, 1975.

Bartsch, William, *Everyday a Nightmare: American Pursuit Pilots in the Defense of Java, 1941-1942.* College Station, TX: Texas A&M University Press, 2010.

Bell, Commander Frederick J., *Condition Red: Destroyer Action in the South Pacific* New York: Longmans, Green and Company, 1943.

Bertke, Donald A., Gordon Smith, and Don Kindell, *World War II Sea War, Vol 5: Air Raid Pearl Harbor. This Is Not a Drill (Volume 5)* Dayton, OH: Bertke Publications, 2013.

Bracken, John P., *From the Bridge of the U.S.S. Marblehead: November 25, 1941 – May 4, 1942* Privately Published, 1992.

Campbell, Hugh and Ron Lovell, *So Long, Singapore: Royal Air Force Auxiliary 'Tung Song,' December 1941-March 1942* Hobart, New Zealand: H. Campbell, 2000.

Campbell, John, *Naval Weapons of World War II* Annapolis, MD: Naval Institute Press, 1985.

Chesneau, Roger (ed), *Conway's All the World's Fighting Ships: 1922-1946* London: Conway Maritime Press, 1980.

Churchill, Winston, *Memoirs of the Second World War: An Abridgement of the Six Volumes of the Second World War* Boston: Houghton Mifflin, 1959.

Costello, John, *The Pacific War* New York: Rawson, Wade Publishers, Inc., 1981.

Cox, Jeffrey R., *Rising Sun, Falling Skies: The Disastrous Java Sea Campaign of World War II* Oxford, UK: Osprey Publishing, 2014.

Dull, Paul S., *A Battle History of the Imperial Japanese Navy* Annapolis, MD: Naval Institute Press, 1978.

Dunn, William J., *Pacific Microphone* College Station, TX: Texas A&M University Press, 1988.

Edmonds, Walter Dumaux, *They Fought with What They Had: The Story of the Army Air Forces in the Southwest Pacific, 1941-1942* Washington, DC: Center for Air Force History, 1992.

Edwards, Bernard, *Japan's Blitzkrieg: The Allied Collapse in the East 1941-42* Barnsley, England: Pen and Sword, 2006.

Farndale, General Sir Martin, *History of the Royal Regiment of Artillery: The Far East Theatre, 1941-1946* London, England: Brassey's, 2002.

Fetridge, William Harrison, *The Navy Reader* Indianapolis, New York: The Bobbs-Merrill Company, 1943.

Francillon, Dr Rene J., *Japanese Navy Bombers of World War II* New York: Doubleday & Company, 1969, 43.

Friedman, Norman, *U.S. Cruisers: An Illustrated Design History* Annapolis, MD: Naval Institute Press, 1984.

Friedman, Norman, *U.S. Destroyers: An Illustrated Design History* Annapolis, MD: Naval Institute Press, 1982.

Gill, G. Hermon, *Royal Australian Navy, 1939-1942* Canberra: Australian War Memorial, 1957.

Hammond, John, *A James Hilton Companion: A Guide to the Novels, Short Stories, Nonfiction Writings and Films* Jefferson, NC: McFarland, 2010.

Hilton, James, *The Story of Doctor Wassell* Boston: Little, Brown and Company, 1943.

Holbrook, Stewart H., *None More Courageous* New York: MacMillan Co., 1942.

Hornfischer, James D., *Ship of Ghosts: The Story of the USS Houston, FDR's Legendary Lost Cruiser, and the Epic Saga of Her Survivors* New York: Bantam Dell, 2007.

Hoyt, Edwin P., *The Lonely Ships: The Life and Death of the U.S. Asiatic Fleet* New York: McKay, 1976.

Kehn, Donald M., *A Blue Sea of Blood: Deciphering the Mysterious Fate of the USS Edsall* Minneapolis, MN: MBI, 2008.

Kehn, Donald M., *In the Highest Degree Tragic: The Sacrifice of the U.S. Asiatic Fleet in the East Indies During World War II* Lincoln, NE: Potomac Books, 2017.

Leutze, James R., *A Different Kind of Victory: A Biography of Admiral Thomas C. Hart* Annapolis, MD: Naval Institute Press, 1981.

Manchester, William R., and Paul Reid. *The Last Lion: Winston Spencer Churchill Defender of the Realm, 1940-1965* Boston: Little, Brown and Company, 2012.

Mawdsley, Edward, *December 1941: Twelve Days that Began a World War* New Haven, CT: Yale University Press, 2011.

Messimer, Dwight R., *Pawns of War: The Loss of the USS Langley and the USS Pecos* Annapolis, MD: Naval Institute Press, 1983.

Michel, John, *Mr Michel's War: From Manila to Mukden: An American Navy Officer's War with the Japanese, 1941-1945* Novato, CA: Presidio, 1998.

Miller, Edward S., *War Plan Orange: The U.S. Strategy to Defeat Japan, 1897–1945* Annapolis, MD: Naval Institute Press, 1991.

Morison, Samuel Eliot, *History of United States Naval Operations in World War II Volume I: The Battle of the* Atlantic Edison, NJ: Castle Books, 2001.

Morison, Samuel Eliot, *History of United States Naval Operations in World War II Volume III: The Rising Sun in the Pacific* Edison, NJ: Castle Books, 2001.

Morison, Samuel Eliot, *History of United States Naval Operations in World War II Volume XI: The Invasion of France and Germany* Edison, NJ: Castle Books, 2001.

Mullin, J. Danial, *Another Six-Hundred* Mt. Pleasant, NC: J. Danial Mullin, 1984.

Perry, George Sessions, John J. Floherty, and Isabel Leighton, *Where Away: A Modern Odyssey* New York: McGraw-Hill Books, 1944.

Prange, Gordon W., Dillon, Katherine V., and Goldstein, Donald M., *At Dawn We Slept: The Untold Story of Pearl Harbor* New York: McGraw-Hill, 1981.

Remmelink, Willem G.J., (eds) *The Invasion of the Dutch East Indies* Leiden, Netherlands: Leiden University Press, 2015. (English translation of *Senshi Sōsho* War History Series.)

Robson, R.W., *The Pacific Islands Handbook* New York: The Macmillan Company, 1946.

Roscoe, Theodore, *United States Submarine Operations in World War II* Annapolis, MD: United States Naval Institute, 1954.

Rottman, Gordon L., *World War II Pacific Island Guide: A Geo-Military Study* Westport, CT: Greenwood Press, 2002.

Routledge, N.W., *Anti-Aircraft Artillery, 1914-55: History of the Royal Regiment of Artillery* London, England: Brassey's, 1994.

Schom, Alan, *The Eagle and The Rising Sun: The Japanese-American War, 1941-1943, Pearl Harbor Through Guadalcanal* New York: W.W. Norton, 2004.

Schultz, Duane, *The Last Battle Station: The Story of the USS Houston* New York: St. Martin's Press, 1985.

Shores, Christopher F., Brian Cull, and Yasuho Izawa. *Bloody Shambles Volume Two: The Defense of Sumatra to the Fall of Burma.* London: Grub Street, 1992.

Spector, Ronald H., *Eagle Against the Sun: The American War with Japan* New York: Vintage Books, 1985.

Spence, Les and Greg Lewis (ed), *From Java to Nagasaki: The Complete Secret Wartime Diaries of a Prisoner of the Japanese* Cardiff, Wales: Magic Rat Books, 2012. Kindle Edition.

Terzibaschitsch, Stefan, *Cruisers of the United States Navy 1922–1962* Annapolis, MD: Naval Institute Press, 1984.

Toland, John, *But Not in Shame: The Six Months After Pearl Harbor* New York: Random House, 1961.

Toll, Ian W., *Pacific Crucible: War at Sea in the Pacific, 1941–1942* New York: W.W. Norton, 2012.

United States Navy, *The Bluejackets Manual* Annapolis, MD: Naval Institute Press, 1944.

Van Der Vat, Dan, *The Pacific Campaign* New York: Simon & Schuster, 1991.

Weller, George, and Anthony Weller, *Weller's War: A Legendary Foreign Correspondent's Saga of World War II on Five Continents* New York: Crown Publishers, 2009.

Williams, Greg, *The Last Days of the United States Asiatic Fleet: The Fates of the Ships and Those Aboard, December 8, 1941 – February 5, 1942* Jefferson, North Carolina: McFarland & Company, 2018.

Winslow, Walter G., *The Fleet the Gods Forgot: The U.S. Asiatic Fleet in World War II* Annapolis, MD: Naval Institute Press, 1982.

Winslow, Walter G., *The Ghost that Died at Sunda Strait* Annapolis, MD: Naval Institute Press, 1984.

Womack, Tom, *The Allied Defense of the Malay Barrier 1941-1942* Jefferson, NC: McFarland & Company, 2015.

Womack, Tom, *The Dutch Naval Air Force Against Japan: The Defense of the Netherlands East Indies, 1941–1942* Jefferson, NC: McFarland & Company, 2006.

Action Reports and Official Documents

Bureau of Ships, Navy Department. 'War Damage Report No. 34: USS *Marblehead* (CL 12) Bomb Damage, 4, February 1942.' November 15, 1943.

Deck Log, *Marblehead*.

CO Destroyer Division Fifty-Nine to Commander in Chief, US Asiatic Fleet. 'Night Destroyer Attack on Enemy Forces off Balikpapan, Borneo, NEI, Commencing at 1915 GCT January 23, 1942 – Report of.' January 26, 1942.

CO Destroyer Division Fifty-Nine to CO Destroyer Squadron Twenty-Nine. 'Notes on Night Action.' February 17, 1942.

CO *Marblehead* to Commander, US Naval Forces Southwest Pacific. 'Information Concerning Collision with Tjilatjap Harbor Tug *Kraus*, February 13, 1942.' February 15, 1942.

CO *Marblehead* to Commander, US Naval Forces Southwest Pacific. 'Report of Action with Japanese Planes North of Lombok Strait on 4 February 1942.' February 17, 1942.

CO *Marblehead* to Chief of Naval Operations, 'Steps Taken to Make USS *Marblehead* Seaworthy Following Action with Japanese Planes in Java Sea, February 4, 1942.' May 4, 1942.

CO *Marblehead*, 'Dispatches: Asiatic Fleet.' College Park, MD: National Archives (Record Group 313).

Combat Narrative: The Java Sea Campaign. Washington, DC: Office of Naval Intelligence, United States Navy, 1943.

Gabriel, Beauford, 'Narrative of Attack on the USS *Marblehead* by Japanese Aircraft on February 4, 1942.' N.d.

Glassford, Admiral William A., 'Narrative of Events in the Southwest Pacific from 14 February to 5 April 1942.' May 16, 1942.

Glassford, Vice Admiral William, 'Supplementary Narrative 1939–1942.' May 16, 1942.

Goggins, William: Biographical Sketch and Service Record. United States Navy: History & Heritage Command.

Hart, Admiral Thomas C., 'Events and Circumstances Concerning the Striking Force.' February 6, 1942.

Hart, Admiral Thomas C., 'Narrative of Events, Asiatic Fleet Leading Up to War and from 8 December 1941 to 15 February 1942.' ND.

Hart, Admiral Thomas C., 'Supplement of Narrative of Events Leading Up to War and from 8 December 1941 to 15 February 1942.' ND.

Mosher, Lieutenant Commander J.S., 'Report on Malaya, Java, and Singapore – March 2, 1941 to March 10, 1942.' Nd.

Muster Rolls, *Marblehead*.

'Narrative by Captain Nicholas B. Van Bergen, USN.' World War II Interviews. College Park, MD: National Archives.

'Narrative by Commander H.H. Keith, USN, Philippine Invasion.' World War II Interviews. College Park, MD: National Archives.

'Narrative by Commander William B. Goggins, Executive Officer – USS *Marblehead*.' World War II Interviews. College Park, MD: National Archives.

Office of Public Relations, U.S. Navy. *Navy Department Communiques 1-300 and Pertinent Press Releases*. Washington, DC: U.S. Government Printing Office, 1943.

Robinson, Arthur: Biographical Sketch and Service Record. United States Navy: History & Heritage Command.

United States Army, Far Eastern Command. *Japanese Monograph No. 31: Air Operations in the Southern Area*. Washington, DC: Office of the Chief of Military History Section, Department of the Army, 1953.

Van Bergen, Nicholas: Biographical Sketch and Service Record. United States Navy: History & Heritage Command.

War Diary, *Marblehead*.
War Diary, Sixteenth Naval District.
Wassell, Corydon: Biographical Sketch and Service Record. United States Navy: History & Heritage Command.

Articles

Abernethy, E. Paul., 'The *Pecos* Died Hard.' *US Naval Institute Proceedings*, December 1969, 74-82.

Arnold, Jeremy. 'The Story of Doctor Wassell.' http://www.tcm.com/this-month/article/149922%7C0/The-Story-of-Dr-Wassell.html (April 16, 2019).

Brereton, Foster. 'A San Francisco Family, Part II: Triumph, The True Story of Nicholas Van Bergen.' https://medium.com/@fosterbrereton/a-san-francisco-family-part-ii-triumph-8ff2d3d6fb02 (April 8, 2019).

Bridges, Kenneth. 'The Life and Times of Dr. Corydon Wassell, Part 1.' http://www.boonevilledemocrat.com/lifestyle/20180101/life-and-times-of-dr-corydon-wassell-part-1 (December 12, 2018).

Bridges, Kenneth. 'The Life and Times of Dr. Corydon Wassell, Part 2.' http://www.arkansasnews.com/lifestyle/20180108/life-and-times-of-dr-corydon-wassell-part-2 (December 12, 2018).

'Capt. Robinson of *Marblehead* Gets Navy Cross.' *Chicago Tribune*, May 15, 1942.

'Captain Tells How 37 Planes Hit *Marblehead*.' *Chicago Tribune*, May 9, 1942.

'Chicagoan Back on *Marblehead* Phones Family.' *Chicago Tribune*, May 8, 1942.

Cole, Captain Bernard D. 'America's Asiatic Fleet.' *Naval History*, October, 2011.

Corpening, Captain M.M., 'Tells Lone Dive Bomber's Raid on Marblehead.' *Chicago Tribune*, May 20, 1942.

'Crisis in Tsingtao.' *New York Times*, December 20, 1937.

'Cruiser Bombed in Indies Home with Many Wounds.' *New York Times*, May 7, 1942.

'Escape from Java.' *Cairns Post* (Australia), March 17, 1942. http://nla.gov.au/nla.news-article42336354 (August 19, 2019).

Fischer, Robert. 'Ghost Ship *Marblehead*.' *Sea Classics*, July 1982.

'Gyrocompass.' https://www.britannica.com/technology/gyrocompass (August 27, 2018).

Hailey, Foster, 'War in the Java Sea.' *New York Times* (Book Reviews), December 3, 1944.

Hernandez, Raymond. 'William J. Dunn, CBS Radio Correspondent, 86.' *New York Times*, September 21, 1992.

'History of the Yard' in Brooklyn Navy Yard website. https://brooklynnavyyard.org/about/history (March 10, 2019).

Hull, Michael D., 'Dr. Corydon Wassell's Selfless Effort to Aid Wounded Sailors on Java Earned Him Undying Gratitude and a Navy Cross.' *World War II History*, May 2006, 14-18, 78.

'Japanese Armored Units on Java Island, 1942.' https://dutcheastindies. webs.com/java_armour.html (March 30, 2019).

'Japs Get Borneo Oil Port; Claim U.S. Cruiser Hit.' *Chicago Tribune*, February 7, 1942.

Kingsley, Robert A., 'Hauling Bombs, Bullets, Beer – and MacArthur.' (Blog post). https://thejavagoldblog.wordpress.com/2016/06/13/hauling-bombs-bullets-beer-and-macarthur/ (April 26, 2017).

Mills, Lion G., 'South from Tjilatjap.' *Naval History*, April 2009. https://www.usni.org/magazines/navalhistory/2009-04/south-tjilatjap (February 12, 2018).

Muir, Dan. 'The Night Hawks of Balikpapan: The Balikpapan Raid, January 1942.' http://dutcheastindies.webs.com/BalikpapanRaid.html (April 23, 2017).

'*Marblehead* Hero Gets Navy Cross.' *New York Times*, July 12, 1942.

'*Marblehead*'s Voyage Home an Epic of Heroism, Tragedy.' *New York Times*, May 9, 1942.

'Navy Cross Awarded Eight Heroes of the Marblehead Bombing.' *Chicago Tribune*, August 9, 1942.

'1,308 Marines of the Sixth Regiment Sail from San Diego for Duty in Shanghai.' *New York Times*, August 30, 1937.

'One of Richest Oil Fields on an Island.' *The Oil Weekly*, October 21, 1922.

'Petronella Hospital.' https://historicalhospitals.com/mission-hospitals/petronella-hospital/ (November 19, 2018), 1.

Pinkowski, Edward. 'Dr. Wassell's Boys: The Grim, Unsentimental Story of the Men Who Played in a Famous Drama.' *Our Navy*, January 1945.

'President Gives Gold Star to Admiral Hart; Hails Moral Courage of Asiatic Commander.' *New York Times*, May 23, 1942.

'Saga of Torn U.S. Warship's Voyage Home.' *Chicago Tribune*, May 7, 1942.

'The Bombing of Darwin – Fact Sheet 195.' National Archives of Australia website. http://www.naa.gov.au/collection/fact-sheets/fs195.aspx (January 3, 2019).

'The Conquest of Java Island, March 1942.' https://dutcheastindies.webs (April 13, 2019).

'The Investigations.' https://www.nsa.gov/about/cryptologic-heritage/center-cryptologic-history/pearl-harbor-review/investigations/ (April 24, 2019).

'The wounds of wartime.' http://www.blondmcindoe.com/wartime.html (September 20, 2018).

'Tokyo Claims U.S. Cruiser: Officially Lists *Marblehead* as Sunk – Indies Boot.' *New York Times*, March 12, 1942.

'Two Navy Officers Win High Honor.' *Honolulu Advertiser*, October 27, 1942.

'William B. Goggins, 87, Retired Rear Admiral, Dies.' https://www.washingtonpost.com/archive/local/1986/01/01/william-b-goggins-87-retired-rear-admiral-dies (April 3, 2019).

'Zero Japanese Aircraft.' https://www.britannica.com/technology/Zero-Japanese-aircraft (February 20, 2019).

Other

'Benjamin Hopkins' in World War II Prisoners of War Data File, 12/7/1941 – 11/19/1946 on National Archives Website. https://aad.archives.gov/aad/display-partial-records (April 13, 2019).

'Captain William B. Goggins' in Battleship *Alabama* Website http://www.angelfire.com/va3/bb60/goggins.htm (April 30, 2017).

COFEPOW Website for British PoWs in the Pacific. https://www.cofepow.org.uk/ (Accessed Various Times)

'Crew of the USS *Houston* – CA 30' in USS *Houston* Webpage. http://www.usshouston.org/crewlist/crewroster.htm (February 13, 2019).

'Description of Medals.' https://valor.defense.gov/Description-of-Awards/ (April 16, 2019).

DuBois, David, 'Admiral Thomas C. Hart and the Demise Of The Asiatic Fleet 1941 – 1942' (2014). *Electronic Theses and Dissertations.* Paper 2331. http://dc.etsu.edu/etd/2331

'Experience Over Eight Decades of the Oscars from 1927 to 2019.' https://www.oscars.org/oscars/ceremonies/1945 (April 17, 2019).

'FDR at the Mare Island Hospital.' http://vallejomuseum.blogspot.com/2008/10/fdr-at-mare-island-hospital.html (June 17, 2019).

'Fireside Chats of Franklin D. Roosevelt: On Our National Economic Policy Tuesday, April 28, 1942' in Franklin D. Roosevelt Presidential Library and Museum Website. http://docs.fdrlibrary.marist.edu/firesi90.html (April 8, 2019).

Forgotten Campaign: The Dutch East Indies Campaign 1941-1942 website. https://dutcheastindies.webs.com/ (Accessed Various Times).

Herman Cornelis Jorissen Oral History in Imperial War Museum website https://www.iwm.org.uk/collections/item/object/80011513 (August 14, 2019).

Interview with Raymond Kester. http://www.ussmarblehead.com/kester.html (January 20, 2016).

James August Riddle Collection (AFC/2001/001/83631), Veterans History Project, American Folklife Center, Library of Congress. (Accessed Various Times).

Kehn, Don. 'Corrections to my previous post on CA30/CL12 men, etc.' The Overvalwagen Forum: Pacific War 1941-1945 (Blog Post), https://www.tapatalk.com/groups/theovervalwagenforum/corrections-to-my-previous-post-on-ca30-cl12-men-e-t1330.html (January 29, 2019).

Kehn, Don. 'Numbers + pics' The Overvalwagen Forum: Pacific War 1941-1945 (Blog Post), https://www.tapatalk.com/groups/theovervalwagenforum/numbers-pics-t1324.html (February 13, 2019).

Kester, Raymond. 'Marblehead Ports of Call.' http://ussmarblehead.com/documents/MHDPORTSOFCALL.pdf (December 28, 2017).

National [British] Army Museum Website. https://www.nam.ac.uk/ (August 8, 2019).

Naval History and Heritage Command Website. https://www.history.navy.mil (Accessed Various Times).

Royal Netherlands Navy Warships of World War II. http://www.netherlandsnavy.nl/ (Accessed Various Times).

The Royal Artillery website. https://web.archive.org/web/20090322060614/http://www.ra39-45.pwp.blueyonder.co.uk/index.html (Accessed Various Times).

The Submarines of the Royal Netherlands Navy 1906 - 2005 website http://www.dutchsubmarines.com (August 21, 2019).

University of Houston Libraries Special Collection: Online Exhibit on USS *Houston*. https://exhibits.lib.uh.edu/exhibits (April 1, 2019).

USS *Marblehead* and DR. Wassell Website. http://ussmarblehead.com/ (Accessed Various Times).

'WWII Vet Bob Clark (1) - Amazing Escapes – Pacific.' YouTube Video, 1:48, posted by 'me3tv,' November 22, 2009, https://youtu.be/nRRMKVxteGE.

Wassell, Commander Corydon M., 'The War in the Far East.' https://web.archive.org/web/20061113084858/http://www.empireclubfoundation.com/details.asp?SpeechID=1643&FT=yes (April 16, 2019).

Endnotes

Chapter 1

1. Theodore Roscoe. *United States Submarine Operations in World War II*. (Annapolis, MD: United States Naval Institute, 1954), 24.
2. *Marblehead* Deck Log, November 25, 1941.
3. *Marblehead* Deck Log, December 1, 1941.
4. Lodwick H. Alford. *Playing for Time: War on an Asiatic Fleet Destroyer*. (Bennington, VT: Merriam Press, 2008), 28.
5. Norman Friedman. *U.S. Cruisers: An Illustrated Design History*. (Annapolis, MD: Naval Institute Press, 1984), 79.
6. Al Adcock. *U.S. Light Cruisers in Action*. (Carrollton, TX: Squadron Signal Publications, 1999), 8.
7. Al Adcock. *U.S. Navy Float Planes of World War II in Action*. (Carrollton, TX: Squadron Signal Publications, 2006), 10.
8. United States Navy. *The Bluejackets Manual*. (Annapolis, MD: Naval Institute Press, 1944), 275.
9. *Marblehead* Deck Log, November 28, 1941.
10. Samuel Eliot Morison. *History of United States Naval Operations in World War II Volume III: The Rising Sun in the Pacific*. (Edison, NJ: Castle Books, 2001), 160, *Marblehead* Deck Log, November 28, 1941, and '*Bulmer*' in Dictionary of American Fighting Ships. https://www.history.navy.mil/research/histories/ship-histories/danfs/b/bulmer-dd-222.html (November 9, 2017), 1. Note: Morison incorrectly lists *Blumer* with the *Marblehead* group.
11. *Marblehead* Muster Roll, December 31, 1941.
12. Interview with Raymond Kester. http://www.ussmarblehead.com/kester.html (January 20 2016). Hereafter cited as 'Kester Interview'.
13. *Marblehead* Deck Log, November 29, 1941.

Chapter 2

1. Jeffrey R. Cox. *Rising Sun, Falling Skies: The Disastrous Java Sea Campaign of World War II*: (Oxford, UK: Osprey Publishing, 2014), 29 and Captain Bernard D Cole. 'America's Asiatic Fleet'. *Naval History*, October 2011, 19.
2. *'Marblehead'* in Dictionary of American Fighting Ships. https://www.history.navy.mil/research/histories/ship-histories/danfs/m/marblehead-iii.html (November 7, 2017), 1. Hereafter cited as *'Marblehead.'*
3. Roger Chesneau, ed. *Conway's All the World's Fighting Ships: 1922-1946*. (London: Conway Maritime Press, 1980), 93.
4. Adcock, *Light Cruisers*, 8.
5. Stefan Terzibaschitsch. *Cruisers of the United States Navy 1922-1962*. (Annapolis, MD: Naval Institute Press, 1984), 36.
6. Friedman, *U.S. Cruisers*, 469.
7. *'Marblehead,'* 1.
8. Terzibaschitsch. *Cruisers of the United States Navy*, 49.
9. Ronald H. Spector. *Eagle Against the Sun: The American War with Japan*. (New York: Vintage Books, 1985), 9.
10. '1,308 Marines of the Sixth Regiment Sail from San Diego for Duty in Shanghai.' *New York Times*, August 30, 1937, 3.
11. Edwin P. Hoyt. *The Lonely Ships: The Life and Death of the U.S. Asiatic Fleet*. (New York: McKay, 1976), 4.
12. Raymond Kester. '*Marblehead* Ports of Call.' http://ussmarblehead.com/documents/MHDPORTSOFCALL.pdf (December 28, 2017), 1.
13. Hoyt, *Lonely Ships*, 5.
14. *'Panay'* in Dictionary of American Fighting Ships. https://www.history.navy.mil/research/histories/ship-histories/danfs/p/panay-ii.html (November 21, 2017).
15. 'Crisis in Tsingtao.' *New York Times*, December 20, 1937, 1.
16. James August Riddle Collection (AFC/2001/001/83631), Veterans History Project, American Folklife Center, Library of Congress.
17. *'Ashville'* in Dictionary of American Fighting Ships. https://www.history.navy.mil/research/histories/ship-histories/danfs/a/asheville-gunboat-no-21-i.html (January 11, 2018), 1.

Chapter 3

1. 'Thomas C. Hart' in Naval History and Heritage Command Website https://www.history.navy.mil/research/histories/ship-histories/danfs/t/thomas-c-hart.html (November 15, 2017). Hereafter cited as 'Thomas C. Hart'.
2. Morison, *Rising Sun*, 151.
3. David DuBois. 'Admiral Thomas C. Hart and the Demise of the Asiatic Fleet 1941 – 1942' (2014). *Electronic Theses and Dissertations*. Paper 2331. http://dc.etsu.edu/etd/2331, 19-20.
4. *'Houston'* in Dictionary of American Fighting Ships. https://www.history.navy.mil/research/histories/ship-histories/danfs/h/houston-ii.html (3 January 2018), 1.
5. Spector, *Eagle Against the Sun*, 64.
6. John Toland. *But Not in Shame: The Six Months After Pearl Harbor.* (New York: Random House, 1961), xii.
7. Walter G. Winslow. *The Fleet the Gods Forgot: The U.S. Asiatic Fleet in World War II.* (Annapolis, MD: Naval Institute Press, 1982), 3.
8. Morison, *Rising Sun*, 150.
9. Paul S. Dull. *A Battle History of the Imperial Japanese Navy.* (Annapolis, MD: Naval Institute Press, 1978), 5.
10. Cox, *Rising Sun, Falling Skies*, 35.
11. Ibid.
12. Edward Mawdsley. *December 1941: Twelve Days that Began a World War.* (New Haven, CT: Yale University Press, 2011), 53.
13. Edward S. Miller. *War Plan Orange: The U.S. Strategy to Defeat Japan, 1897-1945.* (Annapolis, MD: Naval Institute Press, 1991), 264-65.
14. Morison, *Rising Sun*, 54.
15. Hoyt, *Lonely Ships*, 134.
16. Morison, *Rising Sun*, 55 and Hoyt, *Lonely Ships*, 134.
17. James R. Leutze. *A Different Kind of Victory: A Biography of Admiral Thomas C. Hart.* (Annapolis, MD: Naval Institute Press, 1981), 200.
18. Hart, Admiral Thomas C. 'Narrative of Events, Asiatic Fleet Leading Up to War and from 8 December 1941 to 15 February 1942.' ND, 8. Hereafter cited as 'Hart Narrative'.

19. Leutze, *Different Kind of Victory*, 198.
20. 'Hart Narrative,' 9.
21. Winslow, *The Fleet the Gods Forgot*, 4.
22. 'Hart Narrative,' 11.
23. Dan Van Der Vat. *The Pacific Campaign*. (New York: Simon & Schuster, 1991), 73, and Winslow, *The Fleet the Gods Forgot*, 5.
24. Van Der Vat, *Pacific Campaign*, 72-73.
25. Spector, *Eagle Against the Sun*, 68-69.
26. Dull, *Battle History*, 7.

Chapter 4

1. Tom Womack. *The Dutch Naval Air Force Against Japan: The Defense of the Netherlands East Indies, 1941-1942*. (Jefferson, NC: McFarland & Company, 2006), 80.
2. *Marblehead* Deck Log, November 29, 1941.
3. 'One of Richest Oil Fields on an Island.' *The Oil Weekly*, October 21, 1922, 72.
4. Alford, *Playing for Time*, 31.
5. 'Hart Narrative,' 30.
6. Terzibaschitsch, *Cruisers of the United States Navy*, 306.
7. Robinson, Arthur: Biographical Sketch and Service Record. United States Navy: History & Heritage Command, 1. Hereafter cited as: 'Robinson Biographical Sketch'.
8. 'Montana' in Dictionary of American Fighting Ships. https://www.history.navy.mil/research/histories/ship-histories/danfs/m/montana.html (July 3, 2019), 1.
9. 'Robinson Biographical Sketch,' 1.
10. Goggins, William: Biographical Sketch and Service Record. United States Navy: History & Heritage Command, 1. Hereafter cited as: 'Goggins Biographical Sketch'.
11. 'Captain William B. Goggins' in Battleship Alabama Website http://www.angelfire.com/va3/bb60/goggins.htm (April 30, 2017). Hereafter cited as 'Captain William B. Goggins'.
12. *Marblehead* Deck Log, December 1, 1941.
13. Tom Womack. *The Allied Defense of the Malay Barrier 1941-1942*. (Jefferson, NC: McFarland & Company, 2015), 20 & 38.

14. Irvine Henry Anderson. *The Standard-Vacuum Oil Company and United States East Asian Policy, 1933-1941.* (Princeton, NJ: Princeton University Press, 1975), 74-75.
15. Womack, *Defense of the Malay Barrier*, 36.
16. Alford, *Playing for Time*, 31.

Chapter 5

1. Spector, *Eagle Against the Sun*, 85.
2. John Costello. *The Pacific War.* (New York: Rawson, Wade Publishers, Inc., 1981), 119.
3. Toland, *But Not in Shame*, 5.
4. Dull, *Battle History*, 7.
5. Spector, *Eagle Against the Sun*, 78-79.
6. Morison, *Rising Sun*, 54.
7. Ibid, 165.
8. Leutze, *Different Kind of Victory*, 199.
9. 'Hart Narrative,' 34.
10. John P. Bracken. *From the Bridge of the U.S.S. Marblehead: November 25, 1941-May 4, 1942.* (Privately Published, 1992), 2.
11. *Marblehead* Deck Log, November 24, 1941.
12. 'Hart Narrative,' 16.
13. Mawdsley. *December 1941*, 133-34.
14. Costello, *Pacific War*, 123.
15. Morison, *Rising Sun*, 157.
16. 'Boise' in Dictionary of American Fighting Ships. https://www.history.navy.mil/research/histories/ship-histories/danfs/b/boise-i.html (January 9, 2018), 1. Hereafter cited as 'Boise'.
17. 'Hart Narrative,' 25.
18. CO *Marblehead*. 'Dispatches: Asiatic Fleet.' College Park, MD: National Archives (Record Group 313). Hereafter cited as 'Dispatches: Asiatic Fleet.'
19. *Marblehead* Deck Log, December 5, 1941.
20. Bracken, *Bridge of the Marblehead*, 5.
21. Van Bergen, Nicholas: Biographical Sketch and Service Record. United States Navy: History & Heritage Command, 2. Hereafter cited as 'Van Bergen Biographical Sketch.'

22. John Campbell. *Naval Weapons of World War II*. (Annapolis, MD: Naval Institute Press, 1985), 132.
23. Hoyt, *Lonely Ships*, 144.
24. George Sessions Perry, John J. Floherty, and Isabel Leighton. *Where Away: A Modern Odyssey*. (New York: McGraw-Hill Books, 1944), 26-27.
25. *Marblehead* War Diary, December 1-7, 1941.
26. *Marblehead* Deck Log, December 7, 1941.

Chapter 6

1. Gordon W. Prange, Katherine V. Dillon and Donald M. Goldstein. *At Dawn We Slept: The Untold Story of Pearl Harbor*. (New York: McGraw-Hill, 1981), 500-501.
2. Dull, *Battle History*, 16.
3. '*Arizona*' in Dictionary of American Fighting Ships. https://www. history.navy.mil/research/histories/ship-histories/danfs/a/arizona-battleship-no-39-ii.html (February 20, 2018), 1.
4. Prange, Dillon, and Goldstein, *At Dawn We Slept*, 517.
5. Morison, *Rising Sun*, 101.
6. 'Remembering Pearl Harbor: A Pearl Harbor Fact Sheet.' https://www.census.gov/history/pdf/pearl-harbor-fact-sheet-1.pdf (February 20, 2018), 1. Hereafter cited as 'Remembering Pearl Harbor'.
7. Dull, *Battle History*, 18.
8. 'Remembering Pearl Harbor,' 1.
9. Alan Schom. *The Eagle and the Rising Sun: The Japanese-American War, 1941-1943, Pearl Harbor Through Guadalcanal*. (New York: W.W. Norton, 2004), 220.
10. Sixteenth Naval District War Diary, December 8, 1941.
11. Leutze, *Different Kind of Victory*, 231.
12. Walter G. Winslow *The Ghost that Died at Sunda Strait*. (Annapolis, MD: Naval Institute Press, 1984), 33.
13. Leutze, *Different Kind of Victory*, 232.
14. *Marblehead* War Diary, December 8, 1941.
15. Bracken, *From the Bridge of the U.S.S. Marblehead*, 5.
16. Ibid, 7.
17. *Marblehead* Deck Log, December 8, 1941.

18. Ibid.
19. Alford, *Playing for Time*, 33.
20. Perry, Floherty, and Leighton, *Where Away*, 29.

Chapter 7

1. '*Wake*' in Dictionary of American Fighting Ships. https://www.history.navy.mil/research/histories/ship-histories/danfs/w/wake.html (March 12, 2018), 1.
2. Van Der Vat, *Pacific Campaign*, 33.
3. *Marblehead* Deck Log, December 9, 1941.
4. *Marblehead* War Diary, December 9, 1941.
5. *Marblehead* Deck Log, December 9, 1941.
6. 'Kester Interview,' 2.
7. Dull, *Battle History*, 40-41.
8. Costello, *Pacific War*, 131.
9. Cox, *Rising Sun, Falling Skies*, 84.
10. Dull, *Battle History*, 39.
11. Morison, *Rising Sun*, 190.
12. Van Der Vat, *Pacific Campaign*, 34.
13. Winslow, *The Fleet the Gods Forgot*, 39.
14. Donald M. Kehn. *In the Highest Degree Tragic: The Sacrifice of the U.S. Asiatic Fleet in the East Indies During World War II.* (Lincoln, NE: Potomac Books, 2017), 44-45.
15. Leutze, *Different Kind of Victory*, 236.
16. Gordon L. Rottman. *World War II Pacific Island Guide: A Geo-Military Study.* (Westport, CT: Greenwood Press, 2002), 197.
17. Womack, *Defense of the Malay Barrier*, 5.
18. Rottman, *Pacific Island Guide*, 200.
19. Cox, *Rising Sun, Falling Skies*, 137.
20. Chesneau, ed. *Conway's All the World's Fighting Ships*, 385.
21. Womack, *Defense of the Malay Barrier*, 5.

Chapter 8

1. Spector, *Eagle Against the Sun*, 108.
2. Morison, *Rising Sun*, 165.

3. Dull, *Battle History*, 29.
4. 'Hart Narrative,' 39.
5. Kehn, *Highest Degree Tragic*, 56.
6. Winslow, *The Fleet the Gods Forgot*, 10.
7. Spector, *Eagle Against the Sun*, 127.
8. Van Der Vat, *Pacific Campaign*, 125.
9. Spector, *Eagle Against the Sun*, 128.
10. Womack, *Dutch Naval Air Force Against Japan*, 78 and Cox, *Rising Sun, Falling Skies*, 140.
11. Dull, *Battle History*, 43.
12. Winslow, *The Fleet the Gods Forgot*, 11.
13. *Combat Narrative: The Java Sea Campaign*. Washington, DC: Office of Naval Intelligence, United States Navy, 1943, 12.
14. *Marblehead* Deck Log, December 9, 1941.
15. *Marblehead* War Diary, December 11, 1941.
16. *Marblehead* War Diary, December 12, 1941.
17. *Marblehead* Deck Log, December 16, 1941.
18. Bracken, *Bridge of the Marblehead*, 10.
19. *Marblehead* Deck Log, January 1, 1942.

Chapter 9

1. Willem G. J. Remmelink, eds. *The Invasion of the Dutch East Indies*. (Leiden, Netherlands: Leiden University Press, 2015), 4.
2. Dull, *Battle History*, 44.
3. Costello, *Pacific War*, 189.
4. Womack, *Defense of the Malay Barrier*, 112-14.
5. Kehn, *Highest Degree Tragic*, 74.
6. Hoyt, *Lonely Ships*, 224.
7. 'Hart Narrative,' 40.
8. Leutze, *Different Kind of Victory*, 256-57.
9. Ibid, 247.
10. Spector, *Eagle Against the Sun*, 129.
11. *Marblehead* War Diary, January 12, 1942.
12. 'Dispatches: Asiatic Fleet.'
13. Bracken, *From the Bridge of the U.S.S. Marblehead*, 13.
14. J. Danial Mullin. *Another Six-Hundred*. (Mt. Pleasant, NC: J. Danial Mullin, 1984), 115.

15. Perry, Floherty, and Leighton, *Where Away*, 85.
16. Roscoe, *United States Submarine Operations*, 65.
17. Winslow, *The Fleet the Gods Forgot*, 151-52.
18. Admiral Thomas C. Hart. 'Events and Circumstances Concerning the Striking Force.' February 6, 1942, 2. Hereafter cited as 'Hart Striking Force Report.'
19. Ibid, 1.
20. Duane Schultz. *The Last Battle Station: The Story of the USS Houston*. (New York: St. Martin's Press, 1985), 51.

Chapter 10

1. *Combat Narrative: The Java Sea Campaign*, 15.
2. *Marblehead* Deck Log, January 18 1942.
3. Leutze, *Different Kind of Victory*, 270.
4. Womack, *Defense of the Malay Barrier*, 116.
5. *Combat Narrative: The Java Sea Campaign*, 17.
6. Remmelink, eds., *Invasion of the Dutch East Indies*, 356.
7. Dan Muir. 'The Night Hawks of Balikpapan: The Balikpapan Raid, January 1942.' http://dutcheastindies.webs.com/BalikpapanRaid.html (April 23, 2017), 2.
8. Womack, *Defense of the Malay Barrier*, 115.
9. Dull, *Battle History*, 62-63.
10. Mullin, *Another Six-Hundred*, 117.
11. Commander Frederick J. Bell. *Condition Red: Destroyer Action in the South Pacific*. (New York: Longmans, Green and Company, 1943), 70.
12. Ibid and Mullin, *Another Six-Hundred*, 118.
13. *Marblehead* Deck Log, January 21, 1942 and 'Dispatches: Asiatic Fleet.'
14. *Marblehead* War Diary, January 21, 1942.
15. Mullin, *Another Six-Hundred*, 117.
16. *'Boise,'* 1.
17. Mullin, *Another Six-Hundred*, 119.
18. Morison, *Rising Sun*, 285.
19. Winslow, *The Fleet the Gods Forgot*, 153.
20. Mullin, *Another Six-Hundred*, 121.

21. CO Destroyer Division Fifty-Nine to Commander in Chief, US Asiatic Fleet. 'Night Destroyer Attack on Enemy Forces off Balikpapan, Borneo, NEI, Commencing at 1915 GCT January 23, 1942 – Report of.' January 26, 1942. Hereafter cited as 'Night Destroyer Attack,' Enclosure A.
22. 'Night Destroyer Attack,' Enclosure B.
23. Norman Friedman. *U.S. Destroyers: An Illustrated Design History.* (Annapolis, MD: Naval Institute Press, 1982), 494-95.
24. Womack, *Defense of the Malay Barrier*, 120.
25. Mullin, *Another Six-Hundred*, 123.
26. Cox, *Rising Sun, Falling Skies*, 156.
27. Morison, *Rising Sun*, 287-88.
28. 'Night Destroyer Attack,' 2.
29. *'Blessman'* in Dictionary of American Fighting Ships. https://www.history.navy.mil/research/histories/ship-histories/danfs/b/blessman-i.html (May 22, 2018), 1
30. Perry, Floherty, and Leighton, *Where Away*, 97.
31. Mullin, *Another Six-Hundred*, 149.
32. Office of Public Relations, U.S. Navy. *Navy Department Communiques 1-300 and Pertinent Press Releases.* (Washington, DC: U.S. Government Printing Office, 1943), 23.
33. Leutze, *Different Kind of Victory*, 271.
34. Womack, *Dutch Naval Air Force Against Japan*, 88.

Chapter 11

1. Womack, *Defense of the Malay Barrier*, 42-43.
2. *Marblehead* Deck Log, January 25, 1942.
3. Ibid.
4. 'Hart Striking Force Report,' 3 and *Combat Narrative: The Java Sea Campaign*, 25.
5. 'Dispatches: Asiatic Fleet.'
6. *Marblehead* Deck Log, January 31, 1942.
7. Alford, *Playing for Time*, 84.
8. Kehn, *Highest Degree Tragic*, 111.
9. Morison, *Rising Sun*, 279, and 'Hart Narrative,' 68.
10. Costello, *Pacific War*, 198.

11. Hoyt, *Lonely Ships*, 225.
12. 'Hart Narrative,' 68.
13. 'Rear-Admiral K.W.F.M. Doorman, RNN' in Royal Netherlands Navy Warships of World War II. http://www.netherlandsnavy.nl/ (June 25, 2018), 1.
14. Schultz, *Last Battle Station*, 77.
15. Womack, *Dutch Naval Air Force Against Japan*, 90.
16. *Combat Narrative: The Java Sea Campaign*, 26.
17. *Marblehead* War Diary, February 2, 1942.
18. Chesneau, ed., *Conway's All the World's Fighting Ships*, 388.
19. 'Narrative by Commander William B. Goggins, Executive Officer – USS *Marblehead*.' World War II Interviews. College Park, MD: National Archives, 2. Hereafter cited as 'Goggins Narrative'.
20. Hoyt, *Lonely Ships*, 228.
21. Womack, *Defense of the Malay Barrier*, 134.
22. Perry, Floherty, and Leighton, *Where Away*, 107.
23. Morison, *Rising Sun*, 298.
24. Doorman, Karel. 'Operation Order No. 1' Enclosure A in CO *Marblehead* to Commander, US Naval Forces Southwest Pacific. 'Report of Action with Japanese Planes North of Lombok Strait on 4 February 1942.' February 17, 1942.
25. *Marblehead* Deck Log, February 4, 1942.

Chapter 12

1. Womack, *Defense of the Malay Barrier*, 138.
2. CO *Marblehead* to Commander, US Naval Forces Southwest Pacific. 'Report of Action with Japanese Planes North of Lombok Strait on 4 February 1942.' February 17, 1942, 1. Hereafter cited as '*Marblehead* Report,' and *Combat Narrative: The Java Sea Campaign*, 27.
3. Christopher F. Shores, Brian Cull, and Yasuho Izawa. *Bloody Shambles. Volume Two: The Defense of Sumatra to the Fall of Burma.* (London: Grub Street, 1992), 158.
4. Cox, *Rising Sun, Falling Skies*, 184.
5. *Marblehead* Deck Log, February 4, 1942.
6. Perry, Floherty, and Leighton, *Where Away*, 109.

7. 'Narrative by Captain Nicholas B. Van Bergen, USN.' World War II Interviews. College Park, MD: National Archives, 2. Hereafter cited as 'Van Bergen Narrative'.
8. Dr Rene J. Francillon. *Japanese Navy Bombers of World War II.* (New York: Doubleday & Company, 1969), 43.
9. 'Marblehead Report,' 2.
10. Schultz, *Last Battle Station*, 89.
11. 'Van Bergen Narrative,' 2.
12. Gabriel, Beauford. 'Narrative of Attack on the USS Marblehead by Japanese Aircraft on February 4, 1942.' N.d., 1-2. Hereafter cited as 'Narrative of Attack'.
13. *Marblehead* Deck Log, February 4, 1942.
14. Womack, *Defense of the Malay Barrier*, 136, and Winslow, *Sunda Strait*, 90.
15. Morison, *Rising Sun*, 300.
16. Winslow, *Sunda Strait*, 91.
17. '*Marblehead* Report,' 5.

Chapter 13

1. 'Goggins Narrative,' 3.
2. '*Heron*' in Dictionary of American Fighting Ships. https://www.history.navy.mil/research/histories/ship-histories/danfs/h/heron-i.html (July 30, 2018).
3. Perry, Floherty, and Leighton, *Where Away*, 116.
4. Winslow, *The Fleet the Gods Forgot*, 159.
5. 'Goggins Narrative,' 4.
6. Stewart H. Holbrook. *None More Courageous.* (New York: MacMillan Co., 1942), 24.
7. 'Gyrocompass.' https://www.britannica.com/technology/gyrocompass (August 27, 2018), 1.
8. 'Narrative of Action by First Lieutenant,' 1. Enclosure H in '*Marblehead* Report.' Hereafter cited as 'First Lieutenant Narrative'.
9. '*Marblehead* Report,' 7.
10. Bureau of Ships, Navy Department. 'War Damage Report No. 34: USS *Marblehead* (CL 12) Bomb Damage, 4, February 1942.' November 15, 1943, 7. Hereafter cited as 'War Damage Report'.

11. *Marblehead* Deck Log, February 4, 1942.
12. 'War Damage Report,' 6.
13. Ibid, 1
14. 'Van Bergen Narrative,' 2.
15. '*Marblehead's* Voyage Home an Epic of Heroism, Tragedy.' *New York Times*, May 9, 1942, 28. Hereafter cited as '*Marblehead's* Voyage Home'.
16. 'List of Casualties, Showing Type of Injury and Location at Time of Injury,' 1-3. Enclosure C in '*Marblehead* Report.' Hereafter cited s 'List of Causalities'.
17. 'Goggins Narrative,' 4.
18. 'List of Casualties,' 7.
19. 'Goggins Narrative,' 5.

Chapter 14

1. 'First Lieutenant Narrative,'1.
2. '*Marblehead* Report,' 6.
3. 'War Damage Report,' 5.
4. United States Navy, *Bluejackets Manual*, 545.
5. Friedman, *U.S. Cruisers*, 469, and 'War Damage Report,' 5.
6. 'War Damage Report,' 7.
7. Perry, Floherty, and Leighton, *Where Away*, 126.
8. Holbrook, *None More Courageous*, 29.
9. Perry, Floherty, and Leighton, *Where Away*, 127.
10. 'Meritorious Conduct During Action,' 6. Enclosure L in '*Marblehead* Report.' Hereafter cited s 'Meritorious Conduct,' 6.
11. Perry, Floherty, and Leighton, *Where Away*, 132.
12. 'Meritorious Conduct,' 3.
13. 'Van Bergen Narrative,' 7.
14. Perry, Floherty, and Leighton, *Where Away*, 152.

Chapter 15

1. 'Captain Tells How 37 Planes Hit *Marblehead*.' *Chicago Tribune*, May 9, 1942, 7. Hereafter cited as '37 Planes Hit *Marblehead*'.

2. 'Communication Record,' 1. Enclosure E in '*Marblehead* Report.' Hereafter cited as 'Communication Record'.
3. Womack, *Defense of the Malay Barrier*, 137.
4. Holbrook, *None More Courageous*, 27.
5. *Marblehead* Deck Log, February 4, 1942.
6. Ibid.
7. Womack, *Defense of the Malay Barrier*, 136.
8. Ibid.
9. 'Communication Record,' 1, and Hoyt, *Lonely Ships*, 232.
10. Winslow, *Sunda Strait*, 89, and Hoyt, *Lonely Ships*, 233.
11. Winslow, *Sunda Strait*, 89.
12. '*Marblehead* Report,' 10.
13. *Marblehead* Deck Log, February 4, 1942, and Schultz, *Last Battle Station*, 97.
14. Womack, *Defense of the Malay Barrier*, 136, and Cox, *Rising Sun, Falling Skies*, 188.
15. Schultz, *Last Battle Station*, 100-101.
16. 'Van Bergen Narrative,' 6.
17. '*Marblehead* Report,' 10.
18. Shores, Cull, and Izawa, *Bloody Shambles*, 160.
19. *Combat Narrative: The Java Sea Campaign*, 31, and Morison, *Rising Sun*, 303.
20. Shores, Cull, and Izawa, *Bloody Shambles*, 160.

Chapter 16

1. 'War Damage Report,' 5.
2. '*Marblehead* Hero Gets Navy Cross.' *New York Times*, July 12, 1942, 8.
3. 'Meritorious Conduct,' 5.
4. '*Marblehead* Report,' 15.
5. 'The Wounds of Wartime.' http://www.blondmcindoe.com/wartime.html (September 20, 2018), 4.
6. Perry, Floherty, and Leighton, *Where Away*, 134-135.
7. Ibid, 143.
8. 'Narrative of Attack,' 2.
9. '*Marblehead* Report,' 16.

10. *Marblehead* Deck Log, February 4, 1942.

11. 'Goggins Narrative,' 5-6.

12. 'Van Bergen Narrative,' 3.

13. Adcock, *Light Cruisers*, 8.

14. 'Narrative of Action by Engineering Officer,' 1. Enclosure I in '*Marblehead* Report.' Hereafter cited as 'Engineering Officer Narrative'.

15. 'Engineering Officer Narrative,' 3.

16. *Marblehead* Deck Log, February 4, 1942.

17. Ibid.

18. 'Damage Sustained by the Construction and Repair Department,' 14, Enclosure G in 'Marblehead Report.' Hereafter cited as 'Construction and Repair Department'.

19. Holbrook, *None More Courageous*, 28.

20. '37 Planes Hit *Marblehead*,' 7.

Chapter 17

1. *Marblehead* Deck Log, February 4, 1942.

2. Womack, *Defense of the Malay Barrier*, 137.

3. '*Marblehead* Report,' 11.

4. 'Communication Record,' 1.

5. 'Van Bergen Narrative,' 3-6.

6. 'War Damage Report,' 3.

7. 'First Lieutenant Narrative,' 2.

8. 'Construction and Repair Department,' 5 and 'Meritorious Conduct,' 6.

9. 'List of Causalities,' 5-6.

10. Perry, Floherty, and Leighton, *Where Away*, 142.

11. Robert Fischer. 'Ghost Ship *Marblehead*.' *Sea Classics*, July 1982, 69.

12. *Marblehead* Deck Log, February 4, 1942.

13. 'War Damage Report,' 9.

14. *Marblehead* Deck Log, February 4, 1942.

15. Alford, *Playing for Time*, 88.

16. '37 Planes Hit *Marblehead*,' 7.

17. '*Marblehead's* Voyage Home,' 28.

18. '*Marblehead* Report,' 14.

19. *'Paul Jones'* in Dictionary of American Fighting Ships. https://www.history.navy.mil/research/histories/ship-histories/danfs/p/paul-jones-iii.html (November 4, 2018), 1.

20. Mullin, *Another Six-Hundred*, 164.

21. Cox, *Rising Sun, Falling Skies*, 441.

22. 'List of Causalities,' 1-7.

23. *Marblehead* Deck Log, February 6, 1942.

24. 'Japs Get Borneo Oil Port; Claim U.S. Cruiser Hit.' *Chicago Tribune*, February 7, 1942, 4A.

Chapter 18

1. Hugh Campbell and Ron Lovell. *So Long, Singapore: Royal Air Force Auxiliary 'Tung Song,' December 1941-March 1942*. (Hobart, New Zealand: H. Campbell, 2000), 156.

2. Ibid.

3. *Marblehead* Deck Log, February 6, 1942.

4. 'Tjilatjap' in Royal Netherlands Navy Warships of World War II. http://www.netherlandsnavy.nl/ (November 19, 2018), 1.

5. 'Marblehead Report,' 13.

6. Womack, *Defense of the Malay Barrier*, 138.

7. Schultz, *Last Battle Station*, 111.

8. Bracken, *From the Bridge of the U.S.S. Marblehead*, 28.

9. Alford, *Playing for Time Playing for Time,* 88.

10. Admiral William A. Glassford. 'Narrative of Events in the Southwest Pacific from 14 February to 5 April 1942.' May 16, 1942, 17. Hereafter cited as 'Glassford Narrative'.

11. Winslow, *Sunda Strait*, 96.

12. Hoyt, *Lonely Ships*, 236.

13. *'Marblehead,'* 2.

14. Kehn, *Highest Degree Tragic*, 138.

15. Winslow, *The Fleet the Gods Forgot*, 163.

16. Perry, Floherty, and Leighton, *Where Away*, 180.

17. *Marblehead* Deck Log, February 6, 1942.

18. 'Glassford Narrative,' 10.

19. CO *Marblehead* to Chief of Naval Operations. 'Steps Taken to Make USS *Marblehead* Seaworthy Following Action with Japanese

Planes in Java Sea, February 4, 1942.' May 4, 1942, 1. Hereafter cited as 'Steps Taken to Make *Marblehead* Seaworthy'.
20. Perry, Floherty, and Leighton, *Where Away*, 178.
21. 'Narrative by Commander H.H. Keith, USN, Philippine Invasion.' World War II Interviews. College Park, MD: National Archives, 5.
22. 'Hart Narrative,' 72.
23. 'Hart Striking Force Report,' 4-5.
24. Morison, *Rising Sun*, 305.
25. Hoyt, *Lonely Ships*, 239.
26. *Marblehead* Deck Log, February 8, 1942.
27. 'Hart Narrative,' 72 and *'Phoenix'* in Dictionary of American Fighting Ships. https://www.history.navy.mil/research/histories/ship-histories/danfs/p/phoenix-iii.html (November 21, 2018), 1.
28. Schultz, *Last Battle Station*, 119-120.

Chapter 19

1. 'Goggins Narrative,' 9.
2. *Marblehead* Deck Log, February 7, 1942.
3. Winslow, *The Fleet the Gods Forgot*, 164.
4. Ibid.
5. 'War Damage Report,' 7.
6. Ibid, 4.
7. 'Steps Taken to Make *Marblehead* Seaworthy,' 1.
8. Cox, *Rising Sun, Falling Skies*, 197.
9. Bracken, *From the Bridge of the U.S.S. Marblehead*, 32.
10. *Marblehead* Deck Log, February 9-10, 1942.
11. 'Steps Taken to Make *Marblehead* Seaworthy,' 2.
12. Bracken, *From the Bridge of the U.S.S. Marblehead*, 31.
13. *Marblehead* Deck Log, February 10, 1942.
14. James D. Hornfischer. *Ship Of Ghosts: The Story Of The USS Houston, FDR's Legendary Lost Cruiser, and the Epic Saga Of Her Survivors.* (New York: Bantam Dell, 2007), 42.
15. DuBois, *Demise Of The Asiatic Fleet*, 56.
16. Toland, *But Not in Shame*, 220.
17. Leutze, *Different Kind of Victory*, 275.
18. Womack, *Defense of the Malay Barrier*, 104.

19. Hoyt, *Lonely Ships*, 241.
20. Toland, *But Not in Shame*, 220.
21. Leutze, *Different Kind of Victory*, 277.
22. Ibid.
23. Hoyt, *Lonely Ships*, 241.
24. Leutze, *Different Kind of Victory*, 277.

Chapter 20

1. Rottman, *Pacific Island Guide*, 214.
2. R.W. Robson. *The Pacific Islands Handbook*. (New York: The Macmillan Company, 1946), 324-328.
3. *Marblehead* Deck Log, February 11, 1942.
4. 'Steps Taken to Make *Marblehead* Seaworthy,' 3.
5. Holbrook, *None More Courageous*, 33.
6. 'Van Bergen Narrative,' 10.
7. 'Dispatches: Asiatic Fleet.'
8. *Marblehead* Deck Log, February 13, 1942.
9. 'Dispatches: Asiatic Fleet.'
10. Bracken, *From the Bridge of the U.S.S. Marblehead*, 33.
11. 'Van Bergen Narrative,' 11.
12. Leutze, *Different Kind of Victory*, 277.
13. Ibid, 284-285.
14. Ibid, 285.

Chapter 21

1. 'Petronella Hospital.' https://historicalhospitals.com/mission-hospitals/petronella-hospital/ (November 19, 2018), 1.
2. 'Goggins Narrative,' 10.
3. Winslow, *The Fleet the Gods Forgot*, 164.
4. Ibid and Michael D. Hull. 'Dr Corydon Wassell's Selfless Effort to Aid Wounded Sailors on Java Earned Him Undying Gratitude and a Navy Cross.' *World War II History*, May 2006, 16.
5. 'List of Causalities,' 4 and Edward Pinkowski. 'Dr Wassell's Boys: The Grim, Unsentimental Story of the Men Who Played in a Famous Drama.' *Our Navy*, January 1945, 12.

6. Pinkowski, 'Dr Wassell's Boys,' 13.
7. *Marblehead* Muster Roll, December 31, 1941.
8. Pinkowski, 'Dr Wassell's Boys,' 13.
9. *Marblehead* Muster Roll, December 31, 1941.
10. 'List of Causalities,' 4.
11. *Marblehead* Deck Log, January 7 1942.
12. '*Chaumont*' in Dictionary of American Fighting Ships. https://www.history.navy.mil/research/histories/ship-histories/danfs/c/chaumont.html (December 11, 2018), 1.
13. 'List of Causalities,' 4
14. Don Kehn. 'Corrections to my previous post on CA30/CL12 men, etc.' The Overvalwagen Forum: Pacific War 1941-1945 (Blog Post), https://www.tapatalk.com/groups/theovervalwagenforum/corrections-to-my-previous-post-on-ca30-cl12-men-e-t1330.html (January 29 2019).
15. Pinkowski, 'Dr Wassell's Boys,' 13.
16. Donald M. Kehn. *A Blue Sea of Blood: Deciphering the Mysterious Fate of the USS Edsall*. (Minneapolis, MN: MBI, 2008), 126-127.
17. Hull, 'Dr Corydon Wassell.' 14
18. Wassell, Corydon: Biographical Sketch and Service Record. United States Navy: History & Heritage Command, 1. Hereafter cited as 'Wassell Biographical Sketch'.
19. Kenneth Bridges. 'The Life and Times of Dr Corydon Wassell, Part 1.' http://www.boonevilledemocrat.com/lifestyle/20180101/life-and-times-of-dr-corydon-wassell-part-1 (December 12, 2018), 1.
20. 'Wassell Biographical Sketch,' 1.
21. Commander Corydon M. Wassell. 'The War in the Far East.' https://web.archive.org/web/20061113084858/http://www.empireclubfoundation.com/details.asp?SpeechID=1643&FT=yes (April 16, 2019). Hereafter cited as 'The War in the Far East'.
22. 'Glassford Narrative,' 17.
23. Vice Admiral William Glassford. 'Supplementary Narrative 1939-1942.' May 16, 1942, 79. Hereafter cited as 'Supplementary Narrative'.
24. James Hilton. *The Story of Doctor Wassell*. (Boston, Little, Brown and Company, 1943), 7-8.

Chapter 22

1. Perry, Floherty, and Leighton, *Where Away*, 193.
2. CO *Marblehead* to Commander, US Naval Forces Southwest Pacific. 'Information Concerning Collision with Tjilatjap Harbor Tug *Kraus*, February 13, 1942.' February 15, 1942, 1.
3. Bracken, *From the Bridge of the U.S.S. Marblehead*, 33.
4. *Marblehead* Deck Log, February 13, 1942.
5. Dull, *Battle History*, 63.
6. Ian W. Toll. *Pacific Crucible: War at Sea in the Pacific, 1941-1942*. (New York: W.W. Norton, 2012), 246.
7. Costello, *Pacific War*, 198-200.
8. Toll, *Pacific Crucible*, 249.
9. William R. Manchester and Paul Reid. *The Last Lion: Winston Spencer Churchill Defender of the Realm, 1940-1965*. (Boston: Little, Brown, and Company, 2012), 482.
10. Costello, *Pacific War*, 198.
11. Van Der Vat, *Pacific Campaign*, 117 and Toland, *But Not in Shame*, 217.
12. Winston Churchill. *Memoirs of the Second World War: An Abridgement of the Six Volumes of the Second World War*. (Boston: Houghton Mifflin, 1959), 535.
13. Toll, *Pacific Crucible*, 252.
14. Hoyt, *Lonely Ships*, 253.
15. Dull, *Battle History*, 64.
16. Morison, *Rising Sun*, 309.
17. Ibid, 310.
18. Womack, *Dutch Naval Air Force Against Japan,* 107.
19. Dull, *Battle History*, 66 and Morison, *Rising Sun*, 309.
20. Womack, *Defense of the Malay Barrier*, 130.
21. Morison, *Rising Sun*, 322.
22. Costello, *Pacific War*, 205.
23. Dull, *Battle History*, 59.
24. Cox, *Rising Sun, Falling Skies*, 216.
25. Dull, *Battle History*, 54.
26. 'The Bombing of Darwin – Fact Sheet 195.' National Archives of Australia website. http://www.naa.gov.au/collection/fact-sheets/fs195.aspx (3 January 2019).

27. Morison, *Rising Sun*, 320.
28. Hoyt, *Lonely Ships*, 257.

Chapter 23

1. Winslow, *The Fleet the Gods Forgot*, 165.
2. Kehn, *Blue Sea of Blood*, 127.
3. William Harrison Fetridge. *The Navy Reader*. (New York: The Bobbs-Merrill Company, 1943), 27.
4. Hull, 'Dr Corydon Wassell,' 16.
5. Winslow, *The Fleet the Gods Forgot*, 165.
6. 'Goggins Narrative,' 10.
7. Lieutenant Commander J.S. Mosher. 'Report on Malaya, Java, and Singapore – March 2, 1941 to March 10, 1942.' Nd, 16.
8. William Bartsch. *Everyday a Nightmare: American Pursuit Pilots in the Defense of Java, 1941-1942*. (College Station, TX: Texas A&M University Press, 2010), 279 and Walter Dumaux Edmonds. *They Fought with What They Had: The Story of the Army Air Forces in the Southwest Pacific, 1941-1942*. (Washington, DC: Center for Air Force History, 1992), 408.
9. Pinkowski, 'Dr Wassell's Boys,' 13.
10. Paul E. Abernethy. 'The Pecos Died Hard.' *US Naval Institute Proceedings*, December 1969, 77.
11. Greg Williams. *The Last Days of the United States Asiatic Fleet: The Fates of the Ships and Those Aboard, December 8, 1941- February 5, 1942*. (Jefferson, North Carolina: McFarland & Company, 2018), 155-157.
12. 'List of Causalities,' 2.
13. 'WWII Vet Bob Clark (1) – Amazing Escapes – Pacific.' YouTube Video, 1:48, posted by 'me3tv,' November 22, 2009, https://youtu.be/nRRMKVxteGE .
14. 'Guestbook Post by Ray Kester' in USS *Marblehead* and DR Wassell Website. http://ussmarblehead.com/ (July 3, 2019).
15. *'Sturgeon'* in Dictionary of American Fighting Ships. https://www.history.navy.mil/research/histories/ship-histories/danfs/s/sturgeon-ii.html (June 20, 2019), 1.
16. 'The Ship' in the MS *Abbekerk* website. http://www.msabbekerk.nl/ (July 3, 2019).

17. 'Stories: A.W. Kik's Memories' in the MS *Abbekerk* website. http://www.msabbekerk.nl/ (July 3, 2019).
18. Edmonds, *They Fought with What They Had*, 409.
19. 'The Crew' in the MS *Abbekerk* website. http://www.msabbekerk.nl/ (July 3, 2019).
20. Edmonds, *They Fought with What They Had*, 409.
21. Bartsch, *Everyday a Nightmare*, 279-280.
22. Ibid, 280.
23. Womack, *Defense of the Malay Barrier*, 157.
24. Edmonds, *They Fought with What They Had*, 414.
25. Womack, *Defense of the Malay Barrier*, 157.

Chapter 24

1. Kehn, *Blue Sea of Blood*, 138.
2. Womack, *Dutch Naval Air Force Against Japan*, 122.
3. United States Army, Far Eastern Command. *Japanese Monograph No. 31: Air Operations in the Southern Area.* (Washington, DC: Office of the Chief of Military History Section, Department of the Army, 1953), 1.
4. Toll, *Pacific Crucible*, 256.
5. Morison, *Rising Sun*, 342-343.
6. Costello, *Pacific War*, 207.
7. Morison, *Rising Sun*, 356.
8. Womack, *Defense of the Malay Barrier*, 229.
9. Winslow, *The Fleet the Gods Forgot*, 210.
10. Hoyt, *Lonely Ships*, 230.
11. 'Goggins Narrative,' 11.
12. Bartsch. *Everyday a Nightmare*, 301.
13. Edmonds. *They Fought with What They Had*, 366-367.
14. Ibid, 432.

Chapter 25

1. Bracken, *From the Bridge of the U.S.S. Marblehead*, 34.
2. *Marblehead* Deck Log, February 13, 1942.
3. Bracken, *From the Bridge of the U.S.S. Marblehead*, 34.

4. *Marblehead* Deck Log, February 15, 1942.
5. 'Steps Taken to Make *Marblehead* Seaworthy,' 4.
6. Perry, Floherty, and Leighton, *Where Away*, 196.
7. *Marblehead* Deck Log, February 15, 1942.
8. Morison, *Rising Sun*, 382.
9. Bracken, *From the Bridge of the U.S.S. Marblehead*, 37.
10. *Marblehead* Deck Log, February 21, 1942.
11. 'Van Bergen Narrative,' 10.
12. *Marblehead* Deck Log, March 1, 1942.

Chapter 26

1. *'Langley'* in Dictionary of American Fighting Ships. https://www. history.navy.mil/research/histories/ship-histories/danfs/l/langley-i. html (January 20, 2019), 1.
2. Bartsch, *Everyday a Nightmare*, 312.
3. DuBois, *Demise of the Asiatic Fleet*, 63.
4. Morison, *Rising Sun*, 363.
5. *Combat Narrative: The Java Sea Campaign*, 81.
6. Morison, *Rising Sun*, 364.
7. Toll, *Pacific Crucible*, 261.
8. Cox, *Rising Sun, Falling Skies*, 350-351.
9. Hoyt, *Lonely Ships*, 291.
10. Winslow, *The Fleet the Gods Forgot*, 215.
11. Costello, *Pacific War*, 205.
12. Charles Robert Anderson. *East Indies*. (Washington, DC: U.S. Army Center of Military History, 1991), 17.
13. Bernard Edwards. *Japan's Blitzkrieg: The Allied Collapse in the East 1941-42*. (Barnsley, England: Pen and Sword, 2006), 110.
14. Kehn, *Blue Sea of Blood*, 138.
15. Toll, *Pacific Crucible*, 255.
16. Abernethy, 'Pecos Died Hard,' 77.
17. Dwight R. Messimer. *Pawns of War: The Loss of the USS Langley and the USS Pecos*. (Annapolis, MD: Naval Institute Press, 1983), 95.
18. *'Pecos'* in Dictionary of American Fighting Ships. https://www. history.navy.mil/research/histories/ship-histories/danfs/p/pecos-i. html (February 5, 2019), 1.

19. Messimer, *Pawns of War*, 116.
20. Ibid, 95.
21. Cox, *Rising Sun, Falling Skies*, 390-391.

Chapter 27

1. Pinkowski, 'Dr Wassell's Boys,' 13.
2. 'Goggins Narrative,' 11.
3. 'The Sailors' in USS *Marblehead* and DR Wassell Website. http://ussmarblehead.com/ (February 6, 2019).
4. Anderson, *East Indies*, 18.
5. Pinkowski, 'Dr Wassell's Boys,' 13.
6. 'Goggins Narrative,' 12.
7. Hilton, *Story of Doctor Wassell*, 81.
8. 'Goggins Narrative,' 12 and Pinkowski, 'Dr Wassell's Boys,' 13.
9. Hull, 'Dr Corydon Wassell,' 18.
10. Hilton, *Story of Doctor Wassell*, 87.
11. Hoyt, *Lonely Ships*, 260.
12. *Combat Narrative: The Java Sea Campaign*, 82.
13. Hoyt, *Lonely Ships*, 303.
14. *Combat Narrative: The Java Sea Campaign*, 82.
15. Bartsch, *Everyday a Nightmare*, 312.
16. Morison, *Rising Sun*, 378.
17. Lion G. Mills. 'South from Tjilatjap.' *Naval History*, April 2009. https://www.usni.org/magazines/navalhistory/2009-04/south-tjilatjap (February 12, 2018), 4.
18. Hoyt, *Lonely Ships*, 303 and Womack, *Defense of the Malay Barrier*, 302.
19. Kehn, *Highest Degree Tragic,* 424.
20. '*Asheville* I (Gunboat No. 21)' in Dictionary of American Fighting Ships. https://www.history.navy.mil/research/histories/ship-histories/danfs/a/asheville-gunboat-no-21-i.html (April 23, 2019).
21. Kehn, *Highest Degree Tragic,* 424.
22. Morison, *Rising Sun*, 379.
23. 'Glassford Narrative,' 29.

Chapter 28

1. Edwards, *Japan s Blitzkrieg*, 110.
2. Womack, *Defense of the Malay Barrier*, 294.
3. Winslow, *The Fleet the Gods Forgot*, 274.
4. 'Goggins Narrative,' 12.
5. Pinkowski, 'Dr Wassell's Boys,' 13.
6. 'Goggins Narrative,' 12.
7. *'Pillsbury'* in Dictionary of American Fighting Ships. https://www.history.navy.mil/research/histories/ship-histories/danfs/l/langley-i.html (February 12, 2019), 1.
8. 'FDR at the Mare Island Hospital.' http://vallejomuseum.blogspot.com/2008/10/fdr-at-mare-island-hospital.html (June 17, 2019).
9. Morison, *Rising Sun*, 378.
10. Don Kehn. 'Numbers + Pics.' The Overvalwagen Forum: Pacific War 1941-1945 (Blog Post), https://www.tapatalk.com/groups/theovervalwagenforum/numbers-pics-t1324.html (February 13, 2019).
11. 'Crew of the USS *Houston* – CA 30' in USS *Houston* Webpage. http://www.usshouston.org/crewlist/crewroster.htm (February 13, 2019).
12. Pinkowski, 'Dr Wassell's Boys,' 13.
13. Womack, *Defense of the Malay Barrier*, 303.
14. Ibid, 304.
15. Robert A. Kingsley. 'Hauling Bombs, Bullets, Beer – and MacArthur.' (Blog post). https://thejavagoldblog.wordpress.com/2016/06/13/hauling-bombs-bullets-beer-and-macarthur/ (April 26, 2017).
16. Hull, 'Dr Corydon Wassell,' 18.
17. Perry, Floherty, and Leighton, *Where Away*, 199.
18. 'Van Bergen Narrative,' 10.
19. 'Tokyo Claims U.S. Cruiser: Officially Lists *Marblehead* as Sunk – Indies Boot.' *New York Times*, March 12, 1942, 6.
20. Holbrook, *None More Courageous*, 34.
21. G. Hermon Gill. *Royal Australian Navy, 1939-1942*. (Canberra: Australian War Memorial, 1957), 367-368.
22. Perry, Floherty, and Leighton, *Where Away*, 200-201.
23. Gill, *Royal Australian Navy*, 451-459.
24. Bracken, *From the Bridge of the U.S.S. Marblehead*, 37.

25. *Marblehead* Deck Log, March 4, 1942.
26. *Marblehead* Deck Log, March 15, 1942.
27. Morison, *Rising Sun*, 383-385.

Chapter 29

1. 'Tender Janssens' in The Submarines of the Royal Netherlands Navy 1906 – 2005 Website http://www.dutchsubmarines.com/tenders/tender_janssens.htm (August 21, 2019). Hereafter cited as 'Tender Janssens'.
2. Womack, *Defense of the Malay Barrier*, 317.
3. 'Tender Janssens.'
4. Womack, *Defense of the Malay Barrier*, 304.
5. Ibid, 18.
6. Donald A. Bertke, Gordon Smith, and Don Kindell. *World War II Sea War, Vol 5: Air Raid Pearl Harbor. This Is Not a Drill (Volume 5)*. (Dayton, OH: Bertke Publications, 2013), 72.
7. Kingsley, 'Hauling Bombs, Bullets, Beer.'
8. Womack, *Defense of the Malay Barrier*, 264 and 279.
9. Herman Cornelis Jorissen Oral History in Imperial War Museum website https://www.iwm.org.uk/collections/item/object/80011513 (August 14, 2019). Hereafter cited as 'Jorissen Oral History'.
10. Womack, *Defense of the Malay Barrier*, 304.
11. Hilton, *Story of Doctor Wassell*, 109.
12. 'Janssens-Class Supply Ship' in Royal Netherlands Navy Warships of World War II Website http://www.netherlandsnavy.nl/.
13. Kingsley, 'Hauling Bombs, Bullets, Beer.'
14. Ibid.
15. 'Goggins Narrative,' 13.
16. Womack, *Defense of the Malay Barrier*, 304.
17. Raymond Hernandez. 'William J. Dunn, CBS Radio Correspondent, 86.' *New York Times*, September 21, 1992, 8.
18. William J. Dunn. *Pacific Microphone*. (College Station, TX: Texas A&M University Press, 1988), 124.
19. Ibid, 125.
20. Campbell and Lovell, *So Long, Singapore*, 197.
21. Dunn, *Pacific Microphone*, 126.

22. George Weller and Anthony Weller. *Weller's War: A Legendary Foreign Correspondent's Saga of World War II on Five Continents.* (New York: Crown Publishers, 2009), 241.
23. Womack, *Defense of the Malay Barrier*, 305.

Chapter 30

1. 'Goggins Narrative,' 14.
2. Ibid, 13.
3. Campbell and Lovell, *So Long, Singapore*, 197.
4. Pinkowski, 'Dr Wassell's Boys,' 14.
5. Dunn, *Pacific Microphone*, 128.
6. 'Zero Japanese Aircraft.' https://www.britannica.com/technology/Zero-Japanese-aircraft (February 20, 2019).
7. Womack, *Defense of the Malay Barrier*, 305.
8. Hilton, *Story of Doctor Wassell*, 133.
9. 'Escape from Java.' *Cairns Post* (Australia), March 17, 1942. http://nla.gov.au/nla.news-article42336354 (August 19, 2019).
10. Weller and Weller, *Weller's War*, 247.
11. Dunn, *Pacific Microphone*, 129.
12. Womack, *Defense of the Malay Barrier*, 305.
13. Dunn, *Pacific Microphone*, 130.
14. 'The War in the Far East.'
15. Womack, *Defense of the Malay Barrier*, 305.
16. Weller and Weller, *Weller's War*, 247.
17. Campbell and Lovell, *So Long, Singapore*, 198.
18. 'The War in the Far East.'

Chapter 31

1. Womack, *Defense of the Malay Barrier*, 305.
2. Dunn, *Pacific Microphone*, 131.
3. 'Goggins Narrative,' 15.
4. Womack, *Defense of the Malay Barrier*, 305.
5. Pinkowski, 'Dr Wassell's Boys,' 14.
6. Campbell and Lovell, *So Long, Singapore*, 198.

7. Winslow, *The Fleet the Gods Forgot*, 170.
8. 'The War in the Far East.'
9. Ibid.
10. 'Jorissen Oral History.'
11. Dunn, *Pacific Microphone*, 133.
12. Pinkowski, 'Dr Wassell's Boys,' 14.
13. Morison, *Rising Sun*, 379.
14. 'The Conquest of Java Island, March 1942.' https://dutcheastindies. webs (April 13, 2019).
15. 'Japanese Armored Units on Java Island, 1942.' https:// dutcheastindies.webs.com/java_armour.html (March 30, 2019).
16. Morison, *Rising Sun*, 379.
17. Anderson, *East Indies*, 21.
18. Bracken, *From the Bridge of the U.S.S. Marblehead*, 39-40.
19. Perry, Floherty, and Leighton, *Where Away*, 212.
20. *Marblehead* Deck Log, March 15, 1942.
21. Perry, Floherty, and Leighton, *Where Away*, 215-216.
22. 'Steps Taken to Make *Marblehead* Seaworthy,' 8.
23. *Marblehead* Deck Log, March 24, 1942.
24. Perry, Floherty, and Leighton, *Where Away*, 221-222.
25. 'Steps Taken to Make *Marblehead* Seaworthy,' 9.
26. 'Van Bergen Narrative,' 11.
27. Perry, Floherty, and Leighton, *Where Away*, 224 and Bracken, *From the Bridge of the U.S.S. Marblehead*, 43.
28. *Marblehead* Deck Log, April 23, 1942.
29. Perry, Floherty, and Leighton, *Where Away*, 225.
30. Samuel Eliot Morison. *History of United States Naval Operations in World War II Volume I: The Battle of the Atlantic.* (Edison, NJ: Castle Books, 2001), 412-413.
31. *Marblehead* Deck Log, May 4, 1942.

Chapter 32

1. *Marblehead* Deck Log, May 4, 1942.
2. 'History of the Yard' in Brooklyn Navy Yard website. https:// brooklynnavyyard.org/about/history (March 10, 2019).
3. *Marblehead* Deck Log, May 5, 1942.

4. 'Chicagoan Back on *Marblehead* Phones Family.' *Chicago Tribune*, May 8, 1942, 6.

5. Terzibaschitsch, *Cruisers of the United States Navy*, 50-51 & 309.

6. 'Fireside Chats of Franklin D. Roosevelt: On Our National Economic Policy Tuesday, April 28, 1942' in Franklin D. Roosevelt Presidential Library and Museum Website. http://docs.fdrlibrary.marist.edu/firesi90.html (April 8, 2019).

7. 'Saga of Torn U.S. Warship's Voyage Home.' *Chicago Tribune*, May 7, 1942, 10.

8. 'Cruiser Bombed in Indies Home with Many Wounds.' *New York Times*, May 7, 1942, 5.

9. '*Marblehead's* Voyage Home,' 28.

10. John Hammond. *A James Hilton Companion: A Guide to the Novels, Short Stories, Nonfiction Writings and Films*. (Jefferson, NC: McFarland, 2010), 144.

11. Ibid.

12. Jeremy Arnold. 'The Story of Doctor Wassell.' http://www.tcm.com/this-month/article/149922%7C0/The-Story-of-Dr-Wassell.html (April 16, 2019).

13. 'The War in the Far East.'

14. Arnold, 'The Story of Doctor Wassell.'

15. 'Experience Over Eight Decades of the Oscars from 1927 to 2019.' https://www.oscars.org/oscars/ceremonies/1945 (April 17, 2019).

16. Kenneth Bridges. 'The Life and Times of Dr Corydon Wassell, Part 2.' http://www.arkansasnews.com/lifestyle/20180108/life-and-times-of-dr-corydon-wassell-part-2 (December 12, 2018).

17. Ibid.

18. Foster Hailey. 'War in the Java Sea.' *New York Times* (Book Reviews), December 3, 1944.

19. 'Description of Medals.' https://valor.defense.gov/Description-of-Awards/ (April 16, 2019).

20. 'Capt. Robinson of *Marblehead* Gets Navy Cross.' *Chicago Tribune*, May 15, 1942, 6.

21. 'Wassell Biographical Sketch,' 1.

22. 'The War in the Far East.'

23. '*Marblehead* Hero,' 8.

24. 'Navy Cross Awarded Eight Heroes of the *Marblehead* Bombing.' *Chicago Tribune*, August 9, 1942, 7.

25. 'Two Navy Officers Win High Honor.' *Honolulu Advertiser*, October 27, 1942, 63.
26. *Marblehead* Deck Log, October 15, 1942.
27. '*Marblehead*,' 2.

Chapter 33

1. *Marblehead* Muster Roll, October 28, 1942.
2. 'Robinson Biographical Sketch,' 2.
3. Morison, *Battle of the Atlantic*, 413.
4. Samuel Eliot Morison. *History of United States Naval Operations in World War II Volume XI: The Invasion of France and Germany.* (Edison, NJ: Castle Books, 2001), 328.
5. 'Robinson Biographical Sketch,' 3.
6. 'Goggins Narrative,' 16.
7. Corpening, Captain M.M. 'Tells Lone Dive Bomber's Raid on *Marblehead*.' *Chicago Tribune*, May 20, 1942, 7.
8. 'Captain William B. Goggins.'
9. Ibid.
10. 'William B. Goggins, 87, Retired Rear Admiral, Dies.' https://www.washingtonpost.com/archive/local/1986/01/01/william-b-goggins-87-retired-rear-admiral-dies (April 3, 2019).
11. 'Van Bergen Biographical Sketch,' 2.
12. Foster Brereton. 'A San Francisco Family, Part II: Triumph, The True Story of Nicholas Van Bergen.' https://medium.com/@fosterbrereton/a-san-francisco-family-part-ii-triumph-8ff2d3d6fb02 (April 8, 2019).
13. 'Van Bergen Biographical Sketch,' 3.
14. Leutze, *Different Kind of Victory*, 277.
15. 'President Give Gold Star to Admiral Hart; Hails Moral Courage of Asiatic Commander.' *New York Times*, May 23, 1942, 5.
16. 'The Investigations.' https://www.nsa.gov/about/cryptologic-heritage/center-cryptologic-history/pearl-harbor-review/investigations/ (April 24, 2019).
17. 'Thomas C. Hart.'
18. 'The War in the Far East.'
19. 'Supplementary Narrative,' 80.

20. 'Wassell Biographical Sketch,' 2.
21. Articles on Benjamin Grover Hopkins in Marblehead Website. http://www.ussmarblehead.com/crew/hopkins.html (April 13, 2019).
22. Ibid.
23. 'Benjamin Hopkins' in World War II Prisoners of War Data File, 12/7/1941 – 11/19/1946 on National Archives Website. https://aad.archives.gov/aad/display-partial-records (April 13, 2019).

Epilogue

1. Womack, *Defense of the Malay Barrier*, 308.
2. Ibid, 309.
3. Morison, *Rising Sun*, 379.
4. Hilton, *Story of Doctor Wassell*, 76.
5. 'Goggins Narrative,' 12.
6. 'Order of battle for Dutch, British, Australian, USA and Japanese Army' in Forgotten Campaign: The Dutch East Indies Campaign 1941-1942 website. https://dutcheastindies.webs.com/ (August 9, 2019).
7. Routledge, N. W. *Anti-Aircraft Artillery, 1914-55: History of the Royal Regiment of Artillery.* (London, England: Brassey's, 1994), 60.
8. 'British Army Organization' in National Army Museum Website https://www.nam.ac.uk/explore/army-organisation (August 8, 2019).
9. Routledge, *Anti-Aircraft Artillery*, 444-447.
10. '77 (Welsh) Heavy AA Regiment RA (TA)' in The Royal Artillery website. https://web.archive.org/web/20090322060614/http://www.ra39-45.pwp.blueyonder.co.uk/index.html (August 5, 2019), and General Sir Martin Farndale. *History of the Royal Regiment of Artillery: The Far East Theatre, 1941-1946.* (London, England: Brassey's, 2002), 330.
11. '21 Light AA Regiment RA(TA)' in The Royal Artillery website. https://web.archive.org/web/20090322060614/http://www.ra39-45.pwp.blueyonder.co.uk/index.html (August 5, 2019).
12. Lewendon, Brigadier R.J. 'Gunners in Java – 1942' in COFEPOW Website www.cofepow.org.uk/armed-forces-stories-list/java-gunners (July 23, 2019). Hereafter cited as 'Java Gunners.'
13. Routledge, *Anti-Aircraft Artillery*, 228.

14. Williams, Bdr A.E. 'The 1942 Java Railway Tragedy' in COFEPOW Website https://www.cofepow.org.uk/armed-forces-stories-list/the-1942-java-railway-tragedy (August 7, 2019) and 'Java Gunners.'

15. 'Timor Gunners' in COFEPOW Website www.cofepow.org.uk/armed-forces-stories-list/timor-gunners (August 7, 2019).

16. 'Java Gunners.'

17. Anderson, *East Indies*, 14-15.

18. Hilton, *Story of Doctor Wassell*, 81.

19. 'The conquest of Java Island, March 1942' in Forgotten Campaign: The Dutch East Indies Campaign 1941-1942 website. https://dutcheastindies.webs.com/ (August 9, 2019).

20. Les Spence and Greg Lewis (Ed). *From Java to Nagasaki: The Complete Secret Wartime Diaries of a Prisoner of the Japanese.* (Cardiff, Wales: Magic Rat Books, 2012), http://a.co/53mv2Va

21. Farndale. *History of the Royal Regiment of Artillery*, 77.

22. 'The POW Camps' in University of Houston Libraries Special Collection: Online Exhibit on USS *Houston*. https://exhibits.lib.uh.edu/exhibits/show/cruiser-houston/the-camps (Accessed August 14, 2019).

23. 'Java Gunners.'

Index